Tolerance in the Twenty-First Century

Tolerance in the Twenty-First Century

Prospects and Challenges

Edited by Gerson Moreno-Riaño

LEXINGTON BOOKS

A division of
ROWMAN & LITTLEFIELD PUBLISHERS, INC.
Lanham • Boulder • New York • Toronto • Oxford

LEXINGTON BOOKS

A division of Rowman & Littlefield Publishers, Inc.
A wholly owned subsidiary of The Rowman & Littlefield Publishing Group, Inc.
4501 Forbes Boulevard, Suite 200
Lanham, MD 20706

PO Box 317
Oxford
OX2 9RU, UK

British Library Cataloguing in Publication Information Available

Library of Congress Cataloging-in-Publication Data

Tolerance in the twenty-first century : prospects and challenges / edited by Gerson
Moreno-Riaño.
    p. cm.
  Includes bibliographical references.
  ISBN-13: 978-0-7391-0868-0 (cloth : alk. paper)
  ISBN-10: 0-7391-0868-9 (cloth : alk. paper)
  1. Toleration. 2. Civil rights. 3. Political psychology. I. Moreno-Riaño, Gerson, 1971- .
II. Title.
HM1271.T65 2006
303.3'8500905--dc22   2005035215

Printed in the United States of America

♾™ The paper used in this publication meets the minimum requirements of American
National Standard for Information Sciences—Permanence of Paper for Printed Library
Materials, ANSI/NISO Z39.48–1992.

In memoriam

David Resnick

and for

Kathy and Nathan

Amicitiae nostrae memoriam spero sempiternam fore

- Cicero

Contents

Acknowledgements

The success of any scholarly endeavor depends on a substantial degree of collaboration and cooperation with a variety of individuals. The present volume is no exception. The leading impetus behind this volume came through the mutual collaboration between my colleague and friend, David Resnick, and I. David passed away unexpectedly in 2002 leaving a deep void not only in the scholarly community but in the lives of all who loved and appreciated him. A brilliant intellectual and political theorist, David pursued an exciting research program in the areas of democratic theory, citizenship, and tolerance. His other chief intellectual interest was the writings of John Locke. But even beyond all of these, David's true love was learning and knowledge. For David, every subject was worthy of discussion and investigation. It is to David's life and memory that this volume is fondly dedicated.

Beyond acknowledging my debt to David, I would like to thank Kathy Resnick, David's wife and partner. In honor of David's life and memory, Kathy volunteered vast amounts of her time to complete the first stage of the copy-editing process of every contribution. Without Kathy's expert eye for detail, language, and orthography, this volume would have suffered. I should also like to thank my administrative assistant, Carla Gaines for her expert contribution in preparing the "camera-ready" copy of each contribution within this volume. Carla's expertise, thoroughness, and sound judgment facilitated a timely delivery of this manuscript to Lexington Books. Thanks are also due to Lexington Books and its editorial staff for their flexibility and understanding when various difficulties were encountered in the preparation of this volume.

In closing, I would like to thank two different groups of individuals- my colleagues and my family. First, thanks to James A. Stever who first pointed me in the direction of tolerance research and to Michael Margolis for his professional support through the years. Without the professional and intellectual encouragement of these two individuals, this project could not have been realized. Thanks also to all of the contributors to this volume, especially to Robert Weissberg who wrote his essay in honor of his friend David Resnick and to Henrik Syse for simply being the kind of friend for which any academic should wish. And lastly, thank you to my friend and partner Ellen whose constant love, support, patience, and unwavering encouragement have allowed me to fulfill so many dreams. And to my five wonderful children, Isaac, Victoria, Abraham, Emma, and Abigail—thank you for all of your love and wonderful ways of being. You make living life and being a father a wonderful and unique experience.

GERSON MORENO-RIAÑO
Springfield, Ohio

Tolerance in the Twenty-First Century: An Introduction

Gerson Moreno-Riaño

The concept of tolerance is a staple in current global political discourse. It is almost impossible to imagine a world in which discussions of politics and public policy would lack talk regarding the importance of tolerance. This, in part, is a testament of the success and flexibility of Liberalism in providing a political and maybe even civic virtue for the continually fluctuating global political milieu. It is also, however, a testament to the conflict-ridden and all too often ideologically incommensurable politics of our times. This tension between incommensurability and virtue, between potential conflict and civility is an essential and fruitful venue that is further explored later in this chapter.

The literature on the subject of tolerance, to say the least, is enormous and only a brief and attenuated survey can be offered here. Perhaps no contemporary theme enjoys the amount of popularity as this one. Popularity, though, is no sign of consensus. As some scholars noted toward the close of the twentieth century:

> Toleration is a central concept in modern political thought, and the practice of toleration is generally recognized as an essential constituent of a free society and a stable polity. Yet there is neither widespread agreement about toleration at the theoretical level, nor is there agreement about either the form or the amount of toleration which should be practiced. . . It would be widely agreed that some toleration is a necessary feature of a good society; but agreement often goes no further. The meaning, grounds and limits of toleration are all to some extent matters of both ideological and practical dispute.[1]

In spite of the lack of agreement, the popularity of tolerance continues well into the twenty-first century. In the last five years, some of the most heated political, social, and religious issues have been framed in regards to the lack of tolerance (intolerance) or the need for tolerance. Whether it is the selection of a new pope for the Roman Catholic church, or the Western understanding of Islam, or the war in Afghanistan and Iraq, or discussions regarding immigration and political ads in Canada, or whether it is conversations regarding primitive versus modern understandings of religion, or collegiate education at military institutions, or theatre performances in Russia, or even sporting events; tolerance or the lack thereof dominates the current socio-political dialogue and exchange of ideas.[2]

The prevalence of tolerance in political discourse is not new. Since the eighteenth century and certainly before, tolerance was central to discussions and debates over religion and conscience. But it was twentieth century social science that spurred an enormous research literature investigating the attitudinal and behavioral structure of tolerance as well as the existence of tolerance amidst various publics and democracies. Perhaps the most important and seminal work in this literature was Samuel Stouffer's *Communism, Conformity, and Civil Liberties*,[3] a work that became the standard bearer for toleration research for almost thirty years. However, long before Stouffer, polls had been conducted in the United States and abroad gauging the toleration of publics on a host of issues from advertising to movies, from communism to the Ku Klux Klan, and beyond. The early years of toleration research spanned a period of over a decade. Polls were conducted on over thirty different topics in an effort to ascertain the public's tolerance or intolerance toward various social issues.[4] Most of these inquiries were driven more by the changing times than by any systematic theory on the subject. While some questions gauged the acceptance of controversial behaviors, others measured everything from support of government intolerance, belief in freedom, and regulation of prostitution. Most of the questions were rudimentary attempts to try to explain a concept that had not yet captured the imagination of social scientists.

Stouffer's work, however, changed this lack of focus. The context for his undertaking was what Stouffer called the "communist threat" or the belief that a communist conspiracy existed both inside and outside of the United States. Consequently, Stouffer was interested in analyzing the extent to which the civil liberties of citizens would be sacrificed in order to prevent the communist advance. Specifically, Stouffer focused on latent individual attitudes and dispositions toward certain types of non-conformists within, as he argued, "the broad context of the communist threat."[5] Stouffer was not interested in behavior nor did he claim that his study assessed this important variable. Rather, he focused on an individual's willingness to extend constitutional rights to social "deviants," on their readiness to limit or restrict other's civil rights.

Beyond the important findings and theories Stouffer's work facilitated, Stouffer's enduring contribution to tolerance research is his conceptualization of tolerance as one's willingness to extend the democratic values of civil rights and liberties to social non-conformists. In much if not all of the research that followed Stouffer, most scholars conceptualized tolerance in politics in terms of a democratic creed of civil rights and liberties and sought to update, refine, and extend Stouffer's work.[6] The centrality of tolerance to democratic theory and polities is well-attested in the literature. As scholars on the subject note:

> The more tolerant citizens are of the rights of others, the more secure the rights of all, their own included; hence the special place of political tolerance in contemporary conceptions of democratic values and democratic citizenship.[7]

While Stouffer's methods implemented this conceptualization of tolerance and continue to be used, other approaches to measuring tolerance arose that continued to view tolerance as a democratic value yet began to challenge Stouffer's methodology and findings. Such approaches began with the Sullivan "least-liked" approach,[8] a rival competing model to Stouffer's, and explored tolerance in a comparative context as well as in connection to other targets of tolerance or intolerance not only leftist groups.

Beyond methodological differences and democratic creeds, tolerance research at the end of the twentieth century also exemplified the search for causes that would yield accurate explanations of and predictions about the *reasons* as to why individuals and polities were tolerant or intolerant. Stouffer had first discovered that a positive relationship existed between education and tolerance—something which continues to be validated in contemporary scholarship. Research also demonstrated that other demographic characteristics such as age, religion, income, and gender were important indicators of one's level of tolerance or its opposite. But was there more? Were there other more "essential" or "enduring" characteristics that could offer better or more robust explanations? A partial answer was provided through a linkage between psychological characteristics, contextual factors, and tolerance levels. Sullivan began this trend and it flourished in *With Malice Toward Some: How People Make Civil Liberties Judgments*.[9] Other contextual factors such as information and socialization along with cognitive sophistication were investigated and yielded important findings regarding the possibilities of educating or not toward tolerance.

As we enter the twenty-first century, it is important to assess contemporary tolerance scholarship both with an eye to the past and to the future. In regards to the past, beyond the very cursory review offered here, Finkel *et al.* suggest that much progress has been accomplished in understanding "the levels and sources of political tolerance and support for democratic values in the mass public."[10] This progress is indebted not only to Stouffer's work and its many extensions but also to various new approaches and methodologies for measuring tolerance and democratic values in the public. Nevertheless, as Finkel *et al.* point out, Stouffer's work as well as the reassessments it engendered left many problems unresolved. These can be summarized as the following:

1. Ignorance regarding the overall structure of democratic values in various polities;
2. Ignorance regarding the stability of democratic attitudes;
3. Ignorance regarding the effects of tolerance upon individuals, cultures, and public policies.

The issues which Finkel *et al.* raise provide an important point of departure for this volume's assessment not only of past and current tolerance research but also for future directions of research into this important subject. In light of this, the present volume has compiled a group of scholars to address not only the promises and limits of tolerance as suggested by previous research but also to consider new areas and initiatives as we move forward in an era of what appears to be increasing conflict as well as democratization. This team of scholars had the unique and difficult task of investigating tolerance within their unique fields of research while at the same time being sensitive to previous work (or the lack thereof) connecting tolerance to their area of inquiry. Some have written extensively in this area while others bring unique and fresh perspectives to develop further our understanding of and applicability of this chief Liberal virtue for the years ahead.

The categories which Finkel *et al.* propose conceptualize tolerance in terms of democratic norms and attitudes. This is of no surprise given the history of research in the subject. And many of the essays in this volume continue this trend through important investigations regarding the comparative nature, structure, stability, and effects of tolerance upon societies and individuals alike. Nevertheless, it may be problematic to conceptualize tolerance solely as a democratic norm since doing so may have given rise to an explosion and perhaps even overpopulation of empirical studies relying on surveys and statistical methodologies. Robert Weissberg, both in his contribution to this volume and elsewhere, has criticized this research trend as providing findings that are highly static as well as offering a portrait of individuals and polities that is at best incomplete and at worst fictional.

Even if one does not accept Weissberg's conclusions regarding the effects of empirical studies upon tolerance research, the empirical framework, with its concentration upon democratic norms, has often clouded other important questions and complexities that underlie questions of tolerance. There is no doubt that empirical studies have yielded much valuable information. But some very important concerns remain to be addressed. The remaining pages of this introduction present some of these concerns in terms of the *challenges* and the *prospects* of tolerance in the century to come.

Beyond the dilemmas raised by Finkel *et al.*, one of the most daunting tasks as we enter a new century and a very different world is that which regards the moral status of tolerance or the question as to whether or not tolerance is a virtue.[11] It is certainly the case that this also raises the question of the moral status of democracy. But both issues should to some degree remain separate. Democratic polities both in developed and under developed countries do not face the same struggles as do polities in which democracy is new, recent, or just introduced. Democratic polities assume democracy as a *sine quo non* of development and therefore do not question the validity or legitimacy of democracy as a principle of government or way of life. For such societies, the deeper struggle is the continual extension of democratic norms amidst social and political pressures to the contrary. Thus, the struggle is to *tolerate or not to tolerate* specific targets not whether or not tolerance is itself a good. In non-democratic societies or newly democratized polities, the struggle is more foundational. In these contexts, the struggle is to reject the entire democratic way of government and life. Tolerance is still an aspect of the problem but the problem is much more comprehensive in scope.

Regardless of the scope of the problem in question, both scenarios present a variety of social and political pressures that reject tolerance or question its value. This rejection is a complicated matter and thus presents a serious challenge to any attempt at the extension of democratic norms or democratic geopolitical reform. Six essays in this volume consider the challenge which the moral status of tolerance presents. Robert Weissberg's essay "The Many Facets of Tolerance," also the volume's starting point, augments his critique of tolerance research which he first published in *Political Tolerance: Balancing Community and Diversity*.[12] Through a critical discussion of the complicated nature of tolerance, Weissberg argues that the current popular consensus regarding the meaning and application of tolerance clouds its complexity and disallows one from arriving at a correct and comprehensive understanding of this concept. To substantiate this claim, Weissberg describes three different understandings of tolerance: historical/theoretical, empirical social scientific (hereafter "empirical"), and social reformist. As suggested earlier, Weissberg holds the empirical approach as characterized by its exclusive focus on individual attitudes, civil liberties, extremists, and its over-reliance on surveys as tools of measurement. Weissberg's criticisms of this approach exemplify some of the classic concerns with quantitative approaches to the study of social problems, namely, the production of highly static, or partial, or artificial results (and in some cases all of these!).

Given the empirical approach's conceptualization of tolerance as support for civil liberties and democratic norms, the rise of what Weissberg terms a "good hearted effort at social reform" is almost a given. It should be noted here that a subtle shift had occurred from the empirical to the reformist understandings of tolerance. The empirical understanding suggested that tolerance constituted respect for democratic norms not a respect for the extremist's views as the object of tolerance. The reformist conceptualization of tolerance, according to Weissberg, blurs the distinction between tolerance as respect for civil liberties and tolerance as respect for those things which civil liberties allow no matter how repugnant. The reformist approach understands tolerance as "appreciation" and a "welcoming" and even "valuing" not only of democratic norms but of the differences which democratic norms seek to protect. This approach is best embodied within a variety of educational and political initiatives and, to some degree, within experimental studies of tolerance and its relation to cognition.

Weissberg's third category (treated first in his contribution to this volume) is what he terms the historical-theoretical. It is within this approach that Weissberg considers the most accurate and instructive understanding of tolerance to reside. Weissberg's contention is that the other two understandings of tolerance consider it as either a global civic virtue and as an important moral trait to acquire and maintain. The historical-theoretical approach holds tolerance to be a political strategy to deal with various types of conflict.[13] As such, tolerance is limited and problem-specific not moral and universal and, one can surmise, it need not be equated with democratic norms and reform.

Following Weissberg, Nick Notion and Jay Budzizsewski undertake two central problems regarding the moral status of tolerance. Fotion considers the meaning of tolerance within the varieties of moral experience. Just what is it that those who ask for tolerance really seek? According to Fotion, tolerance as a moral concept suffers from a semantic vagueness and ambiguity that leads to a misuse and misapplication of the term in social and political discussions. Budziszewski's contribution, modified for this volume, is an excerpt of his *True Tolerance: Liberalism and the necessity of judgment*.[14] Budziszewski offers a spirited critique of an integral part of contemporary understandings of tolerance, namely, that of moral neutrality. For Budziszewski, not only is it morally unrealistic to be ethically neutral, it is not even desirable given the terrible consequences that arise. As Martin Niemoller reminds us:

> First they came for the Communists, and I didn't speak up, because I wasn't a Communist.
> Then they came for the Jews, and I didn't speak up, because I wasn't a Jew.
> Then they came for the Catholics, and I didn't speak up, because I was a Protestant.
> Then they came for me, and by that time there was no one left to speak up for me.[15]

Budziszewski's other concern is also to defend a classical account of tolerance. Similar to Weissberg's historical-theoretical category, Budziszewski also regards tolerance as being limited (one cannot tolerate everything) due to its moral foundation within a distinct and rich Christian tradition. For Budziszewski, then, tolerance correctly understood is deeply moral and circumscribed. Contemporary conceptions of tolerance lack this moral grounding and thus allow society to exist without any moral anchor.

The next two essays assessing the problems surrounding the moral status of tolerance assess the relationship between tolerance, identity, and Liberalism. Both Robert Cummins Neville and Gerson Moreno Riaño investigate these issues from different vantage points. Neville suggests that political tolerance is a democratic requirement that is very much bound up with states and their national identity. Through a comparative analysis of contemporary religions and politics, Neville suggests that the difficulty of tolerance and democratic reforms to take root in various societies, particularly Muslim societies, is due very much in part to the fact that "there is no *body politic* in the Muslim world within which political tolerance of the Euro-American sort fits as an accommodating ideal." For Neville, the deep problem is that of religious identity and how this affects the creation of a body-politic that can sustain moral and political life. Moreno-

Riaño suggests that tolerance, in so far as it is a part of a comprehensive Liberal worldview, is not morally acceptable to individuals from different cultures or worldviews. Tolerance as such is a cultural value and not a moral virtue of universal import. Non-liberal cultures and individuals cannot and do not give their moral assent to tolerance as a principle of Liberal morality. While they may consent to it on non-moral grounds, this consent is at best thin, volatile, and uncertain presenting deep problems for issues of political obligation and citizenship.

Michal Shamir's essay provides some empirical footing to the arguments which Neville and Moreno-Riaño advance. One of the core issues for both of the former is the notion of identity or the self. Tolerance, as these authors suggest, always raises issues of moral and cultural identity. Shamir's essay explores this claim through an empirical assessment of public opinion in Israel. In particular, Shamir's concern is a consideration of the role of threat and conflict as antecedents of intolerance within the most recent intifada. Following Sullivan's "least-liked" method, Shamir further validates the claim that conflict and threat give rise to intolerance. But she goes further to show that the underlying reason for this is the fact that conflict makes one's group identity or "in-group love" more salient and pronounced along with one's "out-group hate." As Shamir points out, this is a conditional and contextual relationship and it is not as constant as one may think. Shamir's work goes a long way to demonstrate the dynamics of intolerance and collective identity and to substantiate the importance of culture and morality in discussions and attempts at political reform.

The challenges which these essays pose regarding the moral status of tolerance should be given serious consideration within any public policy or democratic initiative seeking to reform the sociopolitical fabric of any society. If the moral status of tolerance is ambiguous and vague on account of the varieties of moral experience, worldviews, culture, identity, religion, and historical context, then prescriptions of tolerance and democracy cannot be considered a one-size fits all garment. And, in spite of any suggestion for improvement which the authors may propose, solving these dilemmas may be extremely difficult given the intimately rooted nature of morality, identities, and worldviews.

If the moral challenges facing tolerance initiatives are as difficult as just seen, the prospects for greater understanding, reform, and implementation may be just as encouraging. Ewa Golebiowska leads this section with an insightful and penetrating analysis of the gender gap in tolerance. Beginning with Stouffer and in most studies that followed, significant differences in tolerance levels (i.e., endorsement of civil rights for non-conformists) were found between males and females. The difficulty, as Golebiowska points out in her essay, is that different measures of tolerance have been used with little or no integration of methodological measures or findings. In spite of the different measures and the troubling issues these may raise, Golebiowska suggests that all of these measures are still tapping a more general dimension of tolerance leading to the conclusion that women are still more intolerant than males regardless of the operationalization in question. But Golebiowska does not end her investigation at this point. Through her analysis, she points out that the traditional indicators of tolerance (e.g., education, income) provide a more significant explanation of gender differences in tolerance than gender alone. Golebiowska's analysis helps to clarify one of the most troubling issues in twentieth century tolerance studies and provides the needed empirical impetus not only to clarify the relationship between gender and tolerance but to continue sociopolitical reform in the area of gender equality.

Sociopolitical reform is indeed the topic of consideration for both Patricia Avery and Steve Finkel. For both Avery and Finkel, tolerance is essentially cognitive and thus can be implemented via educational initiatives. Avery's essay considers these initiatives within the United States and, in particular, amidst the pre-collegiate student population. Given the rapid social diversification within this population, educational initiatives that foster appropriate curricula and critical discussion may be tremendously effective both in assisting students to orient themselves toward questions of tolerance and in helping them to apply abstract democratic norms to concrete life situations. Finkel's work examines the effect of adult civic education programs in two developing democracies, the Dominican Republic and South Africa, on the core democratic value of political tolerance. Developing hypotheses about the effects of civic education on tolerance from theories of political culture and democratization, Finkel uses survey data collected on participants in numerous civic education programs as well as control groups in both countries to show that civic education has small but significant effects on tolerance in both South Africa and the Dominican Republic; that the results hold after controlling for other sources of tolerance, as well as for potential biases related to the individual's self-selection into the programs; and that the effects are largely conditional in nature, dependent on the frequency of the civic education "treatment," the individual's prior political dispositions, values, and store of political information. In doing so, Finkel goes a long way in addressing the very same concerns proposed in Finkel *et al.* since his work addresses the implications of civic education and tolerance initiatives for theories of the development of democratic political culture, for theories of attitude change and political persuasion, and for more practical considerations regarding the implementation of civic education programs in democratizing contexts in the future.

The last three essays in this volume present the very first attempts to extend investigations regarding tolerance into new directions. Henrik Syse offers a timely exploration into the relationship between a thick conceptualization of tolerance (i.e., a moral virtue and a political ideal) and the just war tradition. For Syse, since tolerance intimates the acceptance of difference and patience in confronting differences, it is an essential part of the restraint which just war theories have tried to impose on warfare since the time of Augustine. This conclusion is especially relevant in light of the global war on terror. Boettke and Leeson contribute an argument regarding the relationship and effects between tolerance and political economic arrangements. Given the concern which Finkel *et al.* raise regarding the consequences of tolerance upon individuals and societies, Boettke and Leeson argue that political tolerance is essential for robust political economic arrangements that foster the wellbeing of individuals and societies. Such robust arrangements are most in line with market Liberalism since it provides the needed context by which to accommodate multiple and competing ends in a manner that is consistent with the valuations of diverse individuals. The final paper is a posthumous contribution by David Resnick. Prior to David's untimely passing, he had focused his work on the intersections between the Internet and various issues of civic society, in particular, democracy and political tolerance. In this final paper, David considers what type of effect the Internet has upon tolerance or intolerance. To do so, he considers three traditional positions on this issue:

1. Tolerance/intolerance on the Internet mirrors everyday life;
2. The Internet will have an impact on tolerance/intolerance in everyday life;
3. The Internet must be affected to be more tolerant/intolerant through external forces beyond it.

David suggests that the Internet, as it regards issues of tolerance, is not as influential as some initially proposed. In fact, the Internet resembles to a high degree everyday life (position number one) and is more influenced by external factors than itself being an influential agent of political and democratic change.

In closing, it is important to note that a consideration of the *challenges* which tolerance presents is just as instructional as the *prospects* that have just been enumerated. Both should advance our understanding and sensitivity to a very complex concept both in terms of its operationalization, implementation, and its effects. The challenges which the moral status of tolerance raises in light of identity and cultures are extremely relevant given the twenty-first century's struggle with terrorism, genocide, ethnic cleansing, religious conflict, and culture wars. Much more work needs to be conducted in crafting a workable conception of tolerance that takes into account the diversity of cultures and identities as well as the limits of tolerance in light of moral evil. The traditional Liberal separation of political and metaphysical doctrines is no longer effective in cultures and communities that think the separation morally bankrupt. This area is difficult yet holds much promise. As educational initiatives suggest, tolerance can be taught and internalized given the appropriate pedagogical, social, and economic reforms. The solutions, however, must extend beyond academic papers and suggestions. Governments and policy influentials as well as every day citizens must give serious consideration to these challenges and to efforts at implementing the educational, economic, social, and moral prospects for reform. Only then can societies and nation-states acquire a more substantive tranquility of peace.

Notes

1. John Horton and Peter Nicholson, "Philosophy and the practice of toleration," in *Toleration: Philosophy and Practice*, ed. J. Horton and P. Nicholson (Aldershot, England: Avebury Press, 1992), 1.
2. This claim is illustrated in a sampling of news stories for the past three years. Consider, for example, T.R. Reid, "Air Force Removes Chaplain From Post; Officer Decried Evangelicals' Influence," *Washington Post*, 13 May 2005, sec. A, p. 4; David Kelly, "Academy to Get a Checkup on Tolerance; A task force will look into charges that evangelical Christian Air Force staff and cadets are unfair to those with other beliefs," *Los Angeles Times*, 4 May 2005, National Desk, sec. A, p. 14; Letter to *Buffalo News*, 8 May 2005, by Norm R. Allen Jr., Assistant Director, Council for Secular Humanism, Viewpoints Section, p. 15; Tara Dooley and Louis B. Parks, "Pope's outreach both symbolic, tactical; His successor will have to act on his vision, theologians say," *Houston Chronicle*, 11 April 2005, sec. A, p. 1; Arkady Ostrovsky, "Attacks on new Bolshoi opera revive Russia's memories of Stalinism: A rising tide of intolerance towards Russian artists is seen to be linked with a wider nationalistic trend," *The Financial Times*, 5 April 2005, Europe Section, p. 8; "Prime Minister: Reject extremism and intolerance," *New Straits Times* (Malaysia), 25 December 2004, p. 1; Pervez Musharraf, "A Plea for Enlightened Moderation; Muslims must raise themselves up through individual achievement and socioeconomic emancipation," *Washington Post*, 1 June 2004, Editorial A23; Sean Gordon, "Stereotypes stick to Conservatives: Liberals take advantage of mistakes. Tory fundraiser tells party to portray itself as moderate, open-minded and tolerant," *The Gazette* (Montreal, Quebec), 28 February 2004, News A12; Jack Aubry, "Immigrants less welcome here, poll shows: Canadian intolerance on the rise. Quebecers' reluctance to accept newcomers increases by 15 percentage points," *The Gazette* (Montreal, Quebec), 20 December 2003, News A4; and Graham Cornes, "Brave Zimbabwe players hold mirror to our own intolerance," *The Advertiser* (Australia), 15 February 2003, Sports p. 113.
3. Samuel Stouffer, *Communism, Conformity, and Civil Liberties* (New York: Double Day & Company, Inc., 1955)
4. This data can be found in Hadley Cantril, *Public Opinion, 1935-1946* (Princeton: Princeton University Press, 1951)
5. Stouffer, *Communism*, 54.
6. For an excellent review of the literature that addresses this question as well as the various methodologies used to investigate tolerance see Steven E. Finkel, Lee Sigelman, and Stan Humphries, "Democratic Values and Political Tolerance," in *Measures of Political Attitudes*, ed. John P. Robinson, Phillip R. Shaver, and Lawrence S. Wrightsman (San Diego: Academic Press, 1999), 203-96. Other important works exemplifying this claim are, for example, James W. Prothro and Charles W. Grigg, "Fundamental Principles of Democracy: Bases of Agreement and Disagreement," *Journal of Politics* 22 (1960): 276-94; Herbert McClosky, "Consensus and Ideology in American Politics," *American Political Science Review* 58 (1964): 361-82; Herbert McClosky and Alida Brill, *Dimensions of Tolerance: What Americans Believe about Civil Liberties* (New York: Russell Sage Foundation, 1983); Herbert McClosky, Paul J. Hoffman, and Rosemary O'Hara, "Issue Conflict and Consensus Among Party Leaders and Followers," *American Political Science Review* 54 (1960): 406-27; Herbert McClosky and John Zaller, *The American Ethos: Public Attitudes Toward Capitalism and Democracy* (Cambridge: Harvard University Press, 1984); Clyde Z. Nunn, Harry J. Crockett, Jr., and J. Allen Williams, Jr., *Tolerance for Nonconformity* (San Francisco: Jossey-Bass Publishers, 1978); and John L. Sullivan,

James Piereson, and George E. Marcus, *Political Tolerance and American Democracy* (Chicago: University of Chicago Press, 1982).

7. See P. M. Sniderman, et al., "Principled Tolerance and the American Mass Public," *British Journal of Political Science* 19 (1989): 25-45.

8. See Sullivan, Piereson, and Marcus, *Political Tolerance*. For an excellent comparative methodological discussion of both Stouffer and Sullivan see James L. Gibson, "Alternative Measures of Political Tolerance: Must Tolerance Be 'Least-Liked'?" *American Journal of Political Science* 36, no. 2 (1992): 560-77.

9. George E. Marcus, et al., *With Malice Toward Some: How People Make Civil Liberties Judgments* (Cambridge: Cambridge University Press, 1995). Other works were solely rooted in psychological "essentialist" theories. Consider, for example, Stephen D. Johnson, "Model of Factors Related to Tendencies to Discriminate Against People with Aids," *Psychological Reports* 76 (1995): 563-72; Eugene Hightower, "Psychosocial Characteristics of Subtle and Blatant Racists as Compared to Tolerant Individuals," *Journal of Clinical Psychology* 53, no. 4 (1997): 369-74; Karen Bird, et al., "Not Just Lip-Synching Anymore: Education and Tolerance Revisited," *The Review of Education/Pedagogy/Cultural Studies* 16 (1994): 373-86. For a critique of "essentialist" theories of tolerance see G. Moreno-Riano, *Political Tolerance, Culture, and the Individual* (Lewiston, N. Y.: The Edwin Mellen Press, 2002).

10. Finkel, Sigelman, and Humphries, "Democratic Values," 224.

11. On this point, see, for example, David Heyd, *Tolerance: An Elusive Virtue* (Princeton: Princeton University Press, 1997).

12. Robert Weissberg, *Political Tolerance* (Newbury Park, Calif.: Sage, 1998).

13. For an important example, see Andrew Murphy, *Conscience and Community: Revisiting toleration and religious dissent in early modern England and America* (University Park: Pennsylvania State University Press, 2001).

14. Jay Budziszewski, *True Tolerance: Liberalism and the necessity of judgment* (New Brunswick, N. J.: Transaction Publishers, 1992). Copyright permission granted to the author by Transaction Publishers.

15. This quote is attributed to the Lutheran pastor Martin Niemöeller (1892-1984), who spent eight years in Sachenhausen and Dachau concentration camps. Leo Strauss makes a similar argument regarding the unrealistic expectations of moral neutrality as proposed by logical positivism within the social sciences. See Leo Strauss, *What is Political Philosophy and Other Studies* (Chicago: The University of Chicago Press, 1988).

The Many Facets of Tolerance
Robert Weissberg

Few virtues have recently drawn as much celebratory attention as tolerance. Ryszard Legutko once astutely remarked, "the triumph of liberalism has elevated this category [toleration] into the ultimate and almost the only generally accepted litmus test for morality."[1] He added that, "the basic value of the modern pluralist democracy is tolerance." Legutko's remarks did not exaggerate, and this infatuation is neither gratuitous nor confined to the political spectrum's left. Everybody, save a handful of voice-in-the-wilderness academic critics (e.g. Marcuse[2]) or some marginal religious zealots, now covets this virtue. Recall that post-9/11 President George W. Bush fervently and repeatedly appealed for tolerance toward Moslems despite irrefutable evidence that this terrorist attack was provoked by a widespread, often state-sanctioned militant Islam. Imagine Franklin Roosevelt exhorting Americans to display forbearance for Japanese and their peaceful culture post December 7, 1941. We have changed.

Today's upbeat calls for tolerance suggest a consensus, or at least substantial agreement, on what this lofty aim implies. This accord is an illusion that collapses once we proceed beyond glib generalities. Advocates are rarely quizzed about what, exactly, does this *tolerance* mean, nor do these champions feel obliged to differentiate one strain from others. No respectable person publicly opposes heightened tolerance as if present-day levels were woefully inadequate. Even *intolerance* has been generally excommunicated from the common vocabulary, replaced by the seemingly less offensive *zero tolerance*. Achieving ever more tolerance is apparently our new crusade with the Promised Land just about within reach—provided we all make the commitment. Alas, today's pursuit might be more accurately characterized as a helter-skelter enterprise rife with paradoxes pleasantly masked by noble intentions.

To appreciate this uncertain condition, enter *tolerance* and then *toleration*, as I did, into the web search engine, Google. Both exercises predictably elicited hundreds of hits. Nevertheless, and somewhat surprisingly, almost zero overlap existed between these first-cousin concepts.[3] Further, scanning empirical social science citations reveals an almost total ignorance of a rich historical-theoretical literature. Meanwhile, tolerance preoccupied educators—a progressively influential industry—are oblivious to either traditional usage or modern social sci

13

ence inquiry. More than myopic, neglectful scholarship or the technical vagaries of computerized search engines are involved here. We ourselves often slothfully embrace dimly understood ideas whose glittering character often hides pernicious though well-disguised ideological agendas.

Tolerance, correctly grasped, is a wonderful aspect of civic life. This essay argues that today's vacuous tolerance can be haphazardly employed, sometimes for especially perilous uses. It reviews three relevant literatures—historical/ theoretical, social science empirical, and educational—while paying particular attention to diverse conceptualizations, requisite levels, and efficient promotion. The conclusion offers some dire warnings about mindlessly rushing to be ever more tolerant.

The Classical Understanding

A useful starting point is historical usage of the word *tolerance*, a huge, sprawling literature beginning with Milton and Locke through J. S. Mill to modern academics such as T.M. Scanlon and J. Budziszewski.[4] For lack of a better term, this might be labeled the *classical* version. Given centuries of invocation in myriad circumstances, let alone half-hidden political agendas, notable differences of shading and vocabulary inevitably abound. Divergences aside, however, a common (if loose) denotation is readily apparent. The *Oxford English Dictionary* (second edition) ably encapsulates this classic meaning: "The action or practice of tolerating; toleration; the disposition to be patient with or indulgent to the opinions or practices of others; freedom from bigotry or undue severity in judging the conduct of others; forbearance; catholicity of spirit.

This terse definition is a useful beginning, but certain addenda— implied "baggage"—require articulation if the term is to be applied compatibly with its historical roots. Without these sometimes unstated elements, tolerance could simplistically be misinterpreted to mean permitting everything, a bizarre connotation (must one tolerate criminality?) and one inadequate to explore complicated terrain.

The Standard Baggage

What, then, is this vital intellectual baggage that elevates the concept of tolerance above some nebulous plea for greater understanding? Certain themes are indisputable. Most importantly, one can only be tolerant of what one finds objectionable, an implication consistent with the term's Latin roots—*tolerare* or *tolerantia*—meaning to forbear. Bernard Crick put this element forcefully with, "the degree to which we accept things of which we disapprove."[5] This *OED II* definition implies this component of forbearance, but it lies just below the surface and might easily go unnoticed. One must not be unduly severe about the detested but one can still judge harshly. It is this negative element that informs everyday expressions like, "I can put up with (tolerate) lots of pain." A masochist, on the other hand, might relish the hurt, so applying *tolerate* to his or her suffering would be inappropriate. In the political realm, a communist party member is incapable of tolerating the Communist Party, but he or she might be judged tolerant if forbearing a disliked Capitalist Boss Party.

Introducing loathsomeness makes being tolerant an inescapably judgmental enterprise. One must now discriminate among many bad things, some of which are insufferably horrid while others are still nefarious, but bearable. Endless shades of grays must be labeled. As Budziszewski correctly observes, being tolerant is not the suspension of judgment, but it's very opposite.[6] A concrete example might be distinguishing pedophilia from medically risky homosexual intercourse as candidates for criminal sanctions. Is the latter tolerable? In this case, being nonjudgmental is *not* displaying tolerance, though some might insist that this flight from a verdict is the concept's quintessential ingredient. Similarly, today's multiculturalism, which is customarily interpreted as appreciating diverse cultures, is not tolerance unless these assessed cultures are considered flawed.

A capacity to render fine distinctions has major, though often under-appreciated, implications for achieving this classic virtue. Given that satisfactory cognitive capacity (somehow established) cannot be postulated as universal, who, then, can actually exercise this judgment? Children, the mentally feeble, the drug and alcohol impaired, the senile, and others with diminished reasoning may thus be excused from being tolerant in the sense that thoughtful gradations are beyond them.[7] More troublesome are people whose habits of mind, border-line retardation, insufficient schooling, and comparable defects can superficially render distinctions, but whose outcome might be classified as simpleminded or foolish.

Going further down this path might bring us to issues of personal autonomy—should those beholden to others be heeded when dispensing judgments? What if, for example, college professors demanded that, to pass the course, their students display tolerance toward African Americans, and these obedient pupils complied? Does dependency or coercion disqualify the outcome as authentic? Pushed to the extreme, what if tolerance was legally required, and harsh sanctions awaited miscreants? Can we classify this gun-to-the-head version as the genuine article? These are thorny issues that reappear as we consider the nature of forbearance.

Modern scholars offering easy cases flee from the travails of reasoned judgment. Consider, for example, the current academic infatuation with tolerating homosexuality. Exactly how far might one be expected to go? Tolerate an individual's sexuality identity? Suffer their openly gay lifestyle? Are selected non-risky homosexual acts to be tolerated? Should this forbearance be extended to potentially lethal unprotected anal intercourse among consenting adults? Do we draw the line with illegal homosexual behavior whose medical costs potentially burden taxpayers? It is in these devilish details, not in some abstract global sentiment, that tolerance for homosexuality is decided. To thus insist that homosexuality be tolerated is akin to saying that people should suffer contemptible views. Such vacuous pronouncements achieve nothing other than, perhaps, to gain some high moral ground on the cheap.

The classic understanding of tolerance is also inherently fluid. A changing world means that judgments have a short shelf life and require continual adjustment. Interpretations of tolerance will necessarily reflect age, experience, education, and anything else influencing views. An adolescent might find capitalism insufferable but with greater maturity realize that capitalists are not so bad given their eventual contribution to building socialism. Conceivably, in middle age this former radical might embrace capitalism, thus, rendering the issue of tolerance irrelevant. Recall that Locke once denied toleration to Roman Catholics since he believed them subversive Papist agents, a preposterous assertion today.

Mutability acknowledged, if greater tolerance is the aim, it is incomplete to focus only on bestowing or withholding judgment. Tolerance proponents often assume that it is the harsh judgments of the intolerant that require defense. It is, however, certainly fair to scrutinize the loathed to assess whether disdain can be reasonably escaped. Certainly, little prevented Catholics in Locke's day from swearing allegiance to England. During the 1940s and 50s American socialists paid the admission price by cooperating with government in rooting out trade union Communism. If the intolerant can change, objects of this disaffection also can compromise.[8]

To insist that classification is immutable contravenes the spirit of tolerance. And since people everywhere face varying circumstances, conclusions are inevitably provincial, even eccentric. To aver that homosexuals should be tolerated as a civic principle presupposes that homosexuality is permanently static. Not only is such an assertion factually inaccurate, but matters could quickly change. The advent of AIDS, for example, meant that once purely private homosexual behavior could now turn deadly, so certain homosexual acts heretofore tolerated may now be deemed intolerable. The quantity of loathsomeness is also relevant. A scattering of Bierstube anti-Semitic rowdies is one thing; groundswells of officially sanctioned anti-Semites is something else.

Teaching people to be tolerant—to move not-too-dissimilar things from one category to another as complicated circumstances shift—is thus instruction in discrimination. The opposite—teaching intolerance—is equally true. This does not preclude moral instruction, even of absolutes, but such education would be incomplete without the skills necessary to judge tough situations. In terms of today's pedagogical vocabulary, a notable irony now exists: banning *discrimination* in the sense of possessing a capacity to craft fine distinctions renders this mode of tolerance impossible.

When all is said and done, a three-category classification framework emerges. The first consists of totally unacceptable phenomena, the intolerable (e.g., genocide, at least for most people). At the other extreme is the third category, the unqualified laudable. These are the evaluations undeserving of the *tol-*

erated label since nothing can be judged reprehensible. In-between are those entities that are both disliked and accepted, that is, the tolerated.

This classic tripartite classification is by no means universal. Contemporary educators in particular generally favor a two-fold classification in which the middle category, the very heart of classic tolerance, is eliminated. Everything is just a matter of like and dislike, with the former equated to tolerance. Obviously, this *like* cannot be regarded as satisfying the traditional understanding of tolerance since the negative assessment is lacking, and without this ingredient, forbearance is inconceivable. To be fair, nothing outlaws such wordplay, and such connotation shifts are often innocently spontaneous, but it does sow immense conceptual confusion and can produce, as we shall argue, mischievous practical application. In this updated view, to be tolerant of, say, homosexuals, means to expel any lingering homophobia and value homosexuality. To retreat to the centuries old attitude and say, "I abhor gays but we have to put up with them" offers a viewpoint now judged as intolerance. One might speculate that professional pedagogues inclined to this stance are so obsessed with expunging (selected) repugnance no matter how qualified and levelheaded, that disparagement is to be punished by withdrawing the prized tolerance label.

The traditional three-fold framework profoundly differs in its pedagogical implications from a simpler two-category scheme. To instill suffering the disagreeable seldom requires much exertion. Acquiescing to unappealing circumstances is a common human adaptation, and the species would barely have survived without it. Laws or economic incentives regularly accomplish this objective cheaply and unobtrusively. Southern whites in the post civil rights era quickly learned that one did not have to love African Americans, but if they physically attacked blacks, they risked incarceration. One just learned to live with blacks seated nearby at integrated lunch counters. And serving blacks might be good for business—a customer is a customer. By contrast, imposing a newfound appreciation of the once abhorred may be painful and chancy. It also risks being counter-productive by engendering resentment to the point of fermenting even greater hatred toward the tolerated.

Indeed, compared to today's clamor, the more old-fashioned version of tolerance is remarkably generous in permitting cut-rate entrance into a not-very-exclusive club. Turning a blind eye toward one's enemies—not loving them—fully qualifies. As the philosopher John Gray points out, this venerable conception embodies a pessimistic view of human nature.[9] Odium is built into our DNA, and short of brainwashing, cannot be purged regardless of all the efforts by the King's (and Queen's) most able facilitators. At most, coercion can create a hypocritical façade since no one knows what really lurks beneath some public expression. The infatuation of today's Left with refurbishing human nature to construct some everybody-loves-everybody utopia spurns this realistic embrace of human incorrigibility.

Less obvious in this intellectual baggage, but especially pertinent for calibration is what might be deemed the opportunity for actual choice.[10] To be sure, this element is by no means uniformly accepted but to include judgments on limitless, possibly hypothetical menus renders the quest utopian.[11] What if somebody asserted that they were exceptionally tolerant since they put up with such varied despicable creatures as Martians, ghosts, devils, and Rosacrusians but, nevertheless, believed that Catholics should be immolated? This assertion is less a matter of some grand philosophical principle than rendering the enterprise manageable. This narrower view of tolerance also rejects such inventions of modern social science as an enduring intolerant personality apart from any overt act in favor of acting (or believing) intolerantly concretely since it is unclear whether an "intolerant personality" will actually enjoy the opportunity to express this disposition. This may occur, but it cannot be assumed since this alleged pathological type might be a hermit and thus be unable to practice hatefulness.

Rendering a judgment further presupposes that the loathsome element is recognized. An anti-Communist police chief considering a parade permit request from the Communist Party must realize that the organization calling itself Citizens Against War is, indeed, a Communist front despite its innocuous name. If the chief erroneously believes them to be Quakers, or was misled by petitioners, then his parade permit approval would not strictly qualify as tolerance since he or she was not putting up with Communists. Of course, the opposite could happen—the Chief mistakenly assumes that this organization is Communist controlled when it is not, and still awards the permit. The upshot, then, is that the Police Chief congratulates himself on being tolerant when he is objectively not, assuming that he appreciates the Quakers.

This awareness provision can easily play havoc with the concept of tolerance given the possibilities for obliviousness or misrepresentation. People can easily tolerate gays if ignorant of their sexual proclivity while, conversely, showing ill-will to a dark-skinned South Asian in the mistaken view that this person is a reviled African American. Is the latter intolerant of blacks if he or she does not actually display this antipathy toward a bona fide African American? Further, many potentially reviled traits are not readily apparent or, if so, can be temporarily disguised. Orthodox Jews might avoid religious animosity by wearing baseball caps over their yarmulkes. Gays can act straight. Such "disguises" are a far cry from older societies where identities were to be displayed in public (e.g., the mandatory yellow star of ninth century Baghdad Jews).

A further useful addendum is that menu objects are consequential in the sense that choices go beyond personal peccadilloes and imply some collective risk.[12] Again, this element is not unvaryingly accepted among current devotees, but it does resonate with the concept's historical origins—it literally concerned life and death, not harmless personal eccentricities. To open up the debate to every personal predilection, like considering those things beyond personal contact, is a Pandora's Box guaranteeing a world awash in antagonism. By this measure, the average person is probably pathologically intolerant given all the loathed foods, music, clothing and whatnot. Only if such matters of taste spill over into the public realm might these dispositions become relevant to calibrating tolerance.[13]

Compared to today's generous exhortations in everything from personal relationships to every imaginable culture and ethnic group, "classical" appreciation is quite restricted. It rejects tolerance both as a global civic attribute divorced from concrete situations and as a permanent personal trait like having blue eyes. It offers a narrow (and periodically updated) reasoned disposition toward a tiny outcropping, namely those few significant public phenomena over which choice can be exercised. Critically, classic tolerance permits a wide range of reaction to repugnant objects short of embracing or repressing them. This appreciation of nuanced response is quite commendable in a society overflowing with the objectionable. Its aim is modest. According to this conception, the judgment that one can despise gays and mean them harm, but leave them alone, would qualify as tolerant. This understanding is also relatively simple to impose via traditional means such as legal sanctions, physical separation, or subterfuge without any invasive indoctrination or social engineering. No wonder it was so readily embraced to calm violent strife.

Uncertain Baggage

As a prudent and quite realistic recipe, this conception is outstanding. Nevertheless, the basic idea plus all the accompanying baggage (and we have only sampled this collection) are hardly a complete formula. No authoritative classic ideal can be found under controlled conditions at some mythical Bureau of Philosophical Standards. One uncertainty is what social scientists technically call the level of analysis problem. Specifically, what are the precise referents when we speak of this virtue? Individuals? Groups? Society? This is an analytical quandary akin to assessing violence—for example, Japanese are non-violent personally but Japan has had a history of national aggression. Mexico is the opposite—high levels of individual mayhem but a peaceful foreign policy.

This conceptual indeterminacy acknowledged, is a tolerant nation theoretically possible without intolerant people? One could also count up the incidence of tolerance and intolerance without regard to who committed these acts so, for example, society could be awash in enmity thanks to a few energetic bigots when nearly everyone else is exceedingly tolerant.[14] Early proponents, such as John Locke, seemed to emphasize conditions (atmospheres, a zeitgeist) that largely flowed from government or religious edicts apart from popular sentiment though the latter was scarcely irrelevant. In his 1733 *Letters Concerning the English Nation*, Voltaire spoke highly of the air of toleration on London's streets despite an Anglican church that occasionally stirred the passions of zealots. An ideology also can be said to be tolerant (or intolerant) apart from its supporters, as in the statement, "capitalism is generally tolerant" though one might find ample intolerant capitalists.

This multiplicity of levels recognized, on what basis should an assessment be rendered? Do we focus on individuals, or is the polity—a tolerant nation—most relevant? Michael Walzer, a leading writer on the subject, concentrates largely on group-related tolerance, but discussions elsewhere typically speak of tolerant individuals.[15] Might this judgment depend on pragmatic circumstance; might one tolerate the village Marxist but oppose a Communist state? Appraisals can be troublesome since what prevails at one level need not say much about it elsewhere. Individual preferences cannot be monotonically aggregated to assess collective traits. Multiple factors can disrupt this individual to collective property transmission (and vice versa). Influential elites may, for example, be especially tolerant (or intolerant) and impose their views on those below, an argument ("carriers of the creed") once offered to explain certain free-speech paradoxes in the US during the 1950s.[16] Conversely, a single dictator might inflict rigid orthodoxy against an unwilling populace. Something called "pluralistic intolerance" in which antipathy is rampant, but majorities cannot agree on who, precisely, is to be repressed is another possibility. Plausibly, one minuscule group wishes to outlaw communists, another sect seeks to expel Moslems, while a third handful wants to stifle Christian fundamentalists but the upshot is that all three hated groups survive since across-the-board repression is politically unworkable, a condition that might be labeled "intolerance gridlock".[17]

As Kymlicka carefully shows, today's infatuation with individualism obscures a long (and quite successful) history in which the group, not its specific members, constituted the analytical unit.[18] With its multitude of potentially warring religious sects, the Ottoman Empire avoided civil strife by permitting substantial group autonomy at the expense of individual free expression (a "federation of theocracies"). The Muslim Caliph would thus accept the Greek Orthodox Church, but individual followers enjoyed no particular freedom beyond what they were granted as Greek Orthodox adherents. Europe for centuries followed a similar approach—Protestantism might be officially allowed in France, but woe to the Protestant who challenged his or her church's authority. In both instances, then, religious tolerance meant the state permitting an organizational entity, not extending personal freedom to pursue religious aims willy-nilly. Would the Sultan or King of France be truthful if he said, "Yes, we practice religious tolerance"?

Failure to achieve consensus on just where this virtue of tolerance should reside can sow endless confusion when rendering verdicts. Consider just the geographical element in assessing "tolerance of American Communists" during the 1950s. National opinion poll data suggested pervasive personal repressive inclinations (e.g., most wanted communist teachers banned). These popular manifestations were also consistent with a general anti-communist atmosphere expressed in an alarmist mass media and frequent red baiting congressional hearings. Nevertheless, this situation was not true everywhere, at least measured by noticeable outcroppings. In several urban settings, particularly New York City, Communists had several visibly labeled organizations, routinely sold *The Daily Worker,* and occasionally sought public office without any obstacles. Was the US, not just New York City and a few other locales, tolerant of Communism? Or, did tolerance have to be ubiquitous for the US to qualify? Answers depend on where one looks, and reasonable answers can differ.

These myriad possibilities affect how tolerance might be best achieved. Gratuitous rhetoric about ordinary citizens' controlling democratic role aside, surely it is wasteful to insist that remedial training be made universal if ordinary students count for naught given elite domination. Effort should be more wisely invested to convince those closer to power. And if resistance or teacher ineptitude makes training utterly unpromising, perhaps one should heed Voltaire's sage observations when he remarked, "If there were only one religion in England, there would be a danger of tyranny; if there were two, they would cut each other's throats; but if there are thirty, and they live happily in peace."[19] This idea is also akin to Madison's defense of multiple factions to hinder any one from dominating. In other words, encourage proliferating factions or impose structural impediments to breed inertia, rather than seeking futile indoctrination.

Imposters?

A tolerance flourishing divorced from popular cravings might even be its most common variety. If so, this is certainly welcome news for today's frustrated educators bemoaning unheeded lessons. Perchance the abhorred flourish would be due to widespread indifference to anything beyond personal affairs. Potential despots are conceivably too distracted by earning money, family, sports, TV, and similar obsessions to even notice the despised. Indolence or alcohol/drug-induced stupor may further shield those who would otherwise be dispatched to the gulag. In this sense, the US military "solved" an awkward policy dilemma regarding homosexuals via officially enforcing ignorance of an undesired trait—the "don't ask, don't tell" policy which permitted gays to serve by making their sexuality administratively invisible. Forbearance might merely reflect cowardice—racial bigots are just too terrified to harass African Americans. Whether spontaneous or imposed, strict physical separation also may hinder contact, so an intolerance requisite—an opportunity to act—goes unsatisfied. Even if the hated are conveniently nearby or occasionally encountered, other values may prevail. The co-existence of the Israelis and the Palestinians is a familiar situation whereby bitter enemies routinely and civilly interact for economic gain.

The foregoing discussion brings to the fore a problem that might be called *defining the family tree*. That is, are things that sometimes resemble tolerance genuine relatives or merely concepts bearing an accidental family resemblance?[20] One particularly contentious relative who always seems to show up at family reunions but is often asked to leave is indifference. At least some contemporary purists soundly reject indifference from the tolerance pantheon.[21] As Fletcher put it, "Calling my hands-off attitude a matter of tolerance cheapens the virtue and arrogates too much power to myself."[22]

A second potential imposter might be fatalistic acceptance, or what Walzer calls "resigned acceptance."[23] What if somebody said, "I hate the obese, and wish to kill them, and I certainly could bump off a few, but the quest is hopeless since there are just too many, so I have put the matter out of my mind." Surely fatalism is endemic and may well explain most outward forbearance, but is this some legitimate relative on the family tree? Going yet further, might the mere existence of a loathed group, in and of itself, authoritatively certify permissiveness apart from the reasons for this survival?

These dilemmas are hardly trivial conceptually, but their practical resolution may be unreachable. This is largely employment for the philosophically inclined. The origins of beliefs are never self-evident. Probing the matter empirically requires assembling considerable and often difficult to obtain corroborating evidence. Modern surveys face formidable obstacles to rendering a verdict. Imagine a pollster asking if respondents actually knew a gay person, could possibly harm that individual, and whether or not they had done so, in order to calibrate true tolerance toward homosexuals? The pollster would then be obligated to ascertain the authentic motive for this forbearance—was it conscious or just laziness? Further, imagine all the obstacles to defining ambiguous terms like *harm* or verifying claims of obliviousness. A real world taxonomy regarding authentic varieties of tolerance versus pseudo types (e.g., what comes from obliviousness) may be technically impossible.

Is this pseudo versus authentic distinction largely semantic, a matter of curiosity only to the philosophically inclined? From the perspective of unpopular groups dreading suppression, it might be a distinction without a difference: popular permissiveness might be desired but its immediate achievement is secondary to survival. It matters little if this survival depends on popular lethargy or principled forbearance. Winning greater acquiescence may be relevant only if the loathed entity has evangelical ambitions among today's enemies. The same is true for nations on the verge of civil war—they'll gladly take imposters. Still, it is arguable that being tolerant (i.e., consciously forbearing the disliked) is an exceptionally precious civic and personal virtue worthy of steadfast promotion even if a less arduous alleged imposter is more practical.

Compounding this effort to disentangle two overt traits that are quite different in their underlying reasoning is the fact that the authentic article and apathy or fatalism are not alternatives but, possibly, occur in a sequence. Fletcher suggests that the very practice of genuine tolerance could bring indifference.[24] One might, for example, initially put up with some noxious neighbors, but after repeated exasperating experiences, become immune to their once annoying unpleasantness. Human nature itself might encourage this transformation process as an evolutionary survival necessity—the chronically intolerant wind up in the loony bin. The history of Western religious conflict perfectly illustrates this evolving relationship. Bitter seventeenth century life-and-death quarrels gave way to classic tolerance, and by the late twentieth century, few people could even comprehend these once momentous religious divisions. Obviously, this quandary is beyond resolution by scholarly decree, but it should be kept in mind as one campaign after another falls short.

On the other hand, must being tolerant convey anything more than just not interfering with those behaving objectionably? John Horton, one of the leading scholars in this area, certifies passivity as sufficient.[25] Yet it is hardly outrageous to insist that overt action might occasionally be morally required to wear the tolerance badge. In the context of classic understandings, how do we classify somebody who says, "I am tolerant of Catholics" but will refuse to rescue them from persecution? And if mere sentiment is inadequate, how much intervention suffices? Adding behavioral obligations multiplies evaluation problems. What if this ostensibly tolerant person sincerely claims not to know that the persecuted person was actually Catholic, so being tolerant of Catholics was conceptually impossible. Or supposing this person meekly asserts, "I abhor this suppression but only expressed this view privately since anything more was futile."

One possible resolution of this how-far-to-go predicament is to adopt the strategy that US courts apply to religion. Religious beliefs are absolutely protected, but religious behavior can be prohibited. A tolerant person might just claim to be obligated to tolerate the existence of Catholics and nothing more. In this limited understanding, to demand anything more is to require something that is just not tolerance. What if identity and behavior are inexorably linked—those gays who insist that being gay requires engaging in homosexual activity? Or is it legitimate, as in today's Catholic Church view, to tolerate gays, yet still homosexual behavior? These are unresolved issues, and endless intermediate positions are available short of martyrdom. Nobody seriously advocates inserting a willingness to make grand sacrifices into the definition; putting up with something is usually sufficient, even though this might mean little more than thinking good thoughts.[26]

The Hearts and Minds Tolerance of Modern Social Science

Classical tolerance evolved over centuries, and its intellectual ancestry reflected periodic religious carnage and civil wars. Ingrid Creppel, who traces this troubled history, put it this way: "A language of toleration is a collection of ideas, terms, conceptions, reasons, examples, stories, theories and linkages that have been elaborated to address problems of conflict, differences and disagreement."[27] Promoting forbearance at a time of deep divisions was often personally risky—John Locke anonymously wrote in Latin and risked execution for his heresies. Locke even denied authorship of his *Epistola de tolerantia* when it was translated into English while Voltaire twice sojourned in the Bastille. Nor did invocations call for refurbishing society. Aims were always modest, specific, and limited to pleading on behalf of a few officially repressed sects.

From Civil Liberties to Tolerance

Modern social science research displays a remarkably divergent history. The label *tolerance* is in many ways accidental, more reflective of academic fashions and data availability than of the concept of alleviating unwelcome personal repression. Its distinctive character vis-à-vis the classical interpretation lies in its near mechanical calibration. Simply put, tolerance here means only what is expressed to investigators on researcher-determined topics via the fixed format survey. When the sources are sought, these are entirely at the level of personal traits. It is thus technically impossible, as per Voltaire or Adam Smith, to intimate that tolerance might flow from the character of society's commercial marketplace. The attitude-behavior fuzziness that infuses classical musings, let alone worldly events, is entirely absent here: everything is purely a matter of individual psychology. It is scarcely an exaggeration to say that this conceptual cosmology is inseparable from fixed format survey data.

This evolutionary emergence probably reflects today's relative tranquility. The violent civil upheavals are long gone, or in the case of urban riots or terrorism, reduced to mere policing. It is easy to shun reality and delve into psychology when one need not fear Spanish Inquisition clerics lurking nearby. Academic champions flourish in settings (particularly universities) that embrace—if not celebrate—odd-ball proclivities, from the ideological to the sexual, that surely would have flabbergasted the straight-laced John Locke and even the permissive J.S. Mill. The drift toward psychology to mine virgin scholarly territory makes perfect career sense.

The contemporary scholarly infatuation can be traced to polls circa the late 1930s. These early commercial (not academic) polls framed the issue of tolerance in terms of traditional, constitutionally protected civil liberties. Queries haphazardly asked about permitting free speech, the right of unpopular political groups such as Communists and Fascists to hold meetings or be allowed radio time for their election campaigns, and the like. The growing threat to civil liberties instigated by World War II undoubtedly inspired this inquiry. While respondents generally endorsed political openness, they balked when it came to specific acts by hated groups. These data are unmistakably tolerance related, but this honored term never surfaced—everything was a snapshot of here-and-now fleeting civil liberties opinion.

Samuel Stouffer's *Communism, Conformity and Civil Liberties* was a watershed book written by a distinguished Harvard professor that set the foundations for future social science-based explications.[28] Meticulously researched, the book probed the public's acceptance of (assumed) hated groups with a readily executable formula. A random sample plus varied community leaders were asked about members of specific groups such as Communists, Socialists, and Atheists being allowed to engage in certain free-speech-related activities. For example, could such people teach in college or could a library have one of their books in its collection? This disliked group-by-activity grid then revealed the public's civil liberty judgment or, in soon-to-be-adopted terminology, *tolerance*. Once again, the results portrayed considerable hatefulness when problematical choices presented themselves, though tolerance was still abstractly embraced. Stouffer's contribution was more than yet one more snapshot; it authoritatively provided the blueprint for an entire scholarly edifice.

As commercial polling technology infiltrated academic research, this tool was soon applied regularly to the issues raised by Stouffer.[29] Prothro and Grigg added a racial element by asking respondents about permitting Negroes to seek public office to assess support for the democratic creed.[30] McClosky asked about teaching "foreign ideas" in schools to measure popular consensus on democratic ideology but here again the underlying analytical framework, permitting the disliked to pursue common activities, unquestionably continued onward.[31] An entire issue of the well-regarded *Journal of Social Issues* applied the Stouffer framework to push inquiry into myriad puzzles, such as attitude change over the life cycle, that scarcely mattered in by now ancient, almost forgotten, and rarely cited historical/theoretical treatments.[32]

What transformed these sporadic ventures into a robust cottage industry was the University of Chicago's prestigious National Opinion Research Center's (NORC) decision to insert Stouffer-like group/activity queries into its ongoing public opinion monitoring. Though it might be occasionally updated to reflect cultural shifts (e.g., adding homosexuals as a potentially disliked group) the underlying cosmology of tolerance, as it was now named, remained absolutely untouched. Newly emergent computer technology plus readily accessible quality data quickly produced an academic feeding fest. Nunn, Crockett and Williams even replicated Stouffer's work with updated data.[33] An undergraduate political behavior textbook, made the 1977 NORC data its empirical centerpiece.[34] Even those not drawing in the NORC data per se could instantly and authoritatively solve their measurement problems by following this well-established format.

This formula even found its way into highly detailed studies of specific real world tolerance-related conflicts. Gibson and Bingham's landmark analysis, focused on the efforts of the American Nazi Party during 1977 effort to obtain a parade permit in Skokie, Illinois, home of numerous Holocaust survivors.[35] Enormous amounts of data were collected, including the views of those in organizations defending the march plus other liberal group members. Questionnaire items specifically probed views about events and their possible political outcome. The complicated legal issues also received careful scrutiny, so the battle was hardly depicted as one of good versus evil. Nevertheless, the by now familiar Stouffer-like queries, though updated to include the KKK, paramilitarists, and new activities such as marching, remained central to this assessment enterprise. As before, one displayed this virtue by endorsing the right of a certifiably loathsome group such as the Klan to engage in democratic politics.

Fortunately for those who appreciated historic usage, this cookie cutter format did evolve beyond the question of, for example, Communists, who were assumed to be despised, holding meetings with the "no" response being labeled intolerance. Critically, the element of horridness so vital to classic judgment finally explicitly entered this research format. Loathsomeness was to be empirically determined, not just assumed a priori by the investigator as in the past. This shift was perhaps inevitable given that groups once notable for their unpopularity ceased being reviled. After all, by the 1970s the much-dreaded 1950s style Bolshevik had grown toothless, so permitting Marxists to speak publicly hardly evidenced sanctioning the despicable. The same is true for the fear of atheists when secularism was ubiquitous. Critics of this Stouffer approach also noted that the original set of groups assumed to be disliked, such as socialists) all resided on the political spectrum's left, so those also on the left were more likely to be sympathetic than tolerant.

Ascertaining an evaluation prior to rendering an assessment was initially addressed in Lawrence's work[36] but a more full-fledged theoretical framework had to wait until Sullivan, Pierson, and Marcus.[37] In their content controlled methodology, respondents first selected their two most hated groups using a fairly broad ideological menu from John Birchers to Black Panthers. Specific hatred now established, respondents then proceeded to explicit activities such as banning a Black Panther from being President, so the resultant "permit" or "forbid" response could be a bona fide expression of tolerance, intolerance, or acceptance. Interestingly, results contradicted well-documented prior findings showing the better-educated to be more tolerant. The college educated were, indeed, more tolerant when it came to leftist groups, but when judging those on the right, they were decidedly unforgiving. The opposite was true for the less educated. At least in terms of historical continuity, the classic three-fold classification scheme had been restored.

This content controlled method has been incorporated in more contemporary investigations though it has hardly rendered the Stouffer approach extinct. Gibson and Gouws' work in South Africa is particularly striking in its originality.[38] Here respondents were presented with a list of twelve potentially threatening political entities (e.g., right-wing Afrikaners, the African National Congress) and these were then combined with several democratic activities to assess whether South Africans would put up with those they disliked and feared. Vignettes about what might happen if tolerance were permitted, or if respected leaders called for greater understanding, further elucidated these scenarios. Hardly surprising given endemic South African racial strife, tolerance was in dreadfully short supply especially among black South Africans, regardless of how the questions were posed or what the enticements to elicit greater forbearance.

The Hearts and Minds Cosmology

Countless variations in data crunching aside, certain politically relevant assumptions guide the current enterprise. Foremost of these is the exclusive focus on attitudes. It is not that modern scholars overtly reject a behavioral component. Stouffer, among others, is apparently troubled by this lack of corroborating behavioral data, but this absence is always finessed with the assertion that attitudes probably foretell future deeds.[39] Gibson and Anderson take a rather defeatist view, and note that since linkage research is virtually negligible, one can only proceed via an attitude-based inquiry.[40] This neglect is not entirely unreasonable: attitudinally intolerant people might plausibly provide willing accomplices for despots. Still, clever excuses aside, it is impossible to exaggerate the ramifications of this exclusive focus on mere opinion, a decision probably having more to do with the lure of easy-to-execute surveys than explicit theoretical imperatives. Whatever the justification, however, making attitudes central does lead down a troubled trail.

Tolerance Lite might be a more accurate label for this attitude-centered approach, though, to be fair, a few theoretically minded modern scholars emphasize beliefs—not behavior—as the authentic element.[41] Yet it seems quite unlikely that classic enthusiasts would accept a tolerant attitude as the *sine qua non* of tolerance, if an either/or choice were required. The old cliché that actions speak louder than words has much to recommend it especially since sticks and stones can break my bones, but names can never harm me. It is not that attitudes by themselves are irrelevant; rather, this hearts and minds tolerance is insufficient to those of us more concerned about what happens. Moreover, tolerance fans are painfully aware of the human willingness to lie, and would-be tyrants may be unwilling to betray their hand and invite approbation. To rely on outward quiescence when hypocrisy is so inviting is, indeed, little comfort in a world overflowing with hate.

Social science research conducted in other contexts further caution against equating attitude data with authenticity. Opinions about distant, infrequently encountered situations are probably ephemera, and exceedingly few national random sample respondents come across these researcher-concocted possibilities.[42] It is certainly debatable whether the elicited information about, say, permitting Communist teachers is anything more than a flippant reaction to Communism, not some carefully reasoned choice. Such answers are often accurately characterized as non-attitudes that can easily be manipulated by seemingly minor questionnaire details. In an aptly entitled chapter, "Making it up as you go along," Zaller depicts a multitude of response-shaping factors: question ordering, interviewer traits, priming respondents with prior references, how alternatives are posed, among varied other technical but substantively relevant choices.[43]

This attitude-derived universe is also vulnerable to fantasy, or on the other hand, dangerous denial when beliefs are ascertained. Consider, for example, the results of the 1987 NORC survey that found that 55.6 percent of African Americans and 29.6 percent of whites believed that the US government prohibits anti-government speeches.[44] These views are, obviously, grievously mistaken and might be better interpreted as possible paranoia, not evidence of government repression. Nevertheless, to the extent that these mistaken beliefs are real in the sense of impeding action, do these data then demonstrate that feelings of oppression are widespread among African Americans? Is tolerance nothing but subjective psychology? What if Washington actually did squash dissent but did it so secretly that nobody noticed? Do pervasive though erroneous beliefs about tolerance certify that it really does exit? To equate beliefs, no matter how outrageous, with reality is risky business in a world where demagogues fuel paranoia.

Even if the opinion were rock solid and carefully established, no reasons exist to suppose a one-to-one relationship between this expressed viewpoint and behavior. An ample scholarly literature exists going back to the 1930s demonstrating substantial inconsistency between words and actions.[45] An expressed forbearance is better understood as one of several key decision-making factors. Perchance an attitudinally tolerant person will behave intolerantly due to some other, more forceful inclination such as a fear of being ostracized, monetary incentives, or innate shyness. Conversely, the true bigot might act graciously if, for example, that person were in a business firm that demanded it as a condition of employment.

This reliance on surveys also yields a highly static, too unfinished picture. To be sure, periodic NORC-type polls are a far cry from the era when popular sentiment could only be guessed, but they are far too infrequent and partial to be useful in specific circumstances. Peoples' views are often situation dependent, and surveys cannot possible anticipate all of the complicated possibilities. The objects of animus can likewise change their ways. After all, it may be more pleasant to be tolerated than hated, so human nature pushes for some accommodations from those on the outside. Nor can commonplace surveys ascertain value hierarchies. To find tolerance or intolerance per se says little unless we know how these inclinations fit vis-à-vis other values, and this too can shift with time. Everybody might be wonderfully tolerant, but only if this made zero difference.

The gap between what is confessed to the pollster even in gold standard surveys, and what can actually transpire was perfectly illustrated by a simple exercise I performed in the context of the Stouffer data. Specifically, in 1954 he showed that about two-thirds of the US public would forbid libraries to own a Communist authored book. A bare majority of generally tolerant community leaders seconded this intolerance. Nevertheless, *The National Union Catalogue Pre-1956 Imprints*, which lists major library holdings, revealed that Marx's *Communist Manifesto*, the Bolshevik Bible itself, was widely available nationally along with Marx's other tomes. These tracts were also in print and readily obtainable via regular commercial outlets.[46] So much for the power of "dangerous" attitudes to repress unpopular ideas!

Ideological Opportunism

More than just deficient social science research is involved here. Treating tolerance exclusively as an attitude affords innumerable, though barely visible, ideological opportunities. In this survey-centered framework, a virtual reality, so to speak, it is the researcher not public officials, judges, or hoi poloi who single-handedly decides the agenda. Reality can be irrelevant given a modern social science that sanctions wide latitudes in research design. Anti-Semitic pogroms might be everywhere, but views about tolerating Jews might fail to enter the questionnaire. Absolutely nothing requires such inclusion, at least for detached scholars more attuned to disciplinary fashion. This is a far cry from the era when Locke or Voltaire kept a keen eye on clerics anxious to burn heretics.

This near limitless discretion permits researchers to play god and anoint the few worthy to grace the survey. This freedom to express one's bias is deceivingly far-reaching given how research outcomes are treated.[47] In an instant, some people or groups can be scientifically certified as victims of hatefulness or, alternatively, have their claims disallowed. This is surprisingly effortless. If, perchance, the investigator quietly decides that homosexuals might be insufficiently accepted, a query about gays can be inserted into the survey, and with provocative but still professionally acceptable wording, it might be shown that society is, after all, (shamefully) intolerant of gays. By the same token sects, such as fundamentalist Christians, that might legitimately feel wrongly castigated might be rendered invisible in this researcher-created cosmology. After all, how can bad blood exist if survey data fails to document it? That the investigator can provide scientifically certified ammunition in bitter ideological battles might also help explain the popularity of this attitude-based approach.

Surveys also permit the researcher to offer sweeping assessments of society's overall condition, critically disregarding actual events and beyond rebuttal unless disbelievers can marshal their own survey data. Since polls present the investigator's own agenda, assembling only the loathed or labeling things in the most negative way possible virtually guarantees a highly troubling collective portrait. In fact, Marcus, Sullivan, Theiss-Morse, and Wood, authors of a major carefully scientific excursion into today's civic landscape, rather flippantly announce at the beginning of their book that intolerance is an ever-present danger and need not be accepted.[48] What monstrosities are about to befall us? The "frightening" examples offered in the book's Preface, such as vandalizing Jewish cemeteries and conflicts over abortion, are trifling by historical circumstances that inspired calls for tolerance—even more trifling than humdrum political squabbles. It would be hard to imagine these authors awarding America a clean bill of health given how petty events sound the alarm. Discovering ill will is thus tantamount to lifetime employment.

Consider two hypothetical surveys. The first emphasizes groups of actual consequence—Asians, Protestants, Catholics, Jews, and the like some of which have been the objects of past repression. A second survey, by contrast, offers a menu of Nazis, the KKK, skin head militias, and assorted other violent fringe fanatics. Without doubt, the first survey will show the US to be exceptionally tolerant while, equally predictably, the second will reveal vast antagonism. Which is the authentic picture? Both might be accurate by scientific standards, but when put in the context of what really matters in civic life, only the first data are relevant. The second data set might be scientifically interesting but pointless, especially since hardly anybody will ever encounter these extremist groups. But, alas, in a world where uncovering any enmity may sound the alarm, this second study may draw the attention.

The modern survey format also denies the power of individual reasoning. Several studies experimentally manipulate responses to assess decision-making, but this exercise hardly qualifies as autonomy.[49] It is the experimenter who controls an entirely fixed menu, so no substitutions please! This is a Procrustean Bed world as envisioned by professors, not ordinary citizens. If presented with a question about making homosexuality legal, for example, the thoughtful respondent cannot explain that while he or she has nothing against such behavior generally, there are certain limits to this forbearance, and at least some behaviors deserve criminal sanction. Nor could he or she argue with the researcher (impossible anyhow since the interviewer is just an employee) about, say, the distinction between homosexuals as a group versus homosexual acts, some of which may be committed by those not defining themselves as homosexuals. Everything in this assessment is remarkably predetermined, a virtual straightjacket, and for the respondent to quarrel will de facto remove his or her views from the study or encourage non-participation. In a sense, the absence of opportunities to reason freely makes this version of the survey something less than its classical counterpart. It certainly has a low regard for people's capacity to reach nuanced judgments about complicated issues without a researcher-supplied framework.

In important ways the modern survey-based approach unfairly, though perhaps not intentionally, minimizes tolerance and thus paints an unflattering collective portrait. In this scholarly world the bitter strife—religious quarrels, class animosities—that once deeply divided societies is old news and not worth pursuing. Why ask about tolerating Quakers, a sect once persecuted by Puritans, and reasonably so given their disruptive, often lewd behavior. Everybody knows that Quakers today are tolerated, probably appreciated, so any research confirming this trite fact goes unpublished. Savvy inquiry focuses instead on detested marginal extremists. This line of attack will further generate normally distributed variables that permit the complex statistical analysis required of today's contribution to knowledge. In short, the modern appreciation is less about securing a tolerant society than psychologically probing individual likes and dislikes that are probably irrelevant to who gets burned at the stake.

Modern Education

If classic understandings evolved over several centuries, and the social science version took about six decades, what professional educators advance as their ideal has materialized almost overnight. It is also fairly shallow intellectually, often little more than a grab bag of slogans—hardly surprising since professional pedagogues are more attuned to nut and bolts quandaries than arcane theory. It is also a rapidly expanding enterprise given the millions of potential educators wanting simple solutions to their fear of impending tidal waves of hate. All and all, this effort to define tolerance can be accurately depicted as a "goodhearted" effort at social reform.

Nevertheless, despite this disjoined sprawl, certain key elements are readily discernable. By far the most important is conceiving tolerance as unqualified *appreciating*, not just *putting up with* the disliked. That something could be both good and bad and thus be tolerated seems inconceivable to these experts. The Southern Poverty Law Center promotes this viewpoint energetically, and its widely distributed *Teaching Tolerance* defines it as recognition and respect for diverse practices and beliefs. This vision is hardly exceptional. The prestigious *American Heritage Dictionary* published in 2000 offers "The capacity for or the practice of recognizing and respecting the beliefs or practices of others,"[50] and this approbation-free meaning regularly appears in today's educational campaigns. Even the UN has joined this chorus: "Tolerance is respect, acceptance and appreciation of the rich diversity of our world's cultures, our forms of expression and ways of being human."[51]

Even different lifestyles, including homosexuality, are to be tolerated in this sense. One exhortation even called for schools to tolerate, that is, appreciate, fat students, though such early heftiness can be medically devastating.[52] To be sure, it may be ill-advised to expose young children to the unappetizing (e.g., type II diabetic debilitation), and then to portray certain loathsome things as better than others, but as one navigates these incessant calls one cannot help but witness a rather Pollyannaish worldview. The planet is wonderful, overflowing with things to be appreciated, save for a few bigots. An unrefined cultural relativism clearly permeates this worldview.

Consider, for example, a suggested lesson plan offered by the prestigious Public Broadcasting Service (http:www.pbs.org/americaresponds/tolerance. html) directed toward middle and high school students in the wake of 9/11.[53] This training's purpose is to shield Muslims and Arabs from any animosity that these attacks might generate by inculcating "tolerance." That teaching legal obedience goes unmentioned as a solution. Students thus see materials portraying Muslims favorably, post-9/11 anti-Muslim hate crimes are recounted, and the unfair treatment dished out to those of Japanese and Germany ancestry during WW II is similarly described. Effort is also made to separate terrorism from just being a Muslim Arab.

Although factually correct, this is a one-sided exercise. Nothing is said about widespread aggressive anti-western ideology among Muslims; how many Islamic clerics fan this hatred through extensive funding by both Arab governments and private charities to breed anti-Americanism; virulent, often quasi official anti-Semitism; the existence of Muslim jihad directed against Christians in Africa and Asia; and how Islamic theology might justify killing innocent infidels. If anything, this teaching plan depicts Muslims as blameless, wholly innocent victims-in-waiting as if 9/11 had nothing to do with Islam. And, apparently, these lesson planners are unaware that interning those of Japanese ancestry during WW II was constitutionally sanctioned, executed by duly elected officials, and many honestly believed it a prudent wartime policy. That some "innocent" Germans committed sabotage likewise goes unmentioned. To present history's other side hardly counsels incarcerating innocent Muslims; dwelling on the evils of collective guilt and obeying the law are sufficiently strong deterrents against anti-Muslim violence. Rather, the entire issue is more nuanced than what PBS presents. One can certainly acknowledge Islam's unpleasant features and right-fully conclude that Islam deserves tolerance despite these troubling defects. It is all a matter of scrutinizing details and weighing arguments, so showing reproach hardly certifies intolerance. If educators insist that their students cannot grasp this graduated appraisal, perhaps the one-sided lessons should be skipped alto-gether.

Paralleling this condemnation phobia is the enthusiastic welcoming, not just stoic acceptance, of "differences" to certify tolerance commitment. Differences are intrinsically good, and to acknowledge this goodness reflects tolerance, at least in this context. And if these differences reside beyond the kin of naïve stu-dents, at least some educators would aggressively insert them into the class-room.[54] It is here that underlying cultural relativism merges with multicultural-ism.[55] In the above PBS recommendations, the word, *diversity* appears seven times in the plan's aims. This *leitmotiv* obviously applies largely to ethnic and racial traits although homosexuality, gender, and disability are also occasionally included as diversity elsewhere.

Ironically, in light of an infatuation with uniqueness, an equally fervent ef-fort is made to drive out stereotyping of these to-be- appreciated groups. By *stereotyping*, these professional educators mean asserting largely reprehensible traits. For example, to say that African Americans are more criminally violent than Asian Americans makes one guilty of stereotyping, and thus, intolerant, though this statement is factually correct. Even a flattering claim such as assert-ing that students of Chinese ancestry are superior at math may be deemed an adverse stereotype since it reflects poorly on non-Chinese. The underlying mes-sage is that differences should be valued, the more the merrier. However, to ac-knowledge what makes people different in a bad way, even if nominally flatter-ing, risks stereotyping, and this very hint of aversion invalidates tolerance.

An All-Pervasive Tolerance

This strain of tolerance is remarkably encompassing, even totalitarian, in its reach. Recall that classic appreciations sharply focused on what could tear soci-ety apart; even social science research centered on a handful of extremists, not village weirdoes. Equally important, it was the state, not individuals, that was to bestow tolerance. By contrast, today's historically uninformed professional edu-cators seek inculcation everywhere, even in purely personal relations. This is their version of the virtuous society—ubiquitously appreciative of (seemingly) everything. Tolerance is thus to be offered to the disabled, the mentally retarded, the obese, the slothful, old people, and on and on. A lesson plan offered by Tol-erance.org suggests various things parents can do to promote this virtue among their offspring. For example, they could visit a playground to reveal the fullness of "normal," identify mass media "cultural misinformation," or showcase diver-sity in one's home. Predictably, language plays a central role in this project. To use pejorative terms like *lunatic* or *nut case* reveals bias against those who are just different. What was once lack of tact or rudeness has now becomes far more insidious.

Like the social science approach, this enterprise awards experts enormous authority to indulge personal whim or heed disciplinary fashions. These specialists can offer admission to the tolerance pantheon to anyone or anything, or just as easily decide that believing that homosexual behavior sinful is inimical to tolerance. The entire process might thus resemble selecting a new Pope though less transparent. Access or refusal by these gatekeepers certainly has not been publicly debated, and criteria are not submitted with sixty days notice for public scrutiny. Nor has law or public expectation granted this authority; compared to teaching reading, everything here is optional.

The bizarre character of this unaccountable authority becomes apparent when we realize the impossibility of appreciating all differences. Choices must be made, and without some explicit standard—whether moral imperatives, utilitarian calculations, or whatever—this entire approach will collapse into gobbledygook. Evil differs from good, but this does not counsel embracing evil. What if the instructed child asks, "Is slavery good since it insures full employment?" How might inquisitive pupils differentiate male circumcision from female genital mutilation? Or dangerous white racial pride from commendable black pride? Obviously, no sane person would insist that all things are equally good or even mainly good, so the rhetoric exhorting people to appreciate difference is just vacuous speech making.[56] Constructing tolerance on this foundation anchors it in quicksand.

This approach also undermines the capacity for reasoned judgments so vital to classical tolerance. To the naïve, instruction is by crude edict not by reason, and smart students will eventually discern this cosmology's intellectual incoherence. Why, for example, should we replace the word *crippled* with *differentially able* as if words altered reality? What separates the acceptable *person of color* from the offensive *colored person*? Bright students will have a field day exposing cultural relativism's inherent contradictions. Why should some groups such as gays be deemed a contribution to diversity though they engender social acrimony while others, such as those believing in racial-related IQ differences, be banished as harmful? Why must the US crave ethnic variety when such hodgepodges often invite civil war? Even clever teachers cannot answer these questions: there are no answers—only shaky, easily rebuked opinions. The upshot, then, will be muddled thinking among the ordinary and cynicism among the more gifted.

Judging Tolerances

These characterizations of tolerance are, admittedly, over-simplifications, if not a tad messy, but they capture quite distinct cosmologies. To insist that any one version is innately superior is obviously absurd; varieties cannot be graded as one might compare French or Italian wines. However, what is possible is to assess their contemporary usefulness and broader implication. What might happen if one version is favored to the exclusion of others?

A useful departure point is to consider how much of this virtue is sufficient, and how we might recognize the Promised Land if it arrived? Surely, to insist that current levels of tolerance are eternally insufficient is pointless. Some evils will always be beyond forbearance, so bad blood is eternal. We certainly cannot appreciate everything. In economics, establishing endpoint benchmarks is routine. For example, if unemployment hovers at 2 percent, government might congratulate itself and energy might be reasonably directed elsewhere. Given the law of diminishing returns, seeking to cut joblessness yet further is excessive and likely counter-productive. But, when do we cease our tolerance mission?

The three versions of tolerance elucidated here handle this quandary quite differently. Classic advocates usually endorse a down-to-earth stance—the substantial but not complete disappearance of civil strife signifies adequacy. A *modus vivendi* suffices, so quelling hypothetical or trivial evils is thus an extravagance. In seventeenth century England, tolerance meant curtailing certain (but not all) contentious religious persecutions that could bring civil war; this might just mean toning down troublesome contemporary racial/ethnic conflicts. Simply leaving gays alone, not celebrating them is enough in this cosmology. It scarcely worries about granting respect, legitimacy, or similar states of acceptance that so infatuate today's ambitious educators. This understanding is not open-ended; hatred is still permissible even if the loathed demonstrate that they are harmless. Nothing about this traditional version requires that, for example, Americans tolerate bigamy, legalized narcotics, public nudity, or any other currently beyond-the-edge disposition. Candidates for inclusion exist in infinite supply, and the admission of one undoubtedly generates two fresh applicants, so one must stop somewhere.

A pragmatic appreciation of community must guide choices. Locke, for example, did not seek to repress Catholics for their unsound theology or peculiar church rituals. That was tolerable. The apprehension was far more pressing, or at least he thought—Catholics were (supposedly) French agents, and schemed to impose a Catholic King on England, all of which presaged civil war. By contrast, accepting Protestant Dissenters and Huguenot refugees from France for their talent added to England's power.[57] Today, of course, matters have evolved. English Catholics are now harmless, and some would anoint Muslim immigrants the new dread. What is key here is not compiling possible inclusionary criteria (hopeless, anyhow) but steering through difficult choices based upon palpable circumstances—not researcher decided hypothetical scenarios—that add or subtract from a nation's well being.

And how are applications for classic tolerance to be adjudicated? There are no majestic principles awaiting resolution by teams of philosophers. It is the political process, warts and all, that decides, be it the King or the multitude. In the latter half of the nineteenth century, for example, it was the federal government that criminalized bigamy when Utah sought statehood. In the late 1930s it was the Congressionally enacted Smith Act that defined the boundaries of permissible radical activity. Today's gay marriage or immigration quarrels just carry on this contentious let-politics-decide tradition.[58] In a democratic political arrangement of the US type, this means that popular sentiment ultimately prevails though, to be sure, eventual implementation may require haranguing government. Still, there is nothing that inherently demands democratic resolution—tyrants can impose their wills, too.

Nevertheless, if we assume the superiority of democratically decided verdicts, it is clear that the two rivals fall short. Despite rhetorical asides about building a better democracy, both involve governance by unaccountable experts. It is they who might decide *ex cathedra*, for example, that homosexuals deserve blanket open-mindedness, but that Christian Fundamentalists espousing moral absolutism do not. It is not that social scientists and professional educators are off in the wilderness blessing creepy things, though this occasionally seems plausible. It is the unaccountability of their choices that draws our ire. One might thus say, "Beware the expert bearing democratic gifts."

In many ways the imbedded pessimistic view of human nature pervading traditional understandings is a great advantage because it permits us to settle for reasonably protecting civil society. It is thus, or tries to be, cost/benefit efficient—to achieve necessary acquiescence without striving for costly utopias. Again, the other two versions fall short. For these latter campaigners, closure is unreachable: there will always be something displaying the dreaded aversion, perhaps a negative stereotype, isolated hooliganism, or a screwball militia patrolling the Montana hills. If nothing can be found, the possibility that something evil is about to happen remains indisputable. Perhaps a minor racial insult might restore slavery. These new champions thus resemble Sisyphus pushing his pet rock.

By far the most pressing question facing all discussions is what should be tolerated? Obviously, answers are not available via papal bull, and disputes are inescapable. One person's insufferable sin is another's charming vice. So long as there are philosophical papers to be written, speculations will flourish. This indeterminacy does not mean, however, that all versions are equally at sea when confronting hard choices. Here again, the classic version has much to recommend it. Key is its stress on reasoned debate guided by actual circumstances with the final choice being made by liable officials. It rejects the search for abstract definitive principles and instead humbly proposes, "When all is said and done, can we live with it?" Its very lingering messiness is an added plus, for it lays things out openly, solicits multiple opinions, and permits endless tinkering. It frankly rejects a grand tolerance *über alles*. Instead, it wisely insists that tolerance cannot exist apart from civil society yet too much tolerance will wreak havoc. Big tent classic advocates, including such tentative family relatives as apathy, fatalism, and cowardice, only benefit civil society at minimal cost.

This ongoing civic engagement is absent when researchers draw up survey questionnaires, or pedagogues devise their lesson plans. Ivory tower denizens need not worry that castigating respondents for their anti-communist sentiment will undermine careers, even if communists do, indeed, endanger society. The adage, "Publish or perish" has evolved considerably from the days when the printer of Voltaire's *Philosophical Letters* was sent to the Bastille—this was publish and perish. Nor do well-meaning teachers suffer the consequences when preaching that all lifestyles are valid even when countenanced behaviors turn dangerous. If there is any responsibility surrounding these pronouncements, it is only scholarly liability, or at least an obligation to honor disciplinary fads, not public accountability.

Elected officials and others publicly beholden rarely enjoy comparable freedom to indulge personal preferences when preaching the tolerance mantra. Lawmakers who insisted that homeless drunks should be tolerated when congregating on sidewalks will be defeated when angry voters sicken of aggressive panhandlers. Taxpayers are not always keen to re-elect those whose generosity towards the sexually marginalized means an over-burdened health care system. You can't argue with the pollster or your fifth grade teacher; you can vote out office holders.

There are also opportunity costs in pursuing a blank-check vision. Hearts and minds oriented researchers and pedagogues all zero in on attitudes, so the pathway to victory must necessarily pass through attitude change. This singularity is both risky and unnecessary. It is easy to envision schools pursuing this agit-prop role to the neglect of more traditional subjects to the point where graduates know that different is good but can barely read or write. Moreover, as noted, transforming beliefs is an exceedingly tough task if only due to the easy opportunities for undetectable hypocrisy. Even if "good" attitudes were instilled, persistence is hardly guaranteed, and even if they linger, they may amount to little in future concrete situations given the multiplicity of diverging forces. If that were insufficient, the success rates of attitude change programs advises pessimism—just ask safe sex educators or those fighting drugs where the wages of sin is death.

Classic tolerance offers bountiful opportunities if one approach fails, particularly if we include second cousins like apathy and distant uncles like stoic acceptance, let alone bastard offspring like cowardice. Civil strife can be quelled by just separating the warring factions, enforcing legal sanctions, and abundant other tactics without ever convincing a Serb to love his Croat neighbor. It is also arguable that these solutions wisely accept human nature. Since time began, in their everyday lives people have been physically distancing themselves from enemies or just ignoring them. In short, if we are searching for flexible remedies with multiple, historically proven options, classic tolerance with all of its extended family easily outshines its rivals.

Some Warnings

This has been an admittedly reactionary analysis to reestablish a vision that has seemingly grown old-fashioned. My advocacy of the classic model of tolerance is motivated less by an appreciation of this time-tested down-to-earth model, and more by the urge to expose the pernicious implications of newly fashioned and seemingly more glamorous rivals. These are ersatz products despite the nomenclature. The road to hell, we are told, is paved with good intentions, and for these academic and educational nostrums, the boulevard is a publicly funded super-highway. Mae West once remarked that too much of a good thing is great but, alas, this does not apply everywhere. Relentless pursuit can bring unexpected catastrophes, not excellence.

In their continued quest for hated groups to justify yet more inclusion, advocates of both of these updated versions of tolerance contribute to the cult of victimization, a grievous defect in a liberal society rightfully commemorating personal autonomy and responsibility.[59] After all, it takes only the slightest hint of aversion, regardless of how qualified or probable, no matter how obscurely expressed, to demonstrate a lurking threat, which, in turn, will excuse self-inflicted misfortune. Worse, to repeat yet one more time, these upstart rivals make transforming thinking the paramount (if not exclusive) pathway to betterment. To resist converting from intolerant to tolerant thus commits an Orwellian thought-crime. Reluctantly accepting the acknowledged disagreeable or even escaping odium via indifference is insufficient; one must mentally embrace the program, and this means appreciating what the academy's experts or professional pedagogues decide. It matters not that sound reasons for resisting can be marshaled or that past events support one's illiberality; there can be no running away. Even saying, "I didn't behave intolerantly" does not certify innocence in this cruel court. It's only the thought that counts. If hectoring children to love their loathsome fat neighbor falls short, and if adults still refuse to extend every civil benefit imaginable to homosexuals, or whoever else is on the menu du jour, sterner education, if not punishment, is the prescription. Professor Robespierre will not be happy with insolence.

Today's quixotic rush to mandated sensitivity training when people express measured distaste foreshadows worse things to come. Just wait until Professor Robespierre is appointed Assistant Secretary of Education to Promote Tolerance. Envision John Locke's reaction if he were shipped off to a workshop to cherish Unitarians, a sect he felt undeserving of tolerance, after carelessly admitting on a survey that Unitarians should be barred from public office. He would, naturally, claim that since nobody could possibly identify his true feelings the re-education exercise was futile. Nor would these enablers listen to his arguments that Unitarians subverted civil society since their sacred oaths were worthless. No matter. The Royal High Pedagogue had decided that Unitarians were different and since Ulster was not yet under the King's reign, and the quirky Scots were dallying about, English diversity came up short. Who knows, say the professors, what slippery slope catastrophe lies ahead if Unitarians are denied full legitimacy? The Unitarians thus deserved unreserved toleration if England was to achieve this Garden of Earthly Delights. Dr. Locke, no doubt, would flee back to Amsterdam, and wisely so.

Notes

1. Ryszard Legutko, "The Trouble with Toleration," *Partisan Review*, 61 (1994): 610-24.
2. E.g. Herbert Marcuse, "Repressive Tolerance," in *A Critique of Pure Tolerance*, ed. Robert Paul Wolff, Barrington Moore, Jr., and Herbert Marcuse (Boston: Beacon Press, 1968), 95-137.
3. To be fair, these two terms do possess somewhat distinct historical meanings, but once subtle distinctions have virtually vanished and seemingly reflect literary style not substance. In his introduction to a book brimming with arcane philosophical hair-splitting, Heyd says that the two terms will be used interchangeably by the assembled authors. David Heyd, introduction to *Toleration: an Illusive Virtue* (Princeton: Princeton University Press, 1996), 17.
4. J. Budziszewski, *True Tolerance: Liberalism and the Necessity of Judgment* (New Brunswick, N.J.: Transaction Publishers, 1992).
5. Bernard Crick, *Political Theory and Practice* (London: Allen Lane the Penguin Press, 1971).
6. J. Budziszewski, "The Illusion of Moral Neutrality," *First Things* 35, (August/September 1993): 32-37.
7. J.S. Mill, today's patron saint of expansive tolerance, freely acknowledged the need to withhold certain "defective" people from enjoying liberty's benefits. In *On Liberty*, ed. Alburey Castel (Arlington Heights, Ill.: AHM Publishing, 1947), 10 he spoke of, for example, denying liberty to those who were "delirious" and people too immature to behave responsibly. This view is light years from today's nearly blank check welcoming of everything imaginable.
8. This other side of the tolerance equation is never addressed in today's admonitions to bestow acceptance on the loathed. Perchance this omission reflects awkwardness in specifying just what is so detested. Imagine the public outcry if, for example, somebody said that whites might better tolerate blacks if blacks refrained from rampant criminality or drug abuse. This discomfiting engendering of tolerance would thus, ironically, be judged offensive and therefore hateful.
9. John Gray, "The Virtues of Toleration." *The National Review* (October 5, 1992): 28-36.
10. See, for example, Susan Mendus, *Toleration and the Limits of Liberalism* (Atlantic Highlands, N.J.: Humanities Press International, 1989), 9.
11. See, for example, John Horton, "Tolerance as a Virtue." in *Toleration: an Illusive Virtue*, ed. David Heyd (Princeton: Princeton University Press, 1996) for a contrary view.
12. See Michael Walzer, *On Toleration* (New Haven: Yale University Press, 1997), 8 for more on this point.
13. The shift from public to private (and vice versa) occurs periodically. Witness the debate over homosexuality. It was once legally prohibited, then almost disappeared from the public realms as strictly private behavior and now has re-emerged as a hot public

issue in the context of gay marriages where gays seek public legitimacy for their sexuality.

14. Calibrating tolerance as distinct from any person raises several intriguing quandaries. For instance, acts of tolerance are sometimes hoaxes, but this might never be discovered without police work and subsequent public announcement. See Laird Wilcox, *Crying Wolf: Hate Crime Hoaxes in America* (Olathe, Kans.: Laird Wilcox Editorial Research Service, 1994). Even more challenging, while it is difficult enough to itemize intolerance, imagine cataloguing tolerance when such behaviors lack any distinctive manifestation. These are no small measurement issues in rendering society-wide judgments.

15. Walzer, *On Toleration*, 8.

16. Samuel A. Stouffer, *Communism, Conformity and Civil Liberties* (New York: Doubleday, 1955).

17. John L. Sullivan, James Piereson, and George E. Marcus, *Political Tolerance and American Democracy* (Chicago: University of Chicago Press, 1982), 77.

18. Will Kymlicka, "Two Models of Tolerance and Pluralism," in *Toleration: an Illusive Virtue*, ed. David Heyd (Princeton: Princeton University Press, 1996).

19. Our analysis of Voltaire's writings also derives from Wendy McElroy, "The Origins of Religious Tolerance: Voltaire" http://www.zetetics.com/mac/volt.htm.

20. Much of the uncertainty regarding how authentic tolerance is to be distinguished from look-alikes flows from how tolerance is established. Many (e.g., Preston King, *Toleration* (New York: St. Martin's Press, 1976), 22-23) concentrate on the origins of this disposition—true tolerance differs from acquiescence since the latter results from a sense of futility, not acceptance. Not only is this inner-thought distinction exceedingly difficult to make in practice, but more important, it may be irrelevant for tolerance assessed generally—people just forbear the loathed regardless of how they arrive at this choice.

21. E.g. George. P. Fletcher, "The Instability of Tolerance," in *Toleration: An Elusive Virtue*, ed. David Heyd, (Princeton: Princeton University Press, 1996), 158-72; Horton, John and Peter Nicholson, eds., "Philosophy and the practice of toleration," in *Toleration: Philosophy and Practice*, (Aldershot, UK: Avebury, 1992), 1-13; Bernard Williams, "Toleration: An Impossible Virtue." in *Toleration: an Illusive Virtue*, ed. David Heyd. (Princeton: Princeton University Press, 1996).

22. Fletcher, "The Instability of Tolerance," 158.

23. Walzer, *On Toleration*, 10.

24. Fletcher, "The Instability of Tolerance."

25. John Horton, ed., "Liberalism, Multiculturalism and Toleration," in *Liberalism, Multiculturalism and Toleration* (New York: St. Martin's, 1993), 4.

26. Nevertheless, some do place a higher burden on those wishing to be labeled tolerant. This "positive tolerance" (see, for example, Lord Scarman, "Toleration and the Law," in *On Toleration*, ed. Susan Mendus and David Edwards (Oxford, England: Clarendon Press, 1987), 49-62), insists that the tolerant person intervene to protect those at risk, especially the weak from the powerful. Hence, those claiming to tolerate Muslims should assist them in, say, securing legal protection against discrimination, but precisely how far this intervention must go still remains uncertain.

27. Ingrid Creppel, *Toleration and Identity: Foundations in Early Modern Thought* (New York: Routledge, 2003), x.

28. Stouffer, *Communism, Conformity and Civil Liberties*.

29. The best overall portrayal of this vast literature, together with many of the actual questionnaire items, can be found in Steven F. Finkel, Lee Sigelman, and Stan Humphries, "Democratic Values and Political Tolerance." in *Measures of Political Atti-*

tudes, ed. John P. Robinson, Phillip R. Shaver, and Lawrence S. Wrightsman (San Diego: Academic Press, 1999), 203-96.

30. James W. Prothro and Charles W. Grigg, "Fundamental Principles of Democracy: Bases of Agreement and Disagreement," *Journal of Politics*, 22 (1960): 276-294.

31. Herbert McClosky, "Consensus and Ideology in American Politics," *American Political Science Review*, 58 (1964): 361-82.

32. *Journal of Social Issues*, 31 (1975).

33. Clyde Z. Nunn, Harry J. Crockett, and J.A. Williams, *Tolerance for Nonconformity* (San Francisco: Jossey-Bass, 1978).

34. Michael Corbett, *Political Tolerance in America: Freedom and Equality in Public Attitudes* (New York: Longman, 1982).

35. James L. Gibson and Richard G. Bingham, *Civil Liberties and Nazis: The Skokie Free Speech Controversy*, (New York: Praeger, 1985).

36. David Lawrence, "Procedural Norms and Tolerance: A Reassessment," *American Political Science Review*, 70 (1976): 80-100.

37. Sullivan, Piereson, and Marcus, *Political Tolerance*, chap. 2.

38. James L. Gibson and Amanda Gouws, *Overcoming Intolerance in South Africa: Experiments in Democratic Persuasion*, (Cambridge: Cambridge University Press, 2003.

39. Stouffer, *Communism, Conformity and Civil Liberties*, 48.

40. James L. Gibson and Arthur J. Anderson "The Political Implications of Elite and Mass Tolerance," *Political Behavior*, 7 (1985): 118-46.

41. E.g. Williams, "Toleration: An Impossible Virtue."

42. Irving Crespi, "What Kinds of Attitude Measures Are Predictive of Behavior?" *Public Opinion Quarterly*, 35 (1971): 327-34.

43. John R. Zaller, *The Nature and Origins of Mass Opinion*, (New York: Cambridge University Press, 1992).

44. Reported in James L. Gibson, "Perceived Political Freedom in the Soviet Union: A Comparative Analysis" (paper presented at the annual meeting of the Western Political Science Association, San Francisco, CA, March 1992), 19-21.

45. See, for example, Richard T. LaPiere, "Attitudes vs. Actions," *Social Forces* 13 (1934): 230-37; Howard Schuman, "Attitudes vs. Actions versus Attitudes vs. Attitudes," *Public Opinion Quarterly* 36 (1972): 347-54; Irwin Deutscher, "Words and Deeds: Social Science and Social Policy," in *The Consistency Controversy*, ed. Allen E. Liska (New York: John Wiley & Sons, 1975).

46. Robert Weissberg, *Political Tolerance: Balancing Community and Diversity* (Thousand Oaks, Calif: Sage, 1998), 75.

47. An especially important impact is in court decisions. Judges increasingly cite poll data to certify community sentiment in cases involving such contentious issues as homosexuality. Evidence of public tolerance (as defined by the poll) that exceeds existent legal standards can justify overturning these standards.

48. George E. Marcus et.al., *With Malice to Some: How People Make Civil Liberties Judgment*, (Cambridge, UK: Cambridge University Press, 1995), 3.

49. See the various citations in Marcus et. al., *With Malice to Some*, chap. 4, and Gibson and Gouws, *Overcoming Intolerance*, chap. 6-9.

50. *American Heritage Dictionary*, 4th ed., On-line version, http://www.bartleby.com/61/31/T0253100.html.

51. UNESCO, *Declaration of Principles of Tolerance*, 1995 http://www.unesco.org/tolerance/declaeng.htm.

52. *NEA Today*, 13 (December 1994): 6.

53. Public Broadcasting Service (http:www.pbs.org/americaresponds/tolerance.html).

54. See, for example, Dennis Carlson, "Gayness, Multicultural Education, and Community," *Educational Foundations* 8, no. 4 (1994): 5-25 regarding how youngsters can learn to value homosexuality.

55. See, for example, Sonia Nieto, "Moving Beyond Tolerance in Multicultural Education," *Multicultural Education*, 1 (1994): 9-12, 35-38.

56. The logical twisting exhibited to weasel out of contradictions can be extraordinary and inadvertently humorous. In one case (Carol Heller and Joseph A. Hawkins, "Teaching Tolerance: Notes from the Front Line," *Teachers College Record*, 95 (1994): 337-68) defenders of encompassing multiculturalism attempt to rebut the charges that the absence of a moral center (hypothetically) permits the embrace of child molesters, drug dealers and similarly loathsome creatures. The rejoinder to this critique is that no educational material endorses tolerance for these despicable behaviors. These defenders are obviously literalists incapable of grasping abstract arguments.

57. Maurice Cranston, "John Locke and the Case for Toleration," in *On Toleration* ed. Susan Mendus and David Edwards (Oxford: Clarendon Press, 1987).

58. The ongoing debate over Muslim headscarves in Europe illustrates that the tolerance wars have not ceased. These quarrels demonstrate our point that classic tolerance proceeds via nitty-gritty details and public debate, not grand principles.

59. The ingenuity in achieving victimhood is often remarkable. Anna Elizabeth Galeotti, *Toleration as Recognition* (Cambridge: Cambridge University Press, 2002), has argued that when marginalized groups are disrespected by society (i.e., those who are white male Christians) for not being normal, they feel impotent and inferior. This disrespect, moreover, can be quite subtle—poll data evidencing public aversion to a group's religious practices. In this Weltanschauung, establishing tolerance becomes a therapeutic exercise in which the now stigmatized must be helped to feel good about their atypical identity. This is a far cry from the era when being victimized meant physical assault or legal prohibitions. By this standard, the quest for tolerance—making everyone feel normal—is totally hopeless.

Understanding Tolerance
Nick Fotion

Some basic definitions of tolerance will provide a good starting point for discussion. The following two definitions are similar, but differ in emphasis. The first comes from the *Encyclopedia of Ethics* and is authored by Susan Mendus: "Toleration is intentionally allowing, or refraining from preventing, actions which one dislikes or believes to be morally wrong."[1] Mendus adds that "toleration requires that the tolerator have the power to intervene, but refrain from using that power."[2] The second definition appears in *The Encyclopedia of Philosophy*, written by Maurice Cranston: "Toleration is a policy of patient forbearance in the presence of something which is disliked or disapproved of."[3]

In its own way, each definition is helpful. The first suggests that the range of toleration is wide, covering everything from dislikes to un-favored moral beliefs. The first definition also emphasizes intentionality. Tolerating someone or some group has to do with choosing to behave in a certain way. The second definition is concerned with a person's behavioral policy. Tolerating is not so much an intentional act as it is a behavior that occurs over a long period of time. We are tolerant when we behave in a certain way today, tomorrow, next week, and so on.

Both definitions make it clear that toleration is not a happy state. The tolerator is in some sense dissatisfied with what is going on, yet does nothing to stop the unwanted behavior. At this point, however, both definitions fail us. The contrasting emphases on attitude and behavior only hint at the complexity inherent in toleration.

Toleration is different from dichotomous ethical concepts such as right and wrong, just and unjust, guilty and not guilty, and even good and bad. Toleration is trichotomous, falling between at least two other concepts.[4] There is intolerance on the one side, and acceptance on the other. In order to understand toleration it is important to understand the concepts that straddle it on either side.

Part of what it means to be intolerant is to have a negative attitude toward someone and to act in some way on that attitude. The formula for intolerance can be expressed as follows:

X is intolerant of Y in ways a, b, c . . . n with respect to features o, p, q . . . w.

This formula makes explicit that to be intolerant requires an object (Y), but also that the intolerance exists not necessarily with respect to Y as a whole. I am not intolerant of Alan because of his baby blue eyes or his habit of eating breakfast every day. Rather, I can't tolerate his loud and boastful behavior, his smoking in the office, and his tendency to demean those beneath him, (o, p, q, and so on). In being intolerant I take certain steps to stop Alan from doing those things that I cannot stand, (a, b, c, and so on). What I do will vary with the circumstances. To be intolerant of certain sorts of behavior does not require that the intolerant behavior be effective. A parent may be effectively intolerant of a child's behavior by punishing it, but a person can be said to be intolerant of the dalliances of Hollywood stars even though he is in no position to do anything about them. We may know him as intolerant by the way he speaks about these people. If he regularly makes disparaging jokes about them, swears at them, and blames them for whatever goes wrong with society, we say he is intolerant. We also say that he is intolerant because we sense that if he were in a position to stop their dalliances, he would (swing) into action.

So far, then, the negative side of toleration is fairly clear cut. To be intolerant, a person or a group can act physically to stop what offends (effectively or not), or merely act linguistically by regularly expressing dislike for whatever is not tolerated. However, on the negative side there is another way of responding that complicates matters somewhat. The complication is hidden from us by expressions such as "I can't stand him," "I can't abide him," or even "I can no longer tolerate him." All of them are ambiguous. They either mean that the speaker is intolerant in one of the ways indicated so far, or they mean that the speaker is going to depart the unhappy scene.

When a lady can no longer stand the crude behavior of her husband, she picks up her things and leaves. Here our language creates difficulties for us. It doesn't seem quite right to say, even though she can *no longer* tolerate him, that she is intolerant. That seems too strong. As we have seen, intolerance usually either carries the meaning of doing something to try to stop the offending behavior, or that those who are intolerant would do something were they in a position to do so. In the past, perhaps, we can say of the wife that she was intolerant when she tried to coerce her husband into compliance by moving into the other bedroom; now, when she merely departs the room to get away from his intolerable behavior, it is tempting to use a somewhat softer term. Her response differs enough from acting to change her husband's ways to be viewed as some variant of intolerance. I will speak of this form of behavior as non-tolerant rather than intolerant.

However, immediately there is a problem. There are degrees of "departing a scene." Consider the following situation. A son has married a woman that his mother does not much care for. The daughter-in-law belongs to what the mother considers an inferior ethnic group. Further, the daughter-in-law behaves in ways that the mother considers inappropriate. The mother does not completely depart the scene, but she restricts her contacts with her son and his wife to a minimum.

A lesser degree of departing the scene might be a case in which the mother visits occasionally or invites the couple over, but rarely. Indeed, she does nothing to put the marriage in jeopardy, so it might be asked, is she non-tolerant toward the couple, or has she crossed the line to tolerance? It is difficult to say. What if the contacts with the mother are more than minimal, but not so frequent as they might be if she were pleased with her daughter-in-law? Is she non-tolerant or tolerant?

It should be noted that the same issues of vagueness arise with tolerance. Consider a somewhat similar situation in which the mother continues to maintain contact with her son and daughter-in-law even though she is quite displeased with her son's choice of a spouse. She is not leaving the scene even to some small degree; however, her displeasure is great enough that on occasion, rarely to be sure, she suggests to her son that he ought to end the marriage. She also, rarely again, makes disparaging comments about the daughter-in-law: "Well, she really doesn't keep a clean house," and "I've seen her flirt with the man next door." Even she recognizes that her efforts to break up the marriage are doomed to fail, but she can't resist. Should we say that she is intolerant, or has she, as well, crossed the line to tolerance? I'll return to these borderline cases later.

So far, looking at the negative side of toleration has helped to delineate that concept. It is time now to turn to the positive side for some further delineation. The word that best identifies this side of the continuum is *acceptance*. The formula for that concept is as follows:

X accepts Y in ways a, b, c, . . . n with respect to features o, p, q, . . . w.

Like intolerance, acceptance occurs in degrees. Formerly, David was tolerant of Catholics, but now he accepts them. What does that mean? It could mean that since marrying Margaret O'Grady, he has joined the Church and is presently a fully participating member. He accepts Catholicism with respect to marriage, baptism, and so on (a, b, and c). I will call this form of acceptance *full acceptance*. Similarly, Bill fully accepts the Republican Party by helping it gather money and voters—and does so with respect to that party's stance on taxation, the role of the government in private affairs, and so on. With full acceptance the nagging displeasures associated with toleration are gone or almost gone.

But acceptance can take another form probably more common than full acceptance. Unfortunately, there is no good name for this form. It could be called *partial acceptance*, except that suggests, wrongly, that the accepting parties are holding back. I will call it *regular acceptance* for lack of a better term. People exercising this form of acceptance embrace a concept, a behavior, or a group of people to the extent that it is possible. If Kevin accepts the Iranians in his community, he can do so by working with them, socializing with them, and so forth. Being Irish, he cannot accept them by joining their group. He cannot become an Iranian.

However, in other cases, the accepting party can do more but chooses not to. If Kevin accepts the Anglicans who also live in his neighborhood, we don't expect him to abandon his religion and become an Anglican. He accepts the Anglicans by being friendly to them, attending many of the social functions at their church, engaging in business transactions with them, celebrating marriages in the Anglican Church, and so on. He is accepting not only in these behavioral ways, but also in not begrudging the Anglicans their religion. Although he believes in the doctrines that the Catholic Church teaches him, he does not do so to the extent that he thinks of Anglicans as holding to an inferior or wrong religion. Were he to have very strong attitudes favoring his own religion we would speak of him as tolerating rather than accepting Anglican neighbors. Instead, he talks in a relativistic way: "Well, yes, I believe, and firmly so, in Catholicism, but religion is a matter of personal choice. For my friends Sally and George, the Anglican religion is best; for my friend Peter, the Orthodox Church is best; for Gerry it is Judaism.

The ways that intolerance (and non-toleration), and acceptance (full or otherwise) bracket toleration are not quite parallel. On the negative side, attitudes are not very helpful in differentiating between toleration and intolerance or non-toleration. Presumably, with intolerance, negative attitudes are stronger than for toleration. Because it is difficult to tell the difference between a strong negative attitude and one that is negative to a somewhat lesser degree, we rely mainly on behavior to distinguish them. Intolerant persons do one or more things to make it clear that they are intolerant while tolerant persons are, relatively speaking, passive.

In contrast, on the positive side, an important attitudinal shift takes place as one moves from tolerating someone to some level of acceptance. Indeed, in many situations the behaviors exhibited while tolerating or accepting are identical. Larry tolerates Joanne in the workplace as if he approves of her being there. He talks to her during breaks, is polite to her in meetings, greets her in the morning, and greets her again as she leaves the office in the evening. He does all these things even though he really doesn't care for her because he believes that women should stay at home caring for their children.

If Larry approved of Joanne in the office, he would do many of the same things. Perhaps there would be a bit more enthusiasm in his voice when greeting her, and his conversational tone during breaks would be somewhat friendlier. Nevertheless, if he tried hard to tolerate Joanne, it would be difficult for Joanne or anyone else to tell whether he was tolerating or accepting her.

There is a related problem in applying the concept of toleration. It is not exactly clear at times what those who plead for toleration are seeking. Take the case of the campaign titled *Wall of Tolerance*.[5] Those in charge of the campaign plan to build a wall in Montgomery, Alabama, a city historically famous for what happened there during the civil rights movement. As planned, the names of the contributors will appear on the wall. The campaign literature says the following to potential contributors:

> This beautiful Wall will be a visible, powerful symbol of unity and the strength of the "Tolerance Movement," the new crusade that is being launched by the National Campaign for Tolerance. Every name added to the Wall will serve as a call to action for other Americans of good will to follow your example and join in this great campaign for tolerance and justice.

Understandably, much of what this campaign literature also says is aimed at intolerance. Steps, it says, need to be taken to stop or curtail crimes and other intolerant acts against those who belong to certain races, ethnic and religious groups.

> I am sure you are well aware that many of our schools are troubled with racial discord and intolerance. Some have called it a national crisis. In many of our communities, Americans of all races and backgrounds are assaulting one another. And now Arab Americans and people with Middle Eastern "look" have become targets of hate crimes.

According to this literature, what we must do is take steps to help us all move away from intolerance and toward tolerance.

How many steps does this movement involve? Is the desired change from intolerance to tolerance supposed to leave one acting in certain ways (e.g., not opposing hiring an Arab computer specialist at the office,) but still acting with dislike in one's heart? Technically, that is what the definitions cited above says tolerance (toleration) is. As we saw, one doesn't tolerate behavior one approves of, so are the leaders of the *Wall of Tolerance* focusing mainly on behavioral changes all the while leaving matters of the heart alone? The following passage suggests otherwise. The following passage suggests otherwise (underlined in the original literature):

> The Civil Rights Movement won a resounding victory in the struggle to change America's laws. Now, through the National Campaign for Tolerance, we can join together in the battle to change American hearts.

The change here might simply be that as people move from being intolerant (or non-tolerant) to tolerant, their hearts soften, even if only a little bit. They still don't like those other people, but the dislike has lessened enough so that, presumably, they no longer are tempted to do anything nasty; however, this passage can be interpreted in another way. What the campaign leaders of the *Wall of Tolerance* may be craving is a change of heart great enough to take those converted from intolerance all the way to acceptance. They may very well hope that their campaign will literally change the hearts of people so they will now love their neighbors rather than harbor some form of dislike for them.

If this is what the campaign supporters of the *Wall of Tolerance* hope for, the concept of toleration is seemingly being stretched beyond what it customarily is taken to mean. People are being urged to transcend toleration and rise to acceptance, but the language being used is still of toleration. It is not difficult to understand why they used the language they did. It has already been noted that, behaviorally, toleration and acceptance are often quite similar, so it is easy to confuse the two. But beyond that, the paradox of the concept of toleration seems to be at work here. On the one side, *toleration, tolerance, tolerating* (the t-words) all project a strong positive image on the level of rhetoric. Politicians, social activists, and preachers can ask for more of this t-stuff and feel that they are on the side of the angels.

On the other side, those who are tolerated do not see this t-stuff in quite such positive terms. They see themselves as vulnerable because of the ever present negative feelings about whoever is tolerated. They sense that those who are tolerant in good times may return to their intolerant ways when times turn bad. For them, toleration is not good enough. Of course, it is important to urge people to be tolerant, but from the side of the one tolerated, that is not enough. The tolerated state is insecure, so it will be tempting to use the t-words hoping to get something more than tolerance. The paradox, then is that toleration will be praised to the hilt and yet, in the end, be rejected in favor of something else.

A bothersome question comes to the fore at this point. How are we to characterize those who use the t-words in order to transcend these "t-concepts?" Are they stretching the meaning of them to the breaking point in order to take advantage of their positive rhetorical flavor? Or are they implying by their uses that the definitions proffered at the beginning of this article by philosophers are wrong? If the latter, then these users of the "stretched" sense of the t-words are telling us that in certain circumstances one does not, after all, always have to feel negatively toward the people or things that one tolerates.

Support for this interpretation can be found in the following argument. Attitudes are not digital in nature. If I had a negative attitude toward Gertrud at one point in my life, it is not likely that later, my attitude would suddenly switch over to the positive side. It could happen that way if she acted bravely in an extremely dangerous situation. However, more than likely, if an attitude change were to take place, it would happen gradually. I could come to like Gertrud a little more after working with her for a while, and then a little more as I observed how she did her work week after week.

What this suggests for toleration is that people could very well experience a range of attitudes under the toleration banner. On the border separating toleration and intolerance (and non-toleration), take John for an example. Because John has some strong negative attitudes, he might tolerate someone only grudgingly. Tolerating under these conditions would be a burden for him. Later he could tolerate more readily as his dislikes lessened little by little. He might even get to the point of indifference to those whom he has been tolerating. If he became indifferent in a laid back sort of way, it would be tempting to say that his is still acting tolerantly. But if he gradually came to mildly approve of those he has tolerated up to now, we get into the vague area where, again, we wonder if the t-words apply at all.

There is another factor that further complicates the use of the word *tolerance* and its relatives. So far vagueness has been the culprit; toleration fades into acceptance. As a result, it is difficult to know when to apply the t-words, and when not. Recall the formula given above for intolerance:

X is intolerant of Y in ways a, b, c, . . . n with respect to features o, p, q, . . . w.

The comparable formula for acceptance looks like this:

X is tolerant of Y in ways a, b, c, . . . n with respect to features o, p, q, . . . w.

Implied in all of these formulas is that the various states they formulate are often situation specific. For example, it is possible for John to be tolerant with respect to Sally's smoking and her tendency to gossip. At the same time it is possible for John to be intolerant of Sally's tendency to tell fibs. In applying the t-words to John in these ways, we are no longer dealing with vagueness, but with ambiguity. John is tolerant of Sally in some ways but not in others.

Take an example from John's life. Let's say Jim is gay. John accepts Jim in the workplace. He does so in such a way that he jokes around with him, discusses the daily ball scores with him, and works well with him in writing company reports. It is tempting to say that John accepts Jim. The situation is not quite the same on the home front. Jim lives with his partner down the street where John lives. John's attitude now varies from indifference to mild disapproval; however, it seems proper to say that he tolerates Jim since he does nothing to encourage Jim to move to some other neighborhood. Indeed on occasion, he even helps "the boys" out when heavy work needs to be done around their house. But John has a son who has just turned sixteen. Fearing perhaps that the son might get too friendly with Jim and his partner, John has made it clear to his 16-year-old that he is not to socialize with those "queers." Now John is being intolerant, or, perhaps, non-tolerant.

I submit that many actions and reactions that we have toward individuals and groups of people is much like John's ambiguous way of reacting to Jim. Of course, there will be others whose reactions are unambiguous. There is no ambiguity in Sam's hate for the Jews. He does all he can to keep them out of his workplace and neighborhood. He even gives money in support of HAMAS. On the other side, Tom's acceptance of Jews is wholehearted. He likes them and even seeks their company in social settings. I surmise, however, that there are more people like John than there are like Sam and Tom. These people can be assessed as being accepting of a person in this way and that, tolerant in this way and that, and even intolerant in this way and that. Thus it will be difficult to call them, as persons, one thing or the other. Is John tolerant of gay people? Well, yes and no.

Exploring the trichotomous nature of *tolerance* and its related words shows that the definitions presented at the beginning of this article are not totally satisfactory. They offer little to help us understand the t-words. Perhaps these definitions do all that one can expect from any definition. Perhaps, then, one should not rely too much on definitions to explain terms like *toleration*. To understand such complex concepts, we need some broader form of explanation.

The broader form adopted in this article takes account of the "geography" of these words. What was discovered is that *tolerance* is situated between two classes of other concepts. On the negative side are *intolerance* and *non-toleration*, while *full acceptance* and *regular acceptance* are situated on the positive side. What was also discovered is that no bold lines separate the t-concepts from those on either side. The t-words suffer from more than their share of vagueness. On the negative side, intolerance and non-tolerance, it is rarely clear whether a policy adopted by a person (or a government) actually falls on the negative side or represents toleration. More than enough vagueness is found also on the positive side. Some policies that are called *tolerant* are backed by an attitude of indifference rather than one of dislike. It may even be that certain very mild attitudes of acceptance are compatible with the t-words as well.

Beyond vagueness, there also are ambiguities that make these words difficult to use. This is especially so when we try to apply them to people. When people have conflicting emotions, it is not easy to say whether they are tolerant or not. With regard to a single individual or thing, people can be accepting in some respects, tolerant in others, and intolerant in still others. In situations which are themselves rich with vagueness and ambiguity, it is no wonder that the t-words are difficult, and perhaps impossible to define.

Notes

1. Susan Mendus, "Toleration," *The Encyclopedia of Ethics*, Vol. 2, ed. Lawrence C. Becker (New York: Garland Publishing, 1992), 1251.
2. Mendus, "Toleration," 1251.
3. Maurice Cranston, "Toleration," *The Encyclopedia of Philosophy*, Vol. 8, ed. Paul Edwards (New York: Macmillan, 1967), 143-46.
4. Nick Fotion and Gerrard Elfstrom, *Toleration* (Tuscaloosa, Ala. and London: The University of Alabama Press, 1992), 61-71.
5. National Campaign for Tolerance, "Wall of Tolerance," (Southern Poverty Law Center, Montgomery, Ala., 2002, mailing).

On Having Done With It: The Death of Modernist Tolerance[1]

J. Budziszewski

Tolerance is a puzzling virtue because the whole point of it lies in putting up with some things that are immoral, offensive, erroneous, in poor taste, or in some other sense bad. In the end the various rationales for tolerance boil down to just two, one of which grounds it on a paradox, the other on an incoherency. Although I briefly describe the former, my concern in this essay is primarily to bury the latter.

Classical and Modernist Tolerance

We owe the classical theory, which grounds tolerance on a paradox, to the ancient Christian writers. In their view, the reason we put up with some bad things is that *the nature of the good demands doing so.* We first find this argument elaborated in reference to religious error by such writers as Tertullian, Hosius of Cordova, Athanasius, Lactantius, Hilary of Poitiers, Gregory of Nazianzus, John Chrysostom, and Isidore of Pelusium.[2] Here, for example, is Lactantius:

> Religion ought to be defended, not by killing but by dying, not by fury but by patience, not by crime but by faith. The former action each time belongs to evil, the latter to good, and it is necessary that good be the practice of religion, not evil. If you wish, indeed, to defend religion by blood, if by torments, if by evil, then it will not be defended, but it will be polluted and violated. There is nothing so voluntary as religion, and if the mind of the one sacrificing in a religious rite is turned aside, the act is now removed; there is no act of religion.[3]

In the classical view, the same good that commands tolerance—in this case the supreme good, fellowship with God—also defines its proper limits. This is why Lactantius holds that although heresy must not be resisted by violence, it ought to be resisted vigorously by argument, example, and the teaching and internal discipline of the Church. Moreover, tolerance for false opinions does not imply tolerance for crimes, such as infanticide, that might result from these opinions. The duty of the state to punish wrongdoing is not impaired by the possibility that their perpetrators may not regard them as wrong.

We owe the competing theory, which grounds tolerance on an incoherency, to early modern thinkers like Samuel Pufendorf and Thomas Hobbes, who were wearied by wars of religion and ready to grasp at straws. In their view, the reason we put up with some bad things is not that the nature of the good demands doing so, but that *we must suspend judgment about the nature of the good.* Starting from this premise it is hard to see why anything should be tolerated, why anything shouldn't be, or how to derive any conclusion at all. Indeed all such arguments smack of getting something from nothing. Hobbes, for example, famously imagines that he is neutral among the various doctrines of the *summum bonum*, because he asserts only a *summum malum.* But, of course, to suppose a greatest evil (in Hobbes' case, death) is to suppose a greatest good (in Hobbes' case, life). Hobbes turns out not to be neutral at all. In his view, people who think there are some things worse than death are simply wrong.

Though Hobbes was no liberal, today's liberal thinkers are his heirs. Not many liberals follow Hobbes in thinking that they can make judgments about evil without making judgments about good,[4] but almost all agree with him that judgments about good should be avoided. The late John Rawls both epitomizes this kind of reasoning and shows why it has reached a dead end.

According to Rawls, modern democratic society is characterized not just by a plurality of opinions, but by a plurality of comprehensive doctrines, all of which are incompatible (here the classical theory of tolerance agrees), yet each of which is reasonable (here it radically disagrees).[5] How then can we agree about what justice requires us to tolerate? His solution is that fundamental disagreements must be privatized. Although citizens and officials may publically defend their political opinions, they should make no appeal to their comprehensive doctrines whatsoever. To Rawls' credit, he recognizes what Hobbes never did: In order to stop talking about what is good, one must stop talking about a great many other things besides. What are we to make of this view?

Before criticizing the Rawlsian theory, let us be sure to understand just how far its demand extends. Consider Abraham Lincoln's *Second Inaugural Address,* widely regarded as the greatest speech by a statesman in the history of the American republic. Rawls would find at least two-thirds of it impermissible. Here is what Lincoln says about the still-ongoing Civil War:

> Both [sides] read the same Bible and pray to the same God, and each invokes His aid against the other. It may seem strange that any men should dare to ask a just God's assistance in wringing their bread from the sweat of other men's faces, but let us judge not, that we be not judged.[6] The prayers of both could not be answered. That of neither has been answered fully. The Almighty has His own purposes. "Woe unto the world because of offenses; for it must needs be that

offenses come, but woe to that man by whom the offense cometh."[7] If we shall suppose that American slavery is one of those offenses which, in the providence of God, must needs come, but which, having continued through His appointed time, He now wills to remove, and that He gives to both North and South this terrible war as the woe due to those by whom the offense came, shall we discern therein any departure from those divine attributes which the believers in a living God always ascribe to Him? Fondly do we hope, fervently do we pray, that this mighty scourge of war may speedily pass away. Yet, if God wills that it continue until all the wealth piled by the bondsman's two hundred and fifty years of unrequited toil shall be sunk, and until every drop of blood drawn with the lash shall be paid by another drawn with the sword, as was said three thousand years ago,[8] so still it must be said "the judgments of the Lord are true and righteous altogether."[9]

God, Bible, prayers, providence, sin, punishment, and repentance: such themes are unendurable. They can no more be expressed in the Rawlsian Newspeak than in the Orwellian, at least not in the public square. Nor is Lincoln the only offender. In fact, appeal to comprehensive doctrines—that is, to shared ideals— is the stuff of American rhetoric from the opening invocation of "the laws of nature and nature's God" in the *Declaration of Independence*, to Martin Luther King's exhortation in his *I Have a Dream* speech to make justice a reality "for all of God's children." Could we satisfy Rawls merely by excising the references to Deity? The answer is no. Suppose we make King's speech more presentable by allowing him to refer only to the brotherhood of man, not the fatherhood of God. Unacceptable; it would still evoke a vision of man. Or suppose we clean up the *Declaration* by allowing it to mention only the laws of nature, not nature's God. Inadmissible; it would still propose a concept of nature. On Rawlsian grounds, we may not permit allusions to any comprehensive doctrine. Should anyone protest that Rawls is at least as controversial as nature, man, or God, Rawls can reply "Yes, but my doctrine is not comprehensive. It is political, not metaphysical."

Here is the problem. Rawls considers his approach tolerant only because it treats every moral, religious and philosophical view the same, but of course it does no such thing. Privatization is compatible with certain comprehensive doctrines, like neo-Kantianism and Millian Utilitarianism. It is incompatible with others, such as Judaism, Christianity, Deism, or for that matter, Benthamite Utilitarianism. True, they are all privatized, but in the case of the former, to be privatized is virtually the same thing as to be enacted. What the Rawlsian policy really does, then, is privilege some comprehensive doctrines at the expense of others. You may publically argue *like* a neo-Kantian, so long as you do not argue explicitly for the doctrine; however you must not even argue *like* a Catholic or a Jew—nor are you allowed to contest the prohibition. You are shut out.

To see how this works in practice, consider abortion. The comprehensive doctrines of one side permit the practice; those of the other prohibit it. Rawlsian privatizers says, "Let's agree to disagree. I won't mention my comprehensive doctrine, and you won't mention yours." But of course, to agree to disagree is precisely to permit abortion. To say that privatization treats all comprehensive views the same is therefore merely a camouflaged grab for power, a fraudulent technique for achieving an outcome without having to defend it. Though Rawls is open to debate among all "reasonable" doctrines, the reasonable ones turn out to be only the ones which accept privatization. These don't even include all liberals, much less conservatives and other non-privatizers. This Rawlsian preference for some comprehensive doctrines over others is incoherent, and could have been rendered coherent only if Rawls had dared resort to comprehensive doctrine himself—if he had frankly pressed claims about moral reality.

But let us not be too hard on liberals, as though they were the only ones guilty of the neutralist fallacy. Consider postmodernists, who imagine themselves beyond all these early-to-late-modern conundrums.

Postmodernists agree with the view this essay has been pressing, that there is no such thing as neutrality. In their view, no claim about what to do, what to tolerate or who should decide can ever be validated except in the context of some Big Story or "meta-narrative." It would seem that in this case they must decide which Big Story is true. But no, they say they have seen through the Big Stories; they are "suspicious of meta-narratives."[10] But suspicion of meta-narratives means suspicion of *all* meta-narratives—which means postmodernists are *outside* all of them and *neutral* among all of them—which, by their own premises, is impossible. Actually postmodernism itself is a meta-narrative, a Big Story about how certain clever intellectuals came to see through the Big Stories of all the rest. Though it pretends to be tolerant in the sense of putting all meta-narratives on an equal footing of suspicion, it is actually intolerant of every meta-narrative but itself. Any opinion may have a seat at the table, but only if it relativizes itself—which is to say, no one has a seat at the table except postmodernists.

Varieties of Neutralist Experience

Motive

To proponents of the classical theory, the zombie-like persistence of the modernist fallacy of neutrality defies credulity. Refuted time after time, its defenders go on proposing suspension of judgment as the very basis of tolerant judgment, seemingly unable to recognize that choice, by its nature, is never neutral. It is in the nature of decision to decide *something* for *some reason*.

A limit of rational argument against any fallacy is that once the fallacy has been exposed, the motives for hanging onto it are irrational. The neutralism of the modernist theory of tolerance is a case in point. It clears the conscience of an age whose convictions are in decay. It gives us something to say when we have nothing to say. It puts opponents on the defensive by defining their opinions as "bias." In a perverse way, its very incoherency has tactical advantages. Consistent arguments are difficult to twist, but from an inconsistent premise, anything can be proven. So it is that neutrality comes in many flavors, shapes, and colors. Besides the liberal and postmodernist proponents whom I have mentioned, there have been conservative neutralists like Michael Oakeshott, Marxist neutralists like Jurgen Habermas and even anarchist neutralists like Robert Paul Wolff. Each supposed that *his* neutrality justified his position. It ought to go without saying that if it makes a difference which version of neutralism one follows, then none of them are actually neutral. Unfortunately, it can't. Each time one must point it out.

In the interests of having done with it, of getting over the long-drawn-out neutralist fallacy, I offer the following modest analysis. The purpose is to exhaustively classify all of the relevant meanings of neutrality, thereby showing in advance the futility of thinking up new varieties.

Analysis

What concerns us is what might be called ethical or world-view neutrality. To be sure, the term *neutrality* is sometimes used in other ways that do not concern us. For instance, when Herbert A. Wechsler famously proposed neutral principles of Constitutional law, he meant only that the reasons given for any judicial decision should be general enough to transcend the outcome of the particular case.[11] A better name for what he was getting at would be *generality*. Although what Wechsler calls neutrality is sometimes confused with ethical or world-view neutrality,[12] Wechsler himself realized that it has nothing to do with it.

Broadly speaking, ethical or world-view neutrality may be regarded as a property of a *policy*, as a property of a *debate* over policy, as a property of *rules for the final choice* of policy, or as some combination of these properties. Each of these senses may be further divided and subdivided. The result of such dissection may be outlined as follows.[13] For the reader's convenience, the headings of the lowest-level entries are in boldface. These are the senses of neutrality that the analysis yields.

I.   Neutrality of Policy.
    A.   Neutrality of Anticipated Impact.
        1.   **Abstract.** A policy is called "neutral" iff its anticipated effects are *equally* desirable no matter the conception of the good by which this desirability is evaluated.
        2.   **Individualistic.** A policy is called "neutral" iff its anticipated application to a person is *unaffected* by the particular conception of the good that the person holds.

B. Neutrality of Language.
   1. **Substantive.**
      a. **Egalitarian.** A policy is called "neutral" iff the language in which it is expressed conveys *equal* esteem for every conception of the good.
      b. **Prohibitive.** A policy is called "neutral" iff the language in which it is expressed does not convey esteem for *any* conception of the good.
   2. **Formal.** A policy is called "neutral" iff the language in which it is expressed does not include any terms or classifications *the application of which would require* an understanding of any conception of the good.

II. Neutrality of Debate.
   A. **Blind.** Debate is called "neutral" iff policy makers refuse to give any consideration to *whether* the anticipated effects of policies under consideration are desirable according to any conception of the good.
   B. **Recursive.** Debate is called "neutral" iff it is limited to *policies* that are neutral, in one of the senses listed under outline division I, Neutrality of Policy.

III. Neutrality of Rules for Final Choice.
   A. As to Policy Makers.
      1. Non-random.
         a. **View-regarding.** Final choice of policy is called "neutral" iff the weight assigned a policy maker's vote does not depend on *the conception of the good that he holds.*
         b. **Fitness-regarding.** Final choice of policy is called "neutral" iff the weight assigned to a policy maker's vote does not depend on *his fitness to make decisions* (by whatever conception of the good this fitness may be evaluated).
         c. **Conduct-regarding.** Final choice of policy is called "neutral" iff only those are allowed to vote whose conduct during *debate* is neutral, in one of the senses listed under Division II, Neutrality of Debate.
      2. **Random.** Final choice of policy is called "neutral" iff the choice among alternatives is made *as in a lottery*, rather than by voting.[14]
   B. As to Alternatives.
      1. **Blind.** Final choice of policy is called "neutral" iff the weight assigned to an alternative in the choice procedure (whatever kind of choice procedure this may be) does not depend on whether the anticipated effects of its implementation are desirable (by whatever conception of the good this desirability may

be evaluated).

2. **Recursive.** Final choice of policy is called "neutral" iff only those *policies* may be enacted that are also neutral, in one of the senses listed under Division I, Neutrality of Policy.

As I mentioned previously, the outline yields exactly thirteen senses of neutrality, having nothing in common except an effort to get rid of the influence of all conceptions of the good. These thirteen senses are the outline's thirteen lowest-level entries, the headings of which are in boldface: I.A.1, I.A.2, I.B.1.a, I.B.1.b, I.B.2, II.A, II.B, III.A.1.a, III.A.1.b, III.A.1.c, III.A.2, III.B.1, and III.B.2.

Figure 4.1

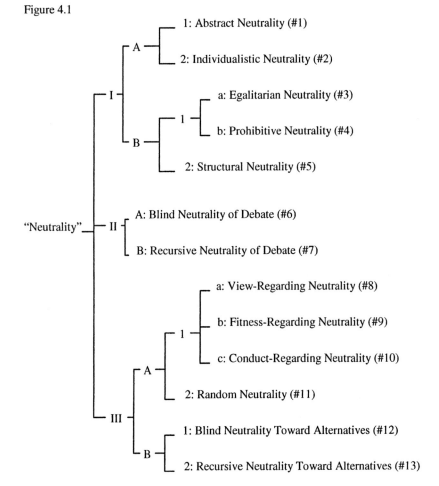

If we convert the outline into a tree diagram (Figure 4.1), they become the thirteen tips of its branches, reading the parenthetical notation #1 as Sense 1, #2 as Sense 2, and so forth.

The higher-level entries in the outline are needed only to show the logical relations among all of these senses of "neutrality," so that the reader can assure himself that they really are mutually exclusive and exhaustive. That task having been accomplished, however, we are now able to discuss the thirteen senses themselves.

Discussion

For convenience, at each step in the following discussion I consider several of the thirteen senses of neutrality at once. The argument makes two different kinds of logical moves—sometimes one, sometimes the other. In each, something is shown about the state of affairs contemplated by a given sense of the term neutrality. One kind of move is to show that the state of affairs could not be brought about at all. The other is to show that whether or not it were brought about, it would not succeed in doing what it is supposed to do—somehow suspending the relevance of world-view, especially conceptions of the good. Either of these logical moves justifies saying that neutrality in the sense in question is impossible. So we begin:

> *Sense 1*: Abstract Neutrality. A policy is called "neutral" iff its anticipated effects are equally desirable, no matter the conception of the good by which this desirability is evaluated.
> *Sense 2*: Individualistic Neutrality. A policy is called "neutral" iff its anticipated application to a person is unaffected by the particular conception of the good that the person holds.

Abstract neutrality can be dismissed easily. It is unachievable because there is no such thing as a policy whose effects are equally desirable no matter by what conception of the good we evaluate them. Anything that can be deemed desirable by one conception of the good can also be deemed undesirable by another. So we eliminate abstract neutrality from further consideration.

Individualistic neutrality presents a slightly more difficult case. The idea is that we should not deny individuals advantages or impose upon them disadvantages just because of the conceptions of the good that they happen to hold. Certainly nothing prevents us from following such a rule; but it presents other difficulties. Let us warm up by considering whether following it would be desirable.

At first it seems that it would be. For instance, certainly it would be wrong to deny welfare payments to poor people whose views about the good agree with the opposition party, while granting them to poor people whose views about the good agree with the party in power. On the other hand, certainly it would be *right* to deny elementary-school teaching appointments to individuals who profess the goodness of sexual relations with children, while granting them to otherwise qualified people who profess no such belief. The question (to take a leaf from Constitutional jurisprudence) should be whether the pattern of penalties and rewards bears a rational relationship to a legitimate governmental purpose; and whenever we speak of legitimate purposes, we must have recourse to conceptions of the good. So individualistic neutrality is not desirable.

Even supposing that it were desirable, would it *deserve* to be called a form of neutrality—would it really "neutralize" conceptions of the good? For even were it proper after all to ignore people's conceptions of the good in order to decide whether to confer advantages or disadvantages upon them, the fact is that conceptions of the good come back like homing pigeons when we try to decide *what counts* as an advantage or a disadvantage. There are two possibilities here. If we are to judge which effects of a policy count as advantages and which as disadvantages *according to the conceptions of the good held by the affected individuals*, this is as much as to reinstate the requirement of abstract neutrality, which we have already found to be impossible. On the other hand, if we are to judge which effects of a policy count as advantages and which as disadvantages *according to the conceptions of the good held by its makers*—for instance, as though policy makers were to regard health as good, enact a health policy, and then decree that its applicability to any individual would be unaffected by whether the individual himself cared about being healthy—well, this is certainly something we can do, but what would be "neutral" about it? It would privilege the policy makers' conceptions of the good over the conceptions of the good of the affected individuals.

> *Sense 3*: Egalitarian Neutrality. A policy is called "neutral" iff the language in which it is expressed conveys equal esteem for every conception of the good.
> *Sense 4*: Prohibitive Neutrality. A policy is called "neutral" iff the language in which it is expressed does not convey esteem for any conception of the good.

Neutrality as to content, whether egalitarian or prohibitive, is easy to deal with. In every social status quo, particular conceptions of the good are held in esteem while others are held in disesteem. The attitude of a content neutralist is like Pontius Pilate: He wants to wash his hands of the matter, to say "I shall neither influence nor be influenced by the prevailing distribution of esteem." One hand-washing strategy is to express equal esteem for every conception of the good; the other is to express no esteem at all for any.

Now there are two difficulties with this. The first is that the very intention of neither influencing nor being influenced by the prevailing distribution of esteem needs justification, but it can be justified only by recourse to particular conceptions of the good. One might, for instance, argue that one should not be influenced *by* the prevailing distribution because it esteems what ought not be esteemed and fails to esteem what ought to be esteemed, and that one should not *influence* the prevailing distribution because however wrong it may be, the good of social cohesion is achieved by customary understandings and not by pure reason. I do not endorse these particular arguments, nor claim that no other arguments could be offered in their place. I only assert that some such arguments are necessary, and that all such arguments must rely on conceptions of the good.

The second difficulty is that it is impossible to *keep* the language of public policy from having an influence on the prevailing distribution of esteem and disesteem. Government is a socializing agent. To the extent that people are impressed with its wisdom they will model their judgments after its own. To the extent that they hold it in contempt their judgments will be shaped by reaction. Let the language of its policies express equal esteem for every conception of the good; this will have the appearance of a judgment that every conception of the good is equally estimable. Let the language of its policies express no esteem for any conception of the good; this will have the appearance of a judgment that every conception of the good is equally beneath estimation. In either case, the message is that one's conception of the good is a matter of indifference, and this message cannot help but alter the status quo.

Altering the status quo is defensible only if the status quo *ought* to be altered. But just as no argument *against* the alteration of the status quo can be made without recourse to particular conceptions of the good, so no argument *for* its alteration can be made without recourse to particular conceptions of the good. We see then that there is nothing neutral about either egalitarian or prohibitive neutrality.

> *Sense 5*: Formal Neutrality. A policy is called "neutral" iff the language in which it is expressed does not include any terms or classifications the application of which would require an understanding of any conception of the good.

Formal neutrality has no interest for the ethical neutralist unless this form is connected with substance: Unless it *abolishes the influence* of conceptions of the good in matters of policy. Thus to show that formal neutrality were really neutral, we would have to show that it promoted neutrality of policy in one of the other, substantive senses of the term. These other senses are neutrality of anticipated effects (Sense 1, abstract neutrality, and Sense 2, individualistic neutrality), and neutrality of content (Sense 3, egalitarian neutrality, and Sense 4, prohibitive neutrality).

However, formal neutrality *couldn't possibly* promote neutrality in any of these other four senses, because, as we have already shown, each of them is incoherent in itself: Either because the state of affairs that it describes is impossible, or because the state of affairs that it describes is possible but does not do what it is supposed to do—does not suspend the relevance of conceptions of the good after all. Formal neutrality enters the same logical drain that they do, and for the same reasons.

Sense 6: Blind Neutrality of Debate. Debate is called "neutral" iff policy makers refuse to give any consideration to whether the antici-pated effects of policies under consideration are desirable according to any conception of the good.

Sense 7: Recursive Neutrality of Debate. Debate is called "neutral" iff it is limited to policies that are neutral in one of the senses listed under Division I, Neutrality of Policy.

Recursive neutrality of debate can be banished right away, because the senses of neutrality to which it "recurs"—senses 1 through 5—have been dis-missed already. Blind neutrality of debate presents a different case.

On the face of it, blind neutrality is gibberish. For to prohibit policy makers from considering whether the anticipated effects of their policies are desirable is to take away the only reason for which we set them to making policies in the first place. Some ethical neutralists, however, would reject this line of reasoning. They would say that whether the anticipated effects of a policy are desirable is beside the point; that what ought to concern us is whether the policy is *right*. In opposition to "teleologists" who maintain that the rightness of right actions has to do with their relationship with what is good for us, they maintain the "deonto-logical" thesis that whatever the rightness of right actions has nothing to do with their relationship with what is good for us. Although this comports odds with the alleged opposition of neutralists to "moralism"—well, it does have the reek of honest moral sweat about it. It suggests disinterestedness.

But all the sweating is for nothing, for the distinction between so-called teleologists and so-called deontologists is artificial and misleading. Right and good depend on each other in much the same way as space and dimension, or light and color; no clear sense can be given to either element of such a pair without the other. Whenever anyone professes that something is right, ask why. To the reply, ask why again. Eventually, unless the professor scurvily takes ref-uge in an infinite regression, the answer will involve a conception of what is good for human beings. (It would make perfectly good sense to knock down all thirteen senses of neutrality at once by this method, but such plain and obvious arguments fail to command scholarly attention, so we will continue the slow way).

Assumptions about the good lurk around every neutralist corner. Even dis-interestedness must be a good in some sense, perhaps a good of character, or promoting it would be unintelligible.[15]

Sense 8: View-Regarding Neutrality. Final choice of policy is called "neutral" iff the weight assigned a policy maker's vote does not de-pend on the conception of the good that he holds."

Sense 9: Fitness-Regarding Neutrality. Final choice of policy is called "neutral" iff the weight assigned a policy maker's vote does not de-pend on his fitness to make decisions (by whatever conception of the good this fitness may be evaluated).

Sense 10: Conduct-Regarding Neutrality. Final choice of policy is called "neutral" iff only those policy makers are allowed to vote whose speech during debate is neutral, in one of the senses listed under Division II, Neutrality of Debate.

Sense 11: Random Neutrality. Final choice of policy is called" neutral" iff the choice among alternatives is made as in a lottery, rather than by voting.

After debate is over, we come down at last to the final choice of policy. How can we make our final choice procedure neutral? Two strategies for doing this have to do with how we treat the policy makers. The non-random strategy is to call for a vote, but make sure that the rules about who votes and how much their votes count are uninfluenced by conceptions of the good. View-regarding, fitness-regarding, and conduct-regarding neutrality—Senses 8, 9, and 10—come under this rubric. The random strategy is to recognize that voting procedures cannot be neutralized, and throw the final outcome to chance instead. This corresponds to Sense 11.

All three non-random senses can be mowed down with a single stroke of the scythe. For it is hardly neutral to prefer the opinions of one group of policy makers over the opinions of another merely because the first group contains more votes.[16] What reasons could we have for doing so? Perhaps we have a high regard for domestic tranquility—we would rather count ballots than bullets. But that reflects a conception of the good. Perhaps we view majority rule as a hedge against tyranny. But that also reflects a conception of the good. Perhaps we think that alternatives ought to be chosen on their merits, and that majorities are less likely to err than minorities. But *that* is a frank repudiation of the neutralist's whole thesis. Need we accept one of these three reasons for adopting a non-random final choice procedure? Not at all; others can be offered. The point is that none will come any nearer to exorcising those devilish conceptions of the good.

The plot thickens. For if non-random procedures for final choice cannot really be neutral, then should we award the palm to random procedures instead? No again. First let us consider lotteries in which each policy alternative has an equal chance of being drawn. As even neutralists are quick to recognize, treating policy alternatives as unequally choice-worthy just because *some* conceptions of the good say that they are is a violation of neutrality. By the same token, treating policy alternatives as *equally* choice-worthy when *not all* conceptions of the good say that they are is also a violation of neutrality. Equal-chance lotteries do just this. So, although they may sometimes be good ideas, they flunk the test of neutrality too.[17]

Could we neutralize the policy lottery by relaxing the requirement of equal chances? No. Either these chances would be assigned under the explicit guidance of a particular conception of the good (better policy alternatives getting better chances), or they would not. Should they be assigned according to a conception of the good, the violation of neutrality would be clear to the even meanest intellect. But should they be assigned in any other fashion, we would have almost the same problem as with equal-chance lotteries: The distribution of chances could be considered neutral only if it were endorsable by every conceivable conception of the good, which is clearly impossible.

We have just been speaking of equal and unequal treatment of policy alternatives. Parallel arguments can be drawn about equal and unequal treatment of policy *makers*, supplementing the arguments against view-regarding and fitness-regarding neutrality offered just earlier. I should not want this to be misunderstood. From the mere fact that neither equal nor unequal treatment is neutral, nothing follows about whether equality has merit. We need only bear in mind that, like any other ideal, equality is affirmed by some conceptions of the good and repudiated by others. One must simply be sure of the conception of the good to which one is committed.

> *Sense 12*: Blind Neutrality Toward Alternatives. Final choice of policy is called "neutral" iff the weight assigned to an alternative in the choice procedure (whatever kind of choice procedure may be is) does not depend on whether the anticipated effects of its implementation are desirable (by whatever conception of the good this desirability may be evaluated).
> *Sense 13*: Recursive Neutrality Toward Alternatives. Final choice of policy is called "neutral" iff only those policies may be enacted that are also in one of the senses listed under Division I, Neutrality of Policy.

Recursive neutrality toward alternatives can be eliminated for the same reason as recursive neutrality of debate (Sense 7): The senses of neutrality to which it recurs (Senses 1 through 5) have already been knocked out of the running.

I might now be expected to say that blind neutrality toward alternatives can be eliminated for the same reason as blind neutrality of debate (Sense 6); however, the parallel this time does not hold. Another parallel does hold: Between blind neutrality toward alternatives and random neutrality (Sense 11). We saw above that no matter how we assign chances to the policy alternatives in a lottery, conceptions of the good still come in the back door. In exactly the same fashion, conceptions of the good come in the back door no matter how we assign weights to the alternatives in a voting procedure. We may assign equal or unequal weights, and either way, we may or may not be doing the right thing. However, we should not delude ourselves that the thing we are doing is neutral.

Concluding Reflections

We have examined all thirteen senses of ethical or world-view neutrality. One may be excused for feeling as though he had just been shown in a geometry marathon that circles can never be squares, whether drawn with chalk, paint or crayons, whether made of felt, paper or plastic, whether represented in literal or figurative idiom or whipped up out of thought. The marathon is over, yet it could begin all over again unless a few more words are added.

Someone might object that the thirteen senses of neutrality do not exhaust the possibilities after all: That because each of them concerns either policy, debate over policy or final choice of policy, my arguments apply only to governmental activism. "You've shown that activist regimes can never achieve neutrality," my opponent might say; "but what about laissez-faire? For that matter, what about anarchy?" The objection is invalid because it depends on an unnecessary limitation of the term *policy*. Let's see how.

As to laissez-faire, it suffices to point out that I have not hurled the accusation of non-neutrality against *nominal* policies that concern the what of social life while excusing *adverbial* policies that concern the how;[18] that I have not hurled it against *first-order* policies that say what is to be done while excusing *meta-policies* that say what kinds of policies are to be allowed; and that I have not hurled it against policy-making by commission, while excusing policy-making by omission.[19] Thus, laissez-faire is a policy in my sense too, and the arguments I have offered already show why it cannot be neutral. The same is true of anarchy, for of course anarchy is merely a meta-policy of *universal* omission. It is a meta-policy of having no policies.[20]

To be sure, all of the distinctions made above—nominal versus adverbial policies and so forth—concern matters of great consequence. There are choices to be made here; it makes a difference whether we live under an activist or under a laissez-faire regime, under anarchy or under *archy*. But where anything makes a difference, neutrality has already flown. The only way to make the choice is to consider the goods involved or affected by the decision.

How often one hears this line: "Perhaps *perfect* neutrality is impossible after all, but shouldn't we get as close to it as we can?"[21] Let us distinguish between possible and impossible varieties of aspiration. In neutrality, we are not speaking of something we can think but never bring about, like a perfect circle; we are speaking of what we *cannot consistently think*, like a square circle. There is no partial neutrality for the same reason that there is no partially square circle.

The modern theory of tolerance is precisely the aspiration for this chimera. Though it can never effect the "neutral" square circles it desires, it certainly does have effects. It has these effects by refusing to call things by their right names and by misunderstanding its own premises. No doubt there is some curious conception of the good according to which such perverse effects are desirable. That conception might be worth learning, if only to help us understand our times.

Notes

1. Copyright ©1992 by Transaction Publishers. Reprinted by permission of the publishers. Original found in *True Tolerance: Liberalism and the Necessity of Judgement* (Piscataway, N. J.: Transaction Publishers, 1992), 103-17. The original has been revised by author for this publication.

2. For discussion, see J. Budziszewski, Appendix 3, "Patristic Sources," in *True Tolerance* (New Brunswick, N.J.: Transaction Publishers, 1992, 2000).

3. Mary Francis McDonald, trans., *Lactantius: The Divine Institutes* (Washington, D.C.: Catholic University of America Press, 1964), 379-80.

4. There are a few exceptions, such as Judith N. Shklar, best known for her view that the *summum malum* is cruelty. See e.g. Judith M. Shklar, *Political Thought and Political Thinkers*, ed. Stanley Hoffman (Chicago: University of Chicago Press, 1998).

5. John Rawls, *Political Liberalism* (New York: Columbia University Press, 1993).

6. Paraphrase of Matthew 7:1; compare Luke 6:37.

7. Quotation of Matthew 18:7; compare Luke 17:1.

8. Allusion to Numbers 35:33, "You shall not thus pollute the land in which you live; for blood pollutes the land, and no expiation can be made for the land, for the blood that is shed in it, except by the blood of him who shed it." In the more distant background is Genesis 9:6, "Whoever sheds the blood of man, by man shall his blood be shed; for God made man in his own image." For both verses I am using the Revised Standard Version.

9. Quotation of Psalms 19:9.

10. Jean-François Lyotard, *The Postmodern Condition: A Report on Knowledge,* trans. Geoff Bennington and Brian Massumi (Minneapolis: University of Minnesota Press, [1979] 1984), xxiv.

11. Herbert Wechsler, "Toward Neutral Principles of Constitutional Law," in *Principles, Politics, and Fundamental Law: Selected Essays* (Cambridge: Harvard University, 1961).

12. E.g. Robert Bork, "Neutral Principles and Some First Amendment Problems," *Indiana Law Journal* 47, 1 (1971).

13. Although still more senses may be constructed from permutations and combinations of the other senses, it would be superfluous to consider them.

14. This introduction of a random element into the procedure for final choice might have been classified as a way of treating policy alternatives rather than as a way of treating policy makers.This is reflected in the character of the rebuttals that I offer later in the text.

15. William A. Galston argues that the most prominent neutralists even depend on the *same* theory of the good: as he claims, a "triadic" theory which assumes "the worth of human existence, the worth of human purposiveness and the achievement of purposes, and the worth of rationality as the chief constraint on social principles and social actions." For Galston's shortest presentation of this view, see his "Defending Liberalism," *American Political Science Review* 76, 621 (1982), 625.

16. Notwithstanding occasional contrary views, e.g. Bruce Ackerman, *Social Justice in the Liberal State* (New Haven: Yale University, 1980), chap. 9; Ronald Dworkin, "Liberalism," in *Public and Private Morality*, ed. Stuart Hampshire (Cambridge: Cambridge University Press, 1978); and Bork, "Neutral Principles and Some First Amendment Problems," cited previously. All three involve either a disguised or modified utilitarianism, a belief that equality is somehow more neutral than the alternative, or both. See, for instance, Bork's discussion of what he half-jokingly calls an "Equal Gratifications Clause," at p. 10. I return later to the question of whether equality guarantees neutrality.

17. I emphasize that I am not suggesting that equal-chance policy lotteries are always bad. An arguably appropriate circumstance is when social peace is so imperiled that we all agree to treat policy alternatives as equally choice-worthy even though no one thinks that they really are. We all know that little boys quarreling over baseball team captaincies sometimes agree to draw straws. Though today most Western political theorists would take a different view, evidently a majority of the U.S. Congress viewed the Compromise of 1850 in similar terms; Congressional factions, deadlocked over the issue of slavery in the new territories, agreed to take their chances as to what the voters in each territory itself would decide. This

essay does not consider whether equal-chance policy lotteries are ever good, but only the question of whether they are ever neutral. They aren't. What drove the lottery in 1850, for example, was a conception of the good according to which social peace trumped all other concerns.

Another argument for an equal-chance lottery—this time for the selection of officials rather than policies—was made in the ancient Greek democracies. The cities were riven by class warfare. Election of magistrates was regarded as an oligarchic procedure; by contrast, selection of magistrates by lot gave "the many" the edge that they desired. See Aristotle, *Politics*, 4.1294b, and Montesquieu, *The Spirit of the Laws*, bk. 2, chap. 2. Of course, this argument depends on a particular conception of the good no less obviously than the last one did. Any such argument must.

18. This distinction is especially crucial to the thinking of the English conservative Michael J. Oakeshott; see esp. *On Human Conduct* (Oxford: University of Oxford Press, 1975).

19. The idea that omission is more neutral than commission is the root fallacy James Buchanan and Gordon Tullock's classic of public choice theory, *The Calculus of Consent* (Ann Arbor, Michigan: University of Michigan, 1962).

20. The last serious political theorist convinced of the neutrality of universal omission may have been Robert Paul Wolff, *In Defense of Anarchism* (New York: Harper, Row, 1970). I may, however, be wrong. Though presently out of favor, anarchism may be experiencing a revival in the anti-globalism movement. It will be interesting to see whether it also revives neutralism.

21. For instance see Charles E. Larmore, *Patterns of Moral Complexity* (Cambridge: Cambridge University Press, 1987), chap. 3; more briefly, "Liberal Neutrality," *Political Theory* 17 (1989).

Culture, Religion, Nation-States, and Reason in the Politics of Tolerance
Robert Cummings Neville

The issue of political tolerance in North Atlantic nations has until recently been associated with diverse tribal, ethnic, cultural, or religious groups under the protections of a nation-state. Distinctions between tribal, ethnic, cultural, and religious groups are notoriously difficult to define. Tolerance is an issue because, however defined, these groups make political demands on the nation-state. The nation-state defines a body politic within which competing groups, especially those identified by religion, need to tolerate one another if they are to flourish together, and which the state itself may (or may not) tolerate, even when the groups put pressure on social stability. Tribal, ethnic, and cultural differences are often understood as religious. Whereas some obvious religious competitions within a body politic are directly concerned with the clash of religions and denominations in theologically significant matters, the broader clash of religious interests to which notions of political tolerance are relevant include tribal, ethnic, and cultural differences that have been given a religious edge.

So long as the body politic is clearly established, certain elements of the issues of political tolerance of diverse religions can be stated in fairly straightforward ways.[1] First, as to religion itself, a distinction needs to be drawn between what might be called its essential function and its functions in civil society, as "civil religion."[2] To speak of the "essential function" of religion is dangerous today because scholars of religious studies know that there is no such thing as an "essence" of religion and that we should probably speak of religions rather than religion.[3] Nevertheless, thinking on the boundary between religion and politics, as this essay attempts, the distinction can be drawn between what religion does in its own sphere, as it were, its "essence," and specific contributions it makes to the political sphere, its function as civil religion.[4] In its own sphere, religion orients people to ultimate matters, and it provides: (1) An understanding of ultimacy, which Peter Berger aptly names a "sacred canopy" and can be expressed in myth, theology, science, the plastic and musical arts, architecture, literature, and philosophy;[5] (2) rituals, formal and informal;[6] and (3) spiritual practices such as prayer, meditation, and more strenuous methods, such as monasticism, to produce religious virtuosity.[7] Ultimacy is defined in vastly different ways by religions of the Axial Age, but they fall into two main camps. What might be called "anthropological ultimacy" refers to the religious quest or path, what the theologian Paul Tillich called "ultimate concern."[8] Ultimacy is also defined ontologically in terms of ultimate realities such as God, Dao, Brahman, Emptiness. Most religions approach ultimacy both ways, although Madhyamika Buddhism denies ontological ultimates, while holding to the ultimate importance of release from suffering.[9] Orienting people to ultimate matters in understanding, social patterns of ritual, and spiritual practices is what religions are essentially about, each in its own ways.

Religions function as civil religion in two ways. First, they are the source of the sense of obligation in people, and hence in the societies where they function. The content of the obligations differs from religion to religion and from society to society sharing the same religion. But the sense of obligatedness, of lying under obligation, comes from religions' definition of human life in the terms of their sacred canopies.[10] In societies where all religions cease to have serious civic functions, the sense of obligatedness itself declines to various kinds of relativism or willfulness.[11]

Second, because religions define obligation within their sacred canopies, they can and should function somewhat critically within any given society, calling the society's moral practices to account in terms of religious bases. Religions, of course, often function so much within societies that they seem to be reduced to expressions of the political culture; sometimes religions feel themselves to be so alienated from their societies as to be reclusive. But from the Islamic califates and Constantinian Christianity of the former sort to the separatist Essene and Branch Davidian communities of the latter, there is always some potential for relevant social criticism that a social or individual practice does not live up to the root obligation.[12] Because of its essential functions, religion has a transcendent character that can never be reduced to social functions; because of its civic functions, it never exists totally outside of civil society and therefore always makes some political demands on the body politic.

Political tolerance of religious diversity in a body politic can be defined as *a prima facie right of individuals and groups to the practice of a religion of their own embrace wherever they live.*[13] To say that people have a religion "of their own embrace" means not only that they can choose their religion but also that they might simply be born into it; the point is that they embrace it. To say the right is "prima facie" is to affirm two qualifications. One is that religions need to recognize in their public behavior the prima facie rights of other religions to be pursued; therefore, if a religion is strongly exclusivistic, believing that other religions are harmful or antithetical to ultimate matters or threatening to one's own, that exclusivism needs to be privatized and kept out of public religious and political behavior. Otherwise the exclusivistic religion cannot be allowed to function within a body politic of tolerance. The other qualification is that where religions come into conflict in political matters, either because of differing views of obligation and its source or because of identifications with competing ethnic or cultural groups, that conflict needs to be set in the framework of a public acknowledgment that the source of obligation transcends the particular religions. In other words, religions need to publicly acknowledge the ultimate civil authority of the state in order to be tolerated within a body politic. Privately, of course, they can worship their own authority.

This view of religions acknowledges their own claims to ultimate transcendence and societies' needs for healthy civic religious functioning. It also acknowledges a kind of historical self-consciousness that characterizes those religions, principally Christianity and Judaism, and perhaps also Hinduism and Buddhism, that have grown through European modernity. Islam does not exhibit much leadership regarding historical self-consciousness, however, and is difficult to explore with the model of political tolerance of religions sketched here.[14] As will be apparent, however, the problem is not primarily with Islam, but with the conception of the body politic.

The modern ideals and institutions of political tolerance have their roots in the seventeenth century European wars over religion. The religious differences between Roman Catholics and Protestants (and Anglicans) were very important, although they were closely allied with cultural, ethnic, and economic differences, bound together in complex ways by a long history predating the Reformation. Although it is commonly said that the European "solution" to religiously focused conflict lay in privatizing religion, that is not entirely true. In fact there would be no need for political tolerance if the competing sides did not make public political demands. However "private" religion was thought to be in Enlightenment thinking, it still had political consequences for which the ideals and institutions of tolerance were developed.

In some cases, political tolerance in Europe now is confronted with a continuation or extension of the early modern problems. In Northern Ireland, for instance, the continuing tensions and violence are focused on the religious differences between Roman Catholics and Protestants. Ethnic differences there are virtually non-existent, and there are few if any cultural differences that are not to be accounted for in terms of economic class difference and religious difference. The history of the eighteenth century political and military victories in Northern Ireland are celebrated by some Protestant groups in such a way as to rub the Catholic noses in the ground, whereas the Catholic identity is closely tied to a political culture of underdog revolution. Of course, Ireland's current Roman Catholic cultural presence, although ancient, stems from the successful eleventh century Norman invasion, the opposition to which has been suppressed for centuries. The current conflict in Northern Ireland stems from no serious *theological* differences (though there are such, to be sure); it stems from political groupings identified by religious differences and marked in many cases by economic and social class differences. No *national* political culture has been found as yet within which the mutual tolerance of the Catholic and Protestant parties has solid institutionalization.

Contemporary Germany is experiencing an unexpected reversion to the seventeenth century situation, this time with regard to the tolerance of a sizable Muslim minority, not only Muslim immigrants but their German-born children. Supersensitive to the Nazi genocidal intolerance of Jews, the German government and majority culture are anxious to institutionalize tolerance of Muslims. Nevertheless, complex problems remain, such as the call for government to support Islamic institutions as it supports Roman Catholic and Evangelical (Protestant) churches. If Christian churches are "established," should Muslim institutions also receive state support? Who provides religious education in the primary and secondary schools when it deals with Islam, or with Christianity where the students are Muslims? To what extent should the Muslim criticism of Christianity and Western culture be tolerated where it can blend into support for terrorist extremists just the way the promotion of Christianity blends into support for Christian skinheads?[15]

In other cases, the situation with regard to political tolerance is quite unlike the earlier European situation. African tribal warfare has perhaps been the bloodiest kind of conflict, after the Nazi-Jewish holocaust, in the twentieth century, and it shows few signs of abating. The nation of Rwanda was the site of a ferocious genocidal war between tribes whose putative territories were not limited to that nation. Burundi and the Congo remain tense with inter-tribal warfare, as is Nigeria. The Sudan is ostensibly at war over religion, with Muslims in the north, controlling the government, in conflict with Christians in the south. Behind this, however, are serious ethnic differences between white North Africans and black sub-Saharan Africans; and among the latter groups are continued tribal conflicts.

The Muslim world has risen recently to the forefront of Western consciousness concerning political tolerance and on terms quite different from the European experience. Political conflicts, as evident in Afghanistan and Iraq, come first from tensions between tribes or clans that are organized around tribal leaders, often called "warlords" in the Western press. Sometimes the tribes differ in ethnicity and culture, as for instance between the Pashtuns and Taqiks in Afghanistan and the Kurds and Arabic peoples in Iraq; even broader differences characterize the tensions and sometimes violence in Indonesia. On top of these differences there are two sorts of traditional religious tensions within Islam, often with quite different boundaries. One is the ancient conflict between Sunni and Shi'ite Islam based on struggles in the second generation of Muhammed's family. The decade long war between Iraq and Iran in the 1980s reflected this tension, even though Iraq, representing Sunni Islam, was by population a majority Shi'ite nation. The other religious conflict within Islam is between the relatively Westernizing governments and purifying, if not puritanical, movements aimed to re-establish a "pure" Islam. The conflict internal to Saudi Arabia, for instance, is between its conservative but Westernizing government of Wahabi Islam and the purifying movement, also within Wahabi Islam, that is critical of the government's Western involvements.

Framing all this, of course, is the conflict between much, if not all, of the Islamic world and Christianity, which Samuel Huntington has called a "clash of civilizations."[16] This conflict began in the earliest days of Islam when it swept out of the Arabian Peninsula conquering the North African and eastern Mediterranean provinces of the Byzantine Empire, pushing to the gates of Constantinople itself. It moved through Spain into Europe where it was finally stopped in the West by Charles Martel in the eighth century. In Eastern Europe Islam's armies broke Constantinople in the fifteenth century and were turned back finally before the gates of Vienna in the sixteenth. Meanwhile Islam spread across Asia through the "Stan-belt" of states along the southern border of what was the Soviet Union and that now are mostly independent states, save for Chechnya, which would like to be independent. These were and are places where Islam and Christianity have been and are in tension or actual conflict. In the 1990s a significant part of the conflict in Indonesia was between Islamic Indonesians and Chinese Christians who are a foreign merchant class. The Indonesian situation indicates that the Muslim-Christian conflict is not a Middle-Eastern versus European conflict alone, although both Europe and the Middle East have histories determined by that conflict.

The salient point to draw from the non-European cases of political tolerance or intolerance is that the boundaries of nation-states established by the retreating colonial powers in the twentieth century make the problems of political tolerance worse rather than better. Generally, they did not draw the boundaries at the natural joints of culture, ethnicity, tribal identity, or religious identity. This holds true of the former Soviet Islamic republics and is especially, though uniquely, troublesome in the case of Israel, which, from the standpoint of the Islamic world, remains a European colony in the territory of the former Ottoman Empire. The European nations have been able to achieve a high level of political tolerance, though without complete success, in large part because there has been a strong sense of national identity. In the Islamic areas, national identity is a twentieth century invention with shallow roots. The soldiers of Islam, who think of themselves engaged in a struggle or jihad to beat back corrupting Christian influences, or more accurately the corrupting influences of global capitalism, move from one country to another according to where the fighting is. Loyalty to a fundamentalist interpretation of Islam is greater than that to any nation within which one might be called to tolerate other ways. In Afghanistan, loyalty to tribal identity and leadership might be greater than that to Islam as a whole.

In short, there is no *body politic* in the Muslim world within which political tolerance of the Euro-American sort fits as an accommodating ideal. To be sure, the tradition of explicit tolerance of the "peoples of the book," Jews and Christians, goes back to the earliest days of Islam. This philosophical tradition, however, supposes that the body politic for which that tolerance is an Islamic ideal and law is the unified Islamic world itself. Such unity has been a fiction since very early in Islamic history. The tolerance of Christians and Jews has worked well only when some caliph, sultan, or emperor was able to establish such hegemony over a portion of the Islamic world as to mimic some of the salient conditions of a modern nation-state, with national or imperial identity overshadowing competing identities of tribes, ethnic groups, and religious denominational differences. The current boundaries of Islamic nations formed by colonial powers as they withdrew does not provide national identities that can override factional identities to the point where political tolerance can be an effective ideal.

How should we think about this? Two powerful, antithetic, political forces are at work. On the one hand is the strong centrifugal tendency for separatism, for the division of mixed social groups into their constituent entities (whatever that means). On the other hand is the centripetal tendency toward pluralistic democracy in which the government and economic systems, and usually the educational system, embrace the constituent entities in a common program. The former force makes political tolerance easier the more the resulting political unit is homogeneous, with "minorities" being tolerated, or not, as guests, rather like the Muslim respect for the peoples of the book. Foreign relations become problematic where one group abuts a very different one. The latter force makes political tolerance all the more important as differences that genuinely count are embraced within a democratic body politic. Both forces have been in tension since the early days of empire in the Axial Age.

The centrifugal strategy was perhaps most forcefully introduced in the late modern situation by Zionism, with the establishment by Europeans and Americans of the State of Israel as a Jewish nation, though democratic and offering citizenship to Palestinian Muslims, Christians, and secular people. The historical reasons behind the establishment of Israel are extremely complicated, having as much to do with Europe and America as with the internal politics of the Middle East. The result, however, is an ethnically defined body politic in the midst of a land that had been otherwise until changed by force. As Palestinians come to outnumber, and hence outvote Jews in Israel, serious questions arise about the very meaning of establishing an ethnic "Jewish" state. In some respects it is the nightmare mirror of the Nazi attempt to establish an ethnic "Aryan" state.

The other prime example of the centrifugal political force was the breakup of Yugoslavia into allegedly pure ethnic states, under the pressure of propaganda as well as military action of the Serbian Orthodox Christians against the Croatian Roman Catholics and the Bosnian Muslims. The term "ethnic cleansing" became popular to describe the Serbian intent in the 1990s to invent pure ethnic groups that were to be separated. In point of historical fact, Orthodox and Roman Catholic Christians, as well as Muslims, had been living together in that general area for centuries, often intermarrying and cooperating in many ways, despite occasional tensions. The so-called ethnic divisions were invented in the late twentieth century, frequently breaking up families. As a result of the Balkan wars of the 1990s, populations were pushed around to make "clean" ethnic areas, building resentments that have been defined and made real ethnically. This situation will remain volatile for a long time unless effective leadership rises to the occasion.

The problem with the centrifugal strategy is that so much fiction is involved in defining the potentially separate groups that group identity is almost impossible to sustain outside the immediacy of conflict. Groups cannot be defined by historical ties to land since no piece of land has belonged forever to any one group, as the history of Jerusalem shows. The great Bantu migration displaced all the tribes of sub-Saharan Africa and the settlements and displacements of the European, South Asian, and East Asian peoples are of historical record. Groups cannot be defined by genetic ethnicity because of millennia of intermarriage. Groups cannot be defined by language and culture because there has been so much borrowing and intermixing. Perhaps the best candidate to define groups that can be separated is religion, because it is in religion that people relate themselves to ultimate matters and take their ultimate identities. But religions themselves are not neatly defined against one another. Are not the Roman Catholics and Orthodox in Yugoslavia both Christian? Are not the serious denominational differences among Muslims reflected widely across the lands dominated by Islam? Do not people fall in love across any of these kinds of boundaries, and establish mixed families? There simply is no stability in defining that which would be separated, however immediate the differences seem to be outside of Catholic and Protestant pubs in Belfast. It's like what the Haitian said to the American when asked what race the Haitians are: "White," he answered. "How could that be?" asked the American, looking at the room full of dark Haitians. "We use the 'one drop of blood rule,'" said the Haitian. "In America, one drop of Negro blood makes a person black; in Haiti, one drop of Caucasian blood makes a person white."

Where there is no clear stable definition of the "pure" group, there is no stopping the fission of division. Furthermore, the fissioning of groups defining the identity of individuals is a religious matter. This need not be so, because there are many aspects of a person's identity that are real but not matters of ultimacy—job, family, ethnic background—all these can be merely relative, though interesting, aspects of identity. Yet when the search for identity takes on the force of cordoning off one's group within the larger whole and searching for political independence from the larger body politic, that identity, however fictional, has become a matter of ultimate concern, a religious matter. Thus divisions that are not explicitly defined in terms of adherence to institutionalized religion take on a religious significance. Often allegiance to institutional religion is itself co-opted to divisions that really are about other things, as is the case in Northern Ireland, whose fights are not about the Eucharist or recognition of the authority of the Pope. In a very important respect, any of the moves to separatism on the basis of tribal, ethnic, cultural, or other differences become religious differences. Political tolerance then, in matters that might divide the body politic, is always tolerance of religious difference, differences that have the heat of ultimate identity.

The force driving for democracy has the virtue of recognizing that no group has exclusive claim on any land, that cultural heritages are mixed, that ethnicity is a fiction in its details, and that any group, no matter how small, is already pluralistic. Recognizing that, what positive motive for democratization would be sufficient to overcome the centrifugal obstacles? Where poverty and rapid social change cause identity problems for large numbers of people, the separatists can always concoct a persuasive identity for the short run, even if it is a fiction. This is especially so when it can be framed in opposition to some threatening opponent: a new identity is made to seem real by defending it against its detractors. Fundamentalisms are extreme examples of this creative narrow identity formation, and they occur in matters of ethnicity, tribal identity, cultural identity, and a host of other potential oppositional blocks.[17] How can the force for democratization overcome these centrifugal motives to separation?

First, the multiple layers of real identity and the complexities of the histories of peoples and lands need to be understood and taught. Perhaps it is always impossible to overcome completely the fictional identities that groups promote for ideological reasons. Nevertheless, an educated population has some power to see through the simplified fictional identities of demagogues.

Second, the conditions of poverty need to be alleviated, for two reasons. One is to lessen the desperate need to find some identity in the conditions of anonymity forced by extreme poverty. The other is to support the settled society within which sophisticated education is possible.

Third, democracy needs to find ways to allow the real differences among people to be recognized and flourish. Family, tribal, ethnic, cultural, and religious differences are all important in their ways, and need to find expression. Otherwise their members would rightly feel that they are under attack by alien forces. All of these elements make up parts of the identity of individuals and the fact that they are highly mixed does not mean that they can be forgotten in a mess of confused homogenized family, tribal, ethnic, cultural, and religious identity.

Democracy is a polity that attempts to harmonize the competing interests of groups and individuals under a sufficiently unified social order that the body politic can be governed by a majority government. The unity has to be so great that a dissatisfied minority has more loyalty to the whole body politic than to the place of its own grievance or, if it does not, that the whole body politic has the means to prevent its secession, as happened in the American Civil War. For this reason among others, the institutions of political tolerance of identity-forming differences are so important in democracies. These institutions need to be backed by power from the democratic government and they need to be supported by the majorities in all the contexts in which the conditions for relevant decision-making are set.

The description of political tolerance of religious diversity above said that those groups who cannot tolerate other groups within the body politic need to privatize that intolerance and keep it from having public force. If they cannot do that, then those intolerant groups cannot be tolerated. Either they must change their ways, emigrate (possibly with considerable loss of investment in the body politic), or suffer public regulation, sanctions, and harassment. It is an old paradox of tolerance that intolerance cannot be tolerated. The solution in Euro-American democracies is to privatize intolerance where possible.

Consider how difficult this is with regard to Muslim communities, either as minority groups within a pluralistic nation-state such as Germany or the United States or as dominant cultures in their own body politic. In the first place, the modern notion of distinguishing private affairs from public ones is very hard to square with the in-principle identity of religious and political law in Islam. In the second place, much Islamic commentary, from conservative to moderate and rather liberal, takes Islam to have the moral high ground relative to the depredations of global capitalism associated with the Western democracies (formerly imperial powers). To much of Islam, democratic "freedom" means only the freedom of avarice, reinforced by laws that protect Western interests and that prevent the protection of interests of Muslim lands. Moreover, at least in intent and self-consciousness if not always in practice, Muslims adhere far more than Jews or Christians to the ancient belief that people should handle wealth the way God does—with great generosity and never so as to impoverish anyone else (Qur'an 2:261-273). This includes the prohibition of lending money for interest, condemned in the Hebrew Bible/Old Testament at Exodus 22:25, Leviticus 25:36-37, and Deuteronomy 23:19-20, and in the Qur'an at 2:275-281.[18] Modern global capitalism is based on lending and investing money with the expectation of an increased return. Judaism and Christianity generally have accepted this and abandoned the prohibition against usury. Islam remains ambivalent if not faithful to its texts. More precisely, Muslims who hold to the Qur'an in these matters condemn the Muslims who do not. They are seen as Westerners who accept avarice as a legitimate way to handle wealth. Of course, the ancient ways were based on economies dominated by trading the products of land and flocks, and the people were generally suspicious of money cultures with mercantile rules. Perhaps the new global economy produces far more wealth than the rural economy of Near Eastern antiquity. Perhaps Islamic cultures will come to see the economic practices of global capitalism as better imitating divine generosity in the long run than merely giving charity. But at the present time this insight is a stretch of imagination when the most conspicuous results of global capitalism for most Muslims are increasing distance between the upper and lower classes, exploitation of non-renewable resources, the destruction of the old tribal authority structure by capitalistic meritocracy, and the undermining of a culture of charity. Of course, the situation is different in each Muslim country, though this is a very wide-spread perception.

How is a moral and religious criticism such as this to be tolerated within a world whose global economy punishes those groups that do not participate and impoverishes those who do not have the strength to participate competitively? According to the three strategies of democracy noted above, there are three conditions under which those criticisms can be tolerated: first, that everyone be educated to understand the extent to which they are true and also the extent to which they fail to appreciate virtues in the economic system; second, that the particular conditions of poverty are alleviated that make some people take the critical view of the economic system to the extreme of rejecting the system itself; and, third, that Islamic cultures of generosity be given honored places in society (which means that no one should be so poor as not to be able to be generous).

None of these conditions is likely to be met in the near future, despite the current efforts of the United States to force something like these three conditions on Iraq. In the short run it seems likely that people in Islamic lands will become secular before feeling integrated into a larger pluralistic culture that honors their contribution as Muslims. The move to secularity itself has many motives, including a recognition that social and economic conditions simply have changed and that insistence on the old ways is irrelevant in ways that were not so in earlier periods. There is also a revulsion against the twin evils of extreme religious authoritarianism and extreme terrorist militancy that characterize a fundamentalist response to the situation. And then, avarice has its attractions if there is hope one can be successful at it. In the short run, those Muslims who do not become secular and who remain uneducated, poor, and denied an honored place will be strongly tempted to terrorism or other alienated resistance. That will not be tolerated.

International terrorism is proof positive that the nation-state is not the body politic within which political tolerance can be institutionalized, especially in Muslim lands. Just as the nation-states are not the units that can control global capitalism effectively, so they cannot be the units that define the limits of tolerance for capitalism's enemies. If the American government honestly believed it was addressing the crimes of terrorism by conquering the nation-states of Afghanistan and Iraq, which is not certain, that belief was politically naïve. The terrorists simply move and rejoice that the wars make their point that capitalist nations are destructive bullies, recruiting more fighters to their cause.

By no means is it certain that the Middle Eastern forces of tribalism, ethnicity, culture, and various forms of Islam will coalesce and evolve into stable nation-states that can internally institutionalize political tolerance of dissident groups identified with religious zeal. The current nations might well divide into smaller units, for instance with the Kurds breaking away from Turkey and Iraq to form their own nation, the Shi'ites in Iraq breaking away to unite with Islam, and so forth. Nigeria and the Congo might break into different tribal units. But in this direction lies continued chaos.

Democracy is the preferable direction because it can institutionalize tolerance of diverse and competing groups, even those in religious opposition to one another. Because large parts of the world do not have effective nation-states, the relevant democracy is the global United Nations. Only the United Nations would be able to draw and enforce boundaries of political tolerance where some of the parties are nation-states and others take tribal, ethnic, cultural, and religious forms. If the United Nations were strong and credible, then the ineffective nation-states created by retreating imperial powers might themselves become more effective through participation as members in the United Nations. The United Nations cannot become strong and credible, however, until the large and very powerful nation-states are willing to cede some of their power to it, and to make themselves subject to the jurisdiction of the United Nations in the courts, in the formation of economic and military policy, and in the development of institutionalized conditions for political tolerance.

A final point brings the argument full circle. It might seem as if the global democracy of an improved United Nations requires a steadfast secularism of political culture, a secularism that transcends the religious and religiously colored oppositions of sectarian differences. This is true in the sense that no religion can be an established religion for the United Nations; diversity of religions, and religiously impassioned tribal, ethnic, and cultural groups, need to have a level playing field if they are all to be allowed to flourish in the global society. Nevertheless, it should be recalled that the essence of religion(s) is to attend to ultimate matters, and political matters simply are not ultimate. Political matters can be associated with infinite religious passions, but in the long run no religion, not even Islam, identifies ultimate loyalty to any actual political program or government. Vital religion is necessary to indicate that politics is not religion. The two principal functions of civil religion are to ground and inculcate the sense of obligation in society, and to serve as a partially transcendent critic of any social arrangement or program. Without a strong sense of obligation, political commitment can in fact be guided by nothing more normative than avarice, getting what one can for oneself and one's group. The courage to sacrifice some of one's self-interest to the greater good of the body politic requires a religiously powerful sense of obligation. Without vital religions, the civic function of grounding obligation will be weakened. As to transcendent criticism of social arrangements and programs, the religions sometimes have difficulty making ancient principles relevant in new circumstances. Banning usury today will not make people more divinely generous, only impoverished upon retirement. Nevertheless, the moral goal of subordinating political and economic expediency to divine standards—the realism of Brahman, the harmony of the Dao—is vital for effective democracy.

In the modern period it has been hard to know whether religions do more good than harm. So much political energy is required to keep them at peace. They feed the worst kinds of ignorant bigotry. Yet they provide an alternative to demagoguery for setting the agenda of life, they ground the sense of obligation required even for the political action of keeping religions within the bounds of tolerance, and they are the primary sources for political change in a moral direction. The best reason for political tolerance of religious diversity is that the diverse vital religions are so important for the body politic.

Notes

1. These remarks summarize the argument made in an essay, "Religion and Politics: Spheres of Tolerance," published as chapter 8 of my *Religion in Late Modernity* (Albany: State University of New York Press, 2002). Portions of the first half of that essay appeared in "Political Tolerance in an Age of Renewed Religious Warfare," in *Philosophy, Religion, and the Question of Intolerance*, ed. Mahdi Amin Razavi and David Ambuel (Albany: State University of New York Press, 1977).
2. The notion of civil religion was made popular by the sociologist of religion, Robert Bellah. See his *The Broken Covenant: American Civil Religion in Time of Trial* (New York: Crossroad, 1975). The civil functions of religion, especially in America, have been recognized since Puritan times and were much discussed in the conversations around the founding of the American republic, for instance the *Federalist Papers*. See also Alexis de Tocqueville's *Democracy in America*, chap. 5-6. The argument in the text here does not adhere closely to any one of these uses in specific theory.
3. On the problems of defining religion and religions, and finding an "essence" of religion, see Walter H. Capps' *Religious Studies: The Making of a Discipline* (Minneapolis: Fortress Press, 1995). See also my *Boston Confucianism: Portable Tradition in the Late-Modern World* (Albany: State University of New York Press, 2000), chap. 4.
4. On the connection between religion and society mentioned here, with a more detailed discussion of the nature of world religions and the distinction between religion and religions, see my *Religion in Late Modernity*, chap. 4. That chapter distinguishes with some care between society, culture, and community, distinctions that are used only informally in the current essay.
5. See Berger's book, *The Sacred Canopy: Element of a Sociological Theory of Religion* (Garden City, N.Y.: Doubleday, 1967). On the contemporary problematic character of theology as sacred canopy, see Wesley J. Wildman's "Theological Literacy: Problem and Promise," in *Theological Education*, ed. Rodney Petersen (Grand Rapids, Mich.: Eerdmans, 2002).
6. Western societies often neglect the pervasiveness of ritual, identifying it only in "church liturgies." Ancient Hinduism had a strong understanding of ritual; see Francis X. Clooney's *Thinking Ritually: Rediscovering the Purva Mimamsa of Jaimini* (Vienna: Indological Institute of the University of Vienna, 1990). Even more thorough has been the Confucian understanding; see Herbert Fingarette's *Confucius: The Secular as Sacred* (San Francisco: Harper, 1972), or my *Normative Cultures* (Albany: State University of New York, 1995), chap. 7.

7. These three characteristics of religion—intellectual, ritual, and practical—have been articulated in many ways in my work, beginning with *Soldier Sage Saint* (New York: Fordham University Press, 1978), in *Boston Confucianism* (Albany: State University of New York Press, 2000), chap. 4, and *Religion in Late Modernity*.

8. See Tillich's introduction to *Systematic Theology*, vol. 1 (Chicago: University of Chicago Press, 1952).

9. The distinction between ontological and anthropological ultimates was drawn carefully by the Comparative Religious Ideas Project after several years of debate, and is reported in its volume, *Ultimate Realities*, ed. Robert Cummings Neville (Albany: State University of New York Press, 2001).

10. On obligation as a partial definition of the religious dimension of the human condition, see the Comparative Religious Ideas Project's volume *The Human Condition*, ed. Robert Cummings Neville (Albany: State University of New York, 2001), 247. That passage summarizes intensive discussions among experts and reports of different senses of obligatedness in Chinese religion, Buddhism, Hinduism, Judaism, Christianity, and Islam.

11. The claim that religion is not grounded in anything providing authentic obligation but is instead only an ideological tool for the pursuit and expression of power was stated forcefully by Plato in the *Republic*, bk. 2, and rejected; Nietzsche made the claim and stuck to it, inspiring many postmodern thinkers in their attitudes toward religion.

12. H. Richard Niebuhr's *Christ and Culture* (New York: Harper and Brothers, 1951), though dealing only with Christianity, offers an effective set of models of the relation between religions and cultures.

13. This is the definition defended in *Religion in Late Modernity*, chap. 8.

14. This is a generally valid observation, though with many exceptions. While attention has been drawn in the West to the resurgent conservative side of Islamic theology, as expressed for instance in the Iranian Revolution of 1979 and in Wahabi Islam, other Islamic scholars have worked hard to engage European Enlightenment thought, scriptural criticism, and history in non-hagiographical modes. Because there is no independent "church" structure to Islam with an ecclesiastical authority to speak for Islam, Islamic thought tends to be identified with its political expressions, even with the sad ideologies of Islamic terrorists. Because of the tendency to identify Islam politically rather than theologically, it is important to look closely at the history of Islam in the recent Middle East. Yasir Arafat's organization, Al Fatah, began as a secular, somewhat socialistic, society to promote Arabic culture. Hamas, by contrast, began as a brotherhood to reclaim Islam from Arab secularists. Each was mainly worried about the other until the establishment of the State of Israel united them in opposition, and the closer a Palestinian State comes to be, the greater that tension within the Palestinian forces. Israel, of course, has a parallel tension between the secular Zionists who founded the state and the religiously conservative Jews whom they welcomed.

15. The Muslim criticism of Christianity and Western culture will be addressed in more detail below.

16. See Samuel P. Huntington, *The Clash of Civilizations and the Remaking of World Order* (New York: Simon and Schuster, 1996).

17. On fundamentalism, see the extraordinary Fundamentalism Project run by the University of Chicago, directed by Martin E. Marty and R. Scott Appleby. See the first volume of its publications, *Fundamentalisms Observed*, ed. Marty and Appleby, especially its (unsigned) introduction and its first chapter by Nancy Ammerman.

18. Deuteronomy condemns lending money for interest to other Israelites, but permits it in the case of lending money to foreigners. That might also be implied in the Exodus and Leviticus passages.

Tolerance, Identity, and the Problem of Citizenship[1]

Gerson Moreno-Riaño

Tolerance as a general political principle was first advanced during the era commonly known as the Enlightenment.[2] Ever since John Locke's *A Letter Concerning Toleration* and John Stuart Mill's *On Liberty*, the concept of toleration has enjoyed a tremendous deal of popularity along with much intellectual and political scrutiny. Popularly understood, tolerance itself is a simple concept—putting up with those things one dislikes or even hates about others. It allows the object of one's tolerance to continue to exist or to be practiced even if the "tolerator" strongly disagrees with it.

It even intimates the religious notion of being long suffering and patient. Practicing tolerance, however, is a bit more complex and is often filled with nuances and pitfalls both for the tolerator and the tolerated.

In spite of the complexities surrounding the practice of tolerance, there is little doubt that it has captivated the imagination of modern academics along with that of everyday people, politicians, journalists, pundits and demagogues alike, and of the world at large. Everyone seems to be concerned with how tolerant they appear and with how intolerant others may be. Many call for philosophical, political, religious, and educational solutions to the intolerance that seems to threaten the possibility of world peace. The problem is that many of these solutions fail to take into account the cultural and communal aspect of morality, politics, and, ultimately, human beings themselves. Too often the solutions (e.g., more tolerance) to the problems of intolerance ignore a vital aspect of human life and are themselves representative, though often unknowingly, of a particular community's view of morality and human well-being.

It is important, then, to understand that human beings have always conducted their affairs as communal or cultural beings, as members of cultures of meaning, not as atomized individuals or in the words of Michael Sandel "unencumbered selves."[3] At its present stage of historical development, politics is the dialogue in conflict and war, between communities, between world-views, between cultures of meaning to which we all belong.[4] This leads to the important conclusion that political values themselves are not universal moral absolutes

81

equally applicable to all. While fire burns here as it does in Persia, political morality does not burn the same everywhere. Insofar as tolerance is such a political
value (and there is sufficient evidence to believe that it is!) it is representative of
a particular community and, therefore, cannot be considered universally and
morally valid for all communities and peoples of the earth. This same observation is applicable to the concept of citizenship. As suggested above, even as
politics and its principles are the outworking of one's communal commitments,
citizenship is the extension of one's communal identity and community-
constructed worldview.[5]

This essay explores the cultural roots of political morality, identity, and citizenship. It is a sympathetic analysis of the fundamental and dynamic relation
between culture, politics, identity, and behavior and a frank consideration of the
opportunities and serious challenges which such an understanding of politics and
behavior poses for humans and their communities in the twenty-first century.
The argument is divided into several segments. Initially, a basic theoretical case
is presented for the relationship between culture, identity, and politics drawing
from the work of John Dewey, among others. Further developing the theoretical
case, tolerance is then presented as the construction of a very peculiar and powerful communal worldview—that of Enlightenment classical Liberalism. The
essay closes with a discussion of the cultural roots of citizenship and the prospect of citizenship in a future of culturally-based politics and political morality.

Culture, Identity, and Politics[6]

Perhaps one of the earliest twentieth century rationales for the bond between
culture, identity, and politics is found within the works of the famous American
pragmatist John Dewey. Several of Dewey's writings address the relationship
between culture and some facet of human life the most telling being found in
Freedom and Culture (1989).[7] In this work, it is Dewey's concern to defend the
relationship between liberty and culture and to suggest the type of culture which
can maintain political freedom. At the simplest level, Dewey argues that culture
is nothing more than the social intercourse existing between persons:

> For we now know that the relations which exist between persons,
> outside of political institutions, relations of industry, of communica-
> tion, of science, art and religions, affect daily associations, and
> thereby deeply affect the attitudes and habits expressed in govern-
> ment and rules of law. . . . For this complex of conditions which taxes
> the terms upon which human beings associate and live together is
> summed up in the word *Culture* [emphasis original].[8]

Dewey's definition of culture directly connects it with a person's attitudes, behaviors, and politics. As such, culture is an all-inclusive *socio-sphere* in which

human beings carry on a whole set of relations affecting themselves, others, and ultimately the *socio-sphere* itself. According to Dewey, all aspects of this environment from art to music to architecture are intimately related to politics, its principles, and its institutions. As Dewey suggests:

> It has not been customary to include the arts, the fine arts, as an important part of the social conditions that bear upon democratic institutions and personal freedom. Even after the influence of the state of industry and of natural science has been admitted, we still tend to draw the line at the idea that literature, music, painting, the drama, architecture, have any intimate connection with the cultural bases of democracy.[9]

Culture helps create a type of political ethos and is a medium of communicating and advancing this ethos. Culture is not a "glittering generality," but rather, a powerful agent stimulating certain types of morals, attitudes, and behaviors. The argument which Dewey forcefully defends is that culture and all of its variants are deeply connected with politics. Any understanding of political principles and institutions, of individual attitudes and opinions, must take into account the cultural bases of these types of activity. More specifically, it must take into account how our cultural commitments affect our politics, identities, morals, and views towards others.[10]

An intervening variable in the relationship between culture and politics is that of the individual. While culture is influential in the formation of political norms and institutions, its most direct influence is on individual actors in the socio-political realm.[11] The power of culture upon individuals has long been an area of research for scholars. In political science, for example, much empirical work has been conducted regarding the "political life history" of individuals in an attempt to understand the development of morals, attitudes, and prejudices in adults within society and groups.[12] More theoretical discussions have birthed the heated debate between contemporary Liberal theorists or *individualists*, and communitarians.[13] Interpreting this debate in the most general form, one can suggest that the basic issue is the nature of the self or the nature and development of one's identity. The individualist vision suggests a radically free human being or the *atomized self*, a person whose responsibility is primarily to him or herself (i.e., rights) and whose responsibility toward others and the community (i.e., obligations) is tertiary.[14] Communitarians defend what they consider to be a more realistic and sensitive view of the socio-political world. It is their contention that individuals are never radically free or "atomized." Rather, human beings are socially constituted by particular communities or cultures of meaning to which they belong. Individuals have very little choice, at least in the beginning of their life history, with regards to which culture of meaning they belong. Mobility to other communities may be more a matter of choice as one increases in age. The central point of communitarians is that a culture of meaning or community is fundamental to the development of individual identity and, thus, to political life.

There is a high degree of validity to the communitarian argument. Liberal theorists have conceded that the framework of society is communitarian, or *pluralist*, in nature; that the community is important for the purposes of self-identification; and that such concepts as identity and recognition are central tenets of contemporary political practice and discussion.[15] In spite of this "theoretical validation," it is much safer, one can suggest, to begin not by presupposing the *a priori* theoretical validity of communitarianism but by accepting its historical reality.[16] It is an indisputable fact that as long as recorded history, human beings have belonged to cultures and communities of meaning. Persons are always born into a culture, into a community with a particular *weltanschauung*. Such communities shape the identity and self-understanding of their members through their structures, norms, and values.[17] Though it often occurs, it is difficult for any culture or community legitimately to defend its principles as universally valid since these are considered by most to be community-relative. This is not to suggest that cultures never attempt to offer universal validation. Every empire, nation-state, tribe, and ideological group portrays its creeds as fact not fiction. But the communal nature of morality, ethics, identity-formation, politics, and art, to name just a few, suggests that no world and life view can escape its social attachment and non-universal character.

The substantive relationship between culture and politics, as well as the deep connection between culture and identity formation, ultimately suggests that the political dimension of life is an outworking of cultural commitments and understandings. Politics is not a neutral nexus where atomized individuals meet and conduct market-style, decontextualized political transactions. Politics is a framework where communal understandings of reality, of the good or the moral, seek priority and realization. As such activity takes place, politics is also the web where communal identities are given voice, where identities seek protection, facilitation, and, most importantly, recognition.[18] In the late twentieth century and especially in the current century in most Western democracies and in other parts of the world, politics is the struggle for recognition if not enthronement of communal identities, ontologies, and cognitions. As one scholar puts it:

> The central questions of identity politics are, first, who decides
> which, if any, identities of the members of a political association are
> unjustly imposed and which are worthy of recognition and some form
> of accommodation? And, second, by what procedures do they decide
> and review their decisions?[19]

Such assessment is magnified when one considers the rapid forces of economic and political globalization. As questions of politics become, to some extent, less local and geographical and, in the minds of some, less rooted within cultures and communities of meaning, the drive toward a global community seems to attenuate if not eliminate the problem of identity and recognition. But as some scholars have observed, the focal issue in the globalization of politics is the "tension between cultural homogenization and cultural heterogenization," so that attempts to homogenize the global political landscape may not be as facile as some suggest.[20] The cultural and communal roots of politics and identity, then, are deeply entrenched within current historical and political reality. This deep-rooted interaction seems to be so fundamental that even the powerful drives of globalization seem powerless to change it anytime soon. Given such a scenario, the politics of identity recognition, and by default, the politics of tolerance, may continue to be the major and defining characteristic of twenty-first century politics.

The "Virtue" of Tolerance and Citizenship

The first part of this essay focused on providing a theoretical and realistic link between culture and politics as well as the crafting of personal identities. This section is concerned with the implications of the cultural basis of politics and identity for the concepts of tolerance and citizenship. Is it possible to apply the "cultural thesis" to such concepts as tolerance and citizenship? If so, what are the implications of this hypothesis as one thinks about tolerance in the current century and beyond?

To begin with, one should consider how tolerance has come to be used in today's environment. To say that tolerance is an important contemporary political value is an understatement. Tolerance has become the only political value that is hailed as a virtue—a universal moral characteristic.[21] It is touted as the premier social and political virtue of the modern era and the modern citizen.[22] Yet, in spite of the broad consensus about how important tolerance is for current politics, many difficulties still exist in clearly defining tolerance and so, effectively implementing a strategy in questions of practical, everyday politics. Beyond these questions, one may still wonder why is it so "good" to be tolerant? Why does a morally vague and ambiguous idea such as tolerance command so much public attention and spirited dialogue?

Part of the answer and the difficulty alike lies in the fact that tolerance is often couched in moral terms appealing to the moral self. Whether we like it or not, modern human beings are just as morally oriented as our ancient predecessors. All of us agree at the most basic level that there are rights and wrongs, though we may substantively disagree on what those may be. The point is that all of us possess concepts of right and wrong by which we conduct our daily lives. Morality, though, is not an individualistic phenomenon—it is a cultural practice. What one considers right and wrong is part and parcel of a particular tradition, a particular culture or inherited way of thinking and acting—a specific culture of meaning. Tolerance is no exception for it too belongs to a particular culture and tradition that values it as a moral virtue.[23] Understanding what is "good" or "virtuous" about tolerance necessitates an understanding of its cultural roots and origins. Only when such an understanding is achieved can much of the apparent ambiguity and confusion surrounding tolerance be cleared, and only then can one be in a better place to understand why issues of tolerance generate so much debate and discussion.[24]

In spite of the "universal" character of modern tolerance, there is very little doubt that it is the creation of the Liberal culture developed and nurtured by the founding fathers of the Liberal worldview—Thomas Hobbes, John Locke, John Stuart Mill, Jeremy Bentham, and Immanuel Kant—and further refined in more recent times by such thinkers as Ronald Dworkin, Bruce Ackerman, and most importantly, John Rawls.[25] Each of these thinkers advocated tolerance for different political and civil reasons. Whether for religious freedom (Locke), utilitarian commitments (Mill), or enlightenment (Kant), tolerance was advanced as a political good due to certain comprehensive Liberal moral commitments. As a principle of political morality, tolerance was a strict derivation of a comprehensive Liberal moral and philosophical core which held individual autonomy to be of fundamental importance.[26] As some scholars remind us, the human being of the Liberal worldview is "the free and rational individual who is capable of self-government but seeks neither to rule others nor to gratify them;" this individual is the "unencumbered self" who is "freed from the dictates of nature and the sanction of social roles, [who is] installed as sovereign, cast as the author of the only moral meanings there are."[27]

This profound and controversial moral vision is at the core of any political or social prescriptions of tolerance. Contemporary Liberal theorists, most notably Rawls, have attempted to distance Liberalism and its political prescriptions from such metaphysical commitments by suggesting that it is possible to advance a concept of justice that is political and not metaphysical or, as Jeremy Waldron puts it, political and not comprehensive.[28] But any such attempt ultimately fails for it ignores the deep and abiding continuity between culture, the individual, and politics. A distinction between political and comprehensive is academic and artificial at best. It does not accurately reflect how human beings live and interact, and therefore, does not stand up to intellectual, political, or public scrutiny. Politics is the outworking of the deepest moral commitments people hold. Politics, as Aristotle reminds us, *is* ethics. Political tolerance is not a unique exception. It is the result of the moral vision of the atomized self, of the Liberal individual articulated by so many since the Enlightenment. And, one should add, that even in cases where individuals do uphold this distinction, they are upholding a communal dictate of political morality not a universal moral prescription.

The discussion thus far has centered on the place of tolerance as a Liberal political prescription within the comprehensive Liberal worldview. And the conclusion reached is that tolerance is a strict derivation of the Liberal metaphysical commitment to individual autonomy. Defending tolerance as a principle of Liberal political morality is unproblematic if the audience whom one addresses is committed in principle and practice to Liberalism. In such cases, defense of, justification of, and obligation to such political prescriptions is simple. The difficulty arises when tolerance is defended to audiences who do not share the principled commitment to a Liberal *weltanschauung*. For these individuals, tolerance is not accepted as legitimate due to its community-relative metaphysical foundations. Therefore, what grounds exist for justifying and defending Liberal tolerance to non-Liberal publics?

The preceding question is a thorny one.[29] Most Liberal answers to this problem expect non-Liberal communities and their members to accept and adopt some thin or "political" version of Liberalism (e.g., Rawls's Political Justice). But this expectation is not only a hypothetical impossibility, it is also unreasonable given the connection between culture, politics, and individuals. Of greater concern is the actual answer which twenty-first century non-Liberal individuals and communities actually *do in fact* live out every day. This *actual* answer or realistic justificatory account is what can be called a prudential and pragmatic validation of tolerance.

The prudential and pragmatic defense of tolerance is based on the seemingly true and accurate observation that being tolerant and advancing policies of tolerance simply works. By using the term *works*, Liberal advocates suggest a two-pronged defense. First, being tolerant allows all to pursue their self-interests since all mutually respect and allow each other this basic civil courtesy. This defense offers a mutually beneficial scenario for all involved: it allows Liberals to entrench individual autonomy in politics, it allows others to live out their autonomy in a number of foreseeable ways including commitment to non-Liberal principles and communities, and it fosters a civil polity. Second, *works* also entails a serious commitment to the politics of the moment, which seems to suggest that extending tolerance to others has produced the current enviable and relatively peaceful polity in which one finds himself or in which others find themselves.[30] Therefore, by default, one's polity should be tolerant.

While both of these defenses seem to avoid, at least on the surface, the problems which metaphysical arguments present, both engender their own set of debilitating difficulties. Prudential justifications are founded on the confidence that individuals not only appropriately discern what is in their interest but also correctly understand that their own self-interest is not dangerous to others and the fabric of society. Furthermore, prudential justifications assume that individuals will not violate the principle of tolerance, even when capable of doing so whenever tolerating others does not appear to suit their own personal interests. Pragmatic justifications of tolerance are perhaps the weakest and most dangerous since they establish the moral validity and political value of tolerance on the grounds of transitory effectiveness, thereby suggesting that momentary success is a sure basis for future stability.

It may be tempting for some to suggest that these are mere academic or theoretical squabbles. But as cited earlier, at least in America, and one could suggest worldwide, individuals are very serious about their communal identities and commitments. As human beings live out their lives, they choose, knowingly or unknowingly, a particular answer that causes the least amount of moral disso-nance. For most, this answer will encompass the prudential and pragmatic de-fense of tolerance, namely that tolerance is good because it serves me and it works! If one does not accept the moral legitimacy of tolerance on its meta-physical grounds, one is left with enlightened self-interest as its proper founda-tion and with what some scholars argue is the only basis for defending any po-litical moral—its apparent temporary success or workability.[31]

As mentioned earlier, both of these prevalent justifications are problematic since they depend on two questionable assumptions: the concern of human be-ings for others above themselves and the longevity and constancy of a society's present success. The overall historical record demonstrates that self-interest al-ways trumps other-regarding interest and that present unprincipled success is never a sound foundation for civic stability and unity.[32] Again the question sug-gests itself as to why tolerance seems to enjoy such fame and universality.

Two discomfiting answers can be suggested to this paradoxical query. One pertains to human nature and the other to the current nature of the modern state. Unfortunately, living without reflecting on our principles (or lack of principles) or their consequences is common among human beings. Careful deliberation and mastication of life, while not necessarily reserved for the elite or privileged, is frequently outside of the realm of most human beings who are busy living life, working, suffering, raising families, etc. Human beings do not always enjoy the luxury of reflecting on their own lives, principles, and civic moral commit-ments.[33] This in turn leads to the conclusion that most citizens of a polity lack a substantial degree of political sophistication and critical evaluation in regards to foundational issues of which tolerance is an example. As such, living out a pru-dential or pragmatic answer, as weak as these may be, is no real problem. It is the option most easily lived, most noticeably successful, and most morally and practically realizable.

The second answer relates to the nature of the modern state. Since its birth, a core principle of the Liberal worldview is the uncontested status of the state as moral umpire.[34] While most theoretical expositions of Liberalism suggest indi-vidual autonomy to be its core, individual autonomy cannot exist apart from a political institution that can defend, articulate, and obligate others to respect (tolerate) it. The chimera of Liberal neutrality is applicable only if one is to sug-gest that modern Liberal states place Liberalism on an equal footing with com-prehensive non-Liberal doctrines. This rarely if ever occurs (thus the chimera of Liberal neutrality!). Most, if not all Liberal states are consistent in treating all non-Liberal worldviews as equal players within the non-neutral context pro-vided by a Liberal moral and political framework. In this role, Liberal states contextualize and frame the terms of debate, policy, and decision-making. Most important, the frontier of possibility, or that which non-Liberal publics can hope to achieve, is structured by the Liberal state itself. As such, Liberal political mo-rality and with it, tolerance, not only provides the context in which all other worldviews can exist but is also forced upon non-Liberal publics that could never accept these as tenets of their own worldview commitments. In short, Liberal states severely limit the very individual autonomy which in principle they claim to protect, and most disconcerting, through their use of institutional force, do not provide a legitimate and lasting foundation to the very principles they cherish.

This realistic scenario undermines the ascribed moral character of tolerance. On the one hand, advocates of tolerance would like to argue that it is a moral claim that is ethically binding while, on the other hand, as we have seen, there are no legitimate moral grounds on which they can defend the morality of tolerance to non-Liberal publics who give their assent to this Liberal ethic either on a prudential, pragmatic, or state power basis. If this is the case, can tolerance really provide the cohesiveness which Liberal polities seek and so desperately need? An affirmative answer is possible only if one is willing to accept a thin account of cohesiveness, one that is based on prudential considerations, self-interest, and political power.[35] But to expect a thick account of cohesiveness, one in which all publics are truly engaged and consider the process and its institutions to be legitimate extensions of themselves may be too much to expect.[36]

Political Tolerance and Citizenship

Given the fact that Liberalism has been foundational to the structure of modern political organizations and processes, citizenship has reflected a Liberal commitment to individual autonomy as expressed by way of rights.[37] As such, most public and academic discussions of citizenship omit the importance of culture as a serious interlocutor in such dialogues.[38] The particularity of culture presents the most serious difficulty in advancing a comprehensive public account of citizenship. Given the cultural account of political morality herein advanced, citizenship is the public outworking of one's basic communal commitments. This can in fact include citizenship as an individualistic phenomenon (i.e., citizenship as rights) but will do so as a Liberal communal conceptualization of citizenship. What is being suggested is that citizenship be considered not as a universal but as a socially-constructed communal product that places particular moral obligations upon its adherents- obligations none of which are universal in nature.[39] Citizenship, then, can be comprehended only as one understands the cultures of meaning which individuals embrace and the moral obligations these place on individuals in regards to social and public action.

If citizenship, then, is nothing more than the public outworking of our basic communal commitments, active citizenship will be conflict prone. Engaged citizens will seek to mobilize and implement their cultures and communities, their moral interests, thus producing fragmentation and conflict and breeding a public sphere of intolerance and more deep-rooted conflict.[40] What one culture advances in the name of tolerance, other cultures will interpret as threat and vice versa.[41] If the culture which advances particular moral positions in the name of tolerance happens to have a monopoly on force, active citizens from other opposing communal traditions have several options: attacking the culture with its own institutions and resources (i.e., legislation, lobbying); going beyond the "rules of the game" and advocating violence; becoming politically non-active and, therefore, passive citizens who follow the basic rules of the game (i.e., law-abiding, apathetic, or doubters of their political efficacy); or, lastly, seeking political office to make Liberalism less absolutist and more pluralistic.

No matter what model of citizenship one opts for (except, perhaps, for the non-active model), it is likely that active citizenship will imply more intense conflict, breeding more and more intolerance. A political life in which different cultures and communities of meaning compete for political leverage will produce nothing more than aggression, hatred, and a lack of civility. Conflict erupting, the only choice left for the dominant culture is to enforce an ambiance of tolerance in the name of morality and civility thereby furthering the intolerance which it desperately wants banished. If this is the current situation or if this is the potential political scenario for the future, perhaps a non-moral, non-communal basis for citizenship can be advanced. This is no easy task. In closing, such a possibility will be minimally sketched.[42]

A non-moral, non-communal account of citizenship can be founded on the principle of economic sufficiency and bureaucratic effectiveness and efficiency. Aristotle first proposed a similar account when he suggested the potential ends of a political community as being mere life, life and the good life. What most of this essay has suggested is that human beings understand political life and citizenship as fostering the good life—a life of social, economic, *and* moral well-being. What if the *moral well-being* in such an account was conflated with economic well-being? In such an account, nation-states would have as their primary moral obligation the implementation of social and economic well-being to all inhabitants. The goal would be the reduction and elimination of poverty and the provision of adequate housing, medical care, employment, and other tangible social and economic benefits. Citizenship would primarily imply engagement to ensure the implementation of such goals as well as institutional mechanisms to ensure governmental efficiency and policy effectiveness.

Political morality would be economic morality—the provision of material and economic well-being to all inhabitants. All communal visions of the good would exist, but only as social concepts. Political institutions would be held accountable to implement a sound and comprehensive economic vision and to foster an adequate framework for all moral visions to exist as private social visions, never public commitments. Further, nation-states would be held accountable to develop and foster a set of norms and laws that would prohibit economic dysfunctionality at the macro, micro, and individual levels alike. Such norms would prohibit and punish all sorts of economic crime from basic theft to complex corporate crime. But no political vision would include *any* communal vision of the moral good. An economic model of politics and citizenship would exclude all such accounts in favor of tangible rewards. This is not to suggest that economic politics and citizenship would be conflict free. But the basis of conflict and the possible solutions are in some sense superior in that empirical validation, and to some extent, control, are within the reach of societies and governments. Conflict will still exist, but the basis and means of agreement are tangible, not ephemeral. As such, economic politics and citizenship may be a more attractive choice for peace and civility than its cultural counterpart.[43]

Notes

1. Aspects of this paper were presented at various academic conferences such as the International Society for the Study of European Ideas, Bergen, Norway (2000) and Aberystwyth, Wales (2002), as well as the Fifty-eighth Midwest Political Science Association Conference, Chicago, Ill. (2000). I would like to thank Walter Schultz, Joel Wolf, Michael Margolis, Michael Sweeney, and (posthumously) David Resnick for their constructive comments during various stages of writing and research. Thanks are also due to the Academic Vice President's office, Cedarville University, for research and travel support.
2. This is not to suggest that previous historical eras, communities, or thinkers did not advance tolerance related arguments. But it is in the Enlightenment that one can find tolerance being advanced as a general and universal principle of politics and the modern state. For a review of important literature addressing this problem see G. Moreno-Riano, "The Roots of Tolerance," *Review of Politics* 65, no. 1 (Winter 2003): 111-29. Other important works are A. Murphy, *Conscience and Community* (University Park: Pennsylvania State University Press, 2001); C. Nederman, *World of Difference: European Discourses of Tolerance in Europe c. 1100-1500* (University Park: Pennsylvania State University Press, 2000); and J.C. Laursen and C. Nederman, eds., *Beyond the Persecuting Society* (Philadephia: University of Pennsylvania Press, 1998).
3. See M. Sandel, "The Procedural Republic and the Unencumbered Self," in *Twentieth Century Political Theory*, ed. S.E. Bronner (New York: Routledge, 1997), 77.
4. On this point see R. George, *The Clash of Orthodoxies* (Wilmington: ISI Books, 2001) and S. Huntington, *The Clash of Civilizations and the Re-making of the World Order* (New York: Simon & Schuster, 1996).
5. For some related treatments of this claim see A.T. Baumeister, "Multicultural Citizenship, Identity and Conflict," in *Toleration, Identity, and Difference*, ed. J. Horton and S. Mendus (London: MacMillan Press, 1999), 87-102.
6. I am indebted for portions of this section to G. Moreno-Riano, *Tolerance, Culture, and the Individual* (Lewiston, N.Y.: The Edwin Mellen Press, 2003).
7. J. Dewey, *Freedom and Culture* (Buffalo, N.Y.: Prometheus Books, 1989). Other suggested works by Dewey are "The Search for the Great Community," in *Twentieth Century Political Theory* ed. S.E. Bronner (New York: Routledge, 1997), 61-65; *Democracy and Education: An Introduction to the Philosophy of Education* (New York: The MacMillan Company, 1933); and *Individualism Old and New* (New York: Minton, Balch and Company, 1930).
8. Dewey, *Freedom and Culture*, 13.
9. Dewey, *Freedom and Culture*, 15.

10. The relationship between culture and politics which Dewey suggests has been given voice as early as G.H. Mead, *Mind, Self and Society* (Chicago: The University of Chicago Press, 1934). This theme was further developed in M. Edelman, *Politics as Symbolic Action* (Chicago: Markham Publishing Company, 1971) and *The Symbolic Uses of Politics* (Urbana: The University of Illinois Press, 1964). More recently, such works as J. Street, *Politics and Popular Culture* (Cambridge: Polity Press, 1997) and Moreno-Riano, *Tolerance, Culture*, have attempted to provide and test empirical referents for a theory linking culture, broadly conceived, and politics. Other important work in this genre is that of Mary Douglas. See, in particular, M. Douglas, *Thought Styles* (Thousand Oaks, Calif.: Sage, 1996); *Risk and Blame: Essays in Cultural Theory* (London: Routledge, 1992); "Introduction to Grid/Group Analysis," in *Essays in the Sociology of Perception*, ed. Mary Douglas (London: Routledge, 1982); and *Natural Symbols: Explorations in Cosmology* (New York: Pantheon Books, 1982); and M. Douglas and A. Wildavsky, *Risk and Culture* (Berkeley: University of California Press, 1982).

11. For an important related treatment of this topic see P. Jones, "Beliefs and Identities," in *Toleration, Identity, and Difference*, ed. J. Horton and S. Mendus (London, MacMillan Press, 1999), 65-86.

12. For some excellent reviews see D.O. Sears and S. Levy, "Childhood and Adult Political Development," in *Oxford Handbook of Political Psychology*, ed. D.O. Sears, L. Huddy, and R. Jervis (Oxford: Oxford University Press, 2003), 60-109; as well as L. Huddy, "Group Identity and Political Cohesion," in *Oxford Handbook of Political Psychology*, ed. D.O. Sears, L. Huddy, and R. Jervis (Oxford: Oxford University Press, 2003), 511-58.

13. The two classic statements of these positions are J. Rawls, "Justice As Fairness: Political Not Metaphysical," in *Twentieth Century Political Theory* ed. S.E. Bronner (New York: Routledge, 1997), 37-58 and Sandel, "The Procedural Republic." For an excellent discussion of these issues see S. Aveneri and A. de-Shalit, eds., *Communitarianism and Individualism* (Oxford: Oxford University Press, 1992).

14. On this point see C. Taylor, "Atomism," in *Communitarianism and Individualism*, ed. S. Aveneri and A. de-Shalit (Oxford: Oxford University Press, 1992), 29-50.

15. See, for example, A. Gutmann, ed., *Multiculturalism: Examining the politics of recognition* (Princeton: Princeton University Press, 1994); J.D. Moon, *Constructing Community: Moral Pluralism and Tragic Conflicts* (Princeton: Princeton University Press, 1993); and R. Dworkin, "Liberal Community," in *Communitarianism and Individualism*, ed. S. Aveneri and A. de-Shalit (Oxford: Oxford University Press, 1992), 205-24. Beyond theoretical affirmation of the communitarian claim there is empirical support such as that indirectly offered in R. Weissberg, *Political Tolerance: Balancing community and diversity* (Thousand Oaks, Calif.: Sage, 1998).

16. Evidence exists, for example, demonstrating that a majority of Americans (58 percent) consider their ethnic group membership to be "important" or "very important." Furthermore, 82 percent of Americans recognize that ethnic groups have a right to maintain their own unique traditions. The source of these figures is the 2002 General Social Survey, National Opinion Research Center, University of Chicago as cited and discussed in *American Attitudes* (Ithaca, N.Y.: New Strategist Publications, Inc., 2005), 209-18.

17. For a fascinating perspective on this point see K. Mannheim, *Ideology and Utopia* (New York: Harcourt, Brace, and Company, 1936).

18. On this point see the important essays C. Taylor, "The Politics of Recognition," in *Multiculturalism: Examining the politics of recognition,* ed. A. Gutmann (Princeton:

Princeton University Press, 1994), 25-74 and J. Habermas, "Struggles for Recognition in the Democratic Constitutional State," in *Multiculturalism: Examining the politics of recognition*, ed. A. Gutmann (Princeton: Princeton University Press, 1994), 107-48. Other important expositions of these themes can be found in A. Phillips, "The Politicisation of Difference: Does this Make for a More Intolerant Society?" in *Toleration, Identity, and Difference*, ed. J. Horton and S. Mendus (London: MacMillan Press, 1999), 126-45.
19. J. Tully, "Identity Politics," in *The Cambridge History of Twentieth-Century Political Thought*, ed. T. Ball and R. Bellamy (Cambridge: Cambridge University Press, 2003), 526. Especially as it regards religious identities, this issue is being confronted anew within various Western states, in particular, Europe and the United States. See, for example, M. Connelly, "How Americans Voted: A Political Portrait," *The New York Times*, 7 November 2004, Week in Review section; and J. Horowitz, "Europe, Seeking Unity, Stumbles Over Issue of Religion," *The New York Times*, 7 November 2004, Front Page International section.
20. A. Appadurai, "Disjuncture and Difference in the Global Cultural Economy," in *The Globalization Reader*, ed. F. Lechner and J. Boli (Malden, Mass.: Blackwell Publishers, 2000), 324. Besides the Lechner and Boli volume, another excellent source regarding this issue is D. Held and A. McGrew, eds., *The Global Transformations Reader* (Cambridge: Polity Press, 2000), especially the essay by F. Halliday, " Global Governance: Prospects and Problems," 431-41.
21. Various case-studies can be offered as examples of this claim. Consider Kofi Annan's keynote address "Role of United Nations Development Programme Much Clearer Now," presented at the Ministerial Meeting on the UN Development Program (UNDP), 11 September 2000 (full address can be found at www.undp.org/execbrd/pdf/sgspeech.pdf), in which Annan linked peace to such "moral" concepts as development, tolerance, and rights. Another excellent example can be found in the UN's treatment of religion as it forcefully defends a policy defending toleration as a primary moral commitment over any religious commitment as well a virtue along side of other religious and moral virtues. On this point see the comments of Bawa Jain in a speech to delegates of the UN's Millennium Peace Summit of Religious and Spiritual Leaders, 28-31 August, 2000, New York City. For this and other information refer to www.millenniumpeacesummit.com as well as to the document unanimously approved by various religious leaders and delegates entitled *The Millennium World Peace Summit of Religious and Spiritual Leaders Commitment to Global Peace* (cf. www.milleniumpeacesummit.com/declaration.html).
22. This certainty regarding the moral value of tolerance is defended in spite of the uncertainty regarding the meaning and application of tolerance. Consider, for example, the collection of essays in D. Heyd, *Tolerance: An Elusive Virtue* (Princeton: Princeton University Press, 1997); M. Walzer, *On Toleration* (New Haven: Yale University Press, 1997); and for example, G. Newey, "Tolerance as a Virtue," in *Tolerance, Identity, and Difference*, ed. J. Horton and S. Mendus (London: MacMillan Press, 1999), 38-64.
23. See, for example, G.F. Newey, *Virtue, Reason, and Toleration* (Edinburgh: Edinburgh University Press, 1999) and S. Kautz, "Liberalism and the Idea of Toleration," *American Journal of Political Science* 37, no. 2 (May 1993): 610-32.
24. See, for example, R. Legutko, "The Trouble with Toleration," *Partisan Review* 61 (1994): 611-23.
25. For an excellent treatment of the Liberal worldview and the problem of tolerance see J. Waldron, "Liberalism, Political and Comprehensive," in *Handbook of Political Theory*, ed. G.F. Gaus and C. Kukathas (Thousand Oaks: Sage Publications, 2004), 89-99. I borrow from Waldron in my comments below.

26. Here I reject the oft-made distinction between political Liberalism and comprehensive Liberalism. On this distinction see Waldron, *Handbook of Political Theory*. For an excellent discussion of the comprehensive Liberal worldview as well as the issues of legitimating tolerance see S. Mendus, *Toleration and the Limits of Liberalism* (Atlantic Highlands, N.J.: Humanities Press International, 1989), especially pp. 69-109.

27. Kautz, "Liberalism and the Idea of Toleration," 611 and Sandel "The Procedural Republic." Sandel cites Rawls' comments of individuals as "self-originating sources of valid claims" in support of his position. See J. Rawls, "Kantian Constructivism in Moral Theory," *Journal of Philosophy* 77 (1980): 543.

28. See Waldron, *Handbook of Political Theory*, 90-94 and J. Rawls, "Justice As Fairness."

29. Besides the possible justifications suggested below, other such justifications exist based on skepticism and neutrality. These are explained and criticized in Mendus, *Toleration and the Limits of Liberalism*.

30. This sort of argument is to some extent implicit in Weissberg, *Political Tolerance*.

31. Here I have in mind the argument advanced by Richard Rorty that political morals are successful only in so far as they achieve the widest intersubjective consensus (i.e., workability) possible. See R. Rorty, *Truth and Progress* (Cambridge: Cambridge University Press, 1998), and *Contingency, Irony, and Solidarity* (Cambridge: Cambridge University Press, 1989).

32. One may raise the objection that a tolerant society's present success is not unprincipled rather, on the contrary, is principled on the notion of tolerance. The difficulty here, however, is that tolerance itself is never firmly grounded on a worldview, but rather, due to diversity and various cultures of meaning, is grounded in its workability and success. Thus, the logic defending the political morals (e.g., tolerance) of any such society is ultimately circular and never foundational.

33. Theories such as "The Elite Theory of Democracy" and other research into the role of the elite did much to suggest the existence of an unthinking public. See T.R. Dye and H.L. Zeigler, *American Politics in the Media Age* (Monterey, Calif.: Brooks/Cole Publishing Company, 1983); T.R. Dye and H.L. Zeigler, *The Few and the Many: Uncommon Readings in American Politics* (Belmont, Calif.: Duxbury Press, 1972); L.J.R. Herson and C.R. Hofstetter, "Tolerance, Consensus, and the Democratic Creed: A Contextual Exploration," *The Journal of Politics* 37 (1975): 1007-32; R.W. Jackman, "Political Elites, Mass Publics, and Support for Democratic Principles," *The Journal of Politics* 34 (1972): 753-73; J.W. Prothro and C.W. Grigg, "Fundamental Principles of Democracy: Bases of Agreement and Disagreement," *Journal of Politics* 22 (1960): 276-94; and C.W. Mills, *The Power Elite* (Oxford: Oxford University Press, 1956).

34. To suggest that the state is the moral umpire is to defend the notion that the Liberal state has been granted and has arrogated to itself the authority to mediate all moral disputes through its principle of Liberal neutrality, and, most important, it is to advance the defensible claim that modern states, in so far as Liberalism is their foundation, exist to advance and defend the Liberal worldview.

35. This problem is not recent. It has been the subject of much debate and controversy in regards to Thomas Hobbes' account of political obligation in *Leviathan*, and perhaps, of modern accounts of political obligation in general. Two classic discussions of the problem are A.E. Taylor, "The Ethical Doctrine of Hobbes," *Philosophy* 13 (1938): xxx; and S.M. Brown, Jr., "Hobbes: The Taylor Thesis," *Philosophical Review* 68 (1959): 303-23.

36. On this point see M. Walzer, *Thick and Thin: Moral Argument at Home and Abroad* (Notre Dame: University of Notre Dame Press, 1994).

37. One of many notable examples is T.H. Marshall, *Citizenship and Social Class* (London: Pluto Press, 1950, reprint 1992).

38. Some recent exceptions are E. Isin and P. Wood, *Citizenship and Identity* (London: Sage, 1999); G. Delanty, *Citizenship in a Global Age* (Buckingham: Open University Press, 2000); C. Lurry, *Cultural Rights* (London: Routledge, 1993); W. Kymlicka and W. Norman, *Citzenship in Diverse Societies* (Oxford: Oxford University Press, 2000); and N. Stevenson, *Culture and Citizenship* (London: Sage, 2001).

39. The social construction of citizenship is evidenced in the various constitutional requirements for naturalization or for natural-born citizenship.

40. On this point see Phillips, "The Politicisation of Difference." The recent election was cast as a conflict between cultures. As one writer reminded us, "The dispute in every contested state is different . . . but the basic contours of the argument are the same throughout the country, and it is an argument infused—like just about every argument in American politics—with race and culture." See M. Bai, "Another Contested Contest?" *The New York Times Magazine*, 31 October 2004, section 6, 20.

41. On the importance of threat and its relation to tolerance see J. Sullivan. We have been reminded of this in the recent presidential election. Given our current passionate and community-motivated electorate, democracy, as Harry C. Boyte reminds us, "seems more like 'a kind of consumer good and spectator sport' than like a workaday commitment in which victors join with vanquished to get things done. 'So the real question is whether this highly charged electoral season can help revive a larger civic culture, and a productive citizenship. . . . Whether people can learn to deal with people they disagree with, or may even hate, for the sake of fixing their neighborhood park or school.'" See T.S. Purdum, "The Year of Passion," *The New York Times*, 31 October 2004, sec. 4, 1.

42. For a different theoretical attempt in this regard see A.N. Eisenberg, "Accommodation and Coherence: In Search of a General Theory for Adjudicating Claims of Faith, Conscience, and Culture," in *Engaging Cultural Differences : the multicultural challenge in liberal democracies*, ed. R.A. Shweder, M. Minow, and H.R. Markus (New York: Russell Sage Foundation, 2002), 147-66.

43. An aspect of this discussion which is not considered here though it is addressed in another paper in this volume is whether or not some moral visions are more conducive to economic wellbeing than others.

Conflict and Political Tolerance in Israel
Michal Shamir and Tamy Sagiv-Schifter

The authors would like to thank the Israel Science Foundation for its research grant 711/99 to the first author, the B.I Cohen Institute of Tel-Aviv University and its director, Noah Lewin-Epstein, for their support for this project, and Yasemin Alkalai for her help in data analysis.

Introduction

War and conflict challenge individuals' and societies' democratic norms. In politics, it boils down to tension between security concerns and democratic principles, and especially, the rule of law, civil liberties, and political toleration. On the social and psychological levels, a situation of conflict affects people's needs, concerns, and priorities. Conflict elicits threat; it also enhances people's identification with the collective; ingroup attachment intensifies, outgroup distrust increases. It is illuminating to theorize about these processes by applying social identity theory, which has become the dominant explanatory framework for the study of intergroup relations,[1] and has also invaded political scientists' work on prejudice and intolerance.[2]

According to this theory, social differentiation to ingroups and outgroups is a universal phenomenon. Individuals define themselves to a large extent in terms of group identities and aspire to a positive social identity. People think in terms of social categories even on the basis of trivial differences, and will favor their ingroup over outgroups even when groups are defined minimalistically and arbitrarily, without any traditional group base or identifiable social anchor (the minimal groups paradigm).[3] Social categorization is thus an important mechanism that cannot be ignored in relation to outgroup distrust, hostility, and conflict.[4]

This mechanism is a deep-rooted part of human and social nature, however the specific social context molds it in different ways:

(1) It determines which categories will become relevant and the basis for social categorization (out of an almost infinite number of such bases);

(2) It affects the salience or importance of the social categorization; and

(3) It affects the relationship between ingroup identity and outgroup orientation.

Each of these stipulations carries with it significant ramifications for group relations in all realms of life. The first provision focuses on the nature of the targets. Thus in political tolerance research we find that the targets for intolerance vary over countries, but also within countries over time.[5] The second specification may be seen in terms of priming effects. Even enduring social categories such as those based upon ethnicity or religion are sometimes salient, and at other times lose their prominence. As we shall see, Arab political groups in Israel are most salient during periods of conflict, but they were much less obtrusive during the 1990s throughout the Oslo peace process and the bitter internal Jewish debate it raised.[6]

The third postulate concerns the relationship of what Marilynn Brewer[7] calls "ingroup love" and "outgroup hate," or in de Figueiredo and Elkins'[8] apt terminology, "pride and prejudice".[9] Ingroup love manifests itself in collective identity, in the image of what the group stands for and how it wishes to be viewed by others. It involves shared representations of the group, and it is positive. Outgroup hate includes the negative orientations toward an outgroup, such as social distance, mistrust, prejudice, hostility, intolerance, and so on. The common view advanced by Sumner was that these are two sides of the same coin, or in other words, the relationship between preference for the ingroup and negative orientation toward the outgroup is strong and constant.[10] Today, a conditional and contextual view of this relationship is gaining prominence.[11]

Personality is one such conditioning factor. Authoritarian personality characteristics, for example, increase the probability of categorizing others as belonging to a group other than one's own, of heightened ingroup attachment, and of bias and hostility toward outgroups.[12] But we focus here on the social context, and more specifically on the situation of conflict.

What Are the Ramifications of Conflict?

A situation of conflict will focus social categorization on categories relevant to the conflict, and will prime these distinctions. Ingroup love will increase; outgroup hate will intensify; and furthermore, the relationship between them will strengthen. Conflict increases the salience of the categorization which differentiates between the ingroup and the outgroup. Given the greater salience of collective identity and the threat to the ingroup's interests, physical well-being, or even existence, identification with and dependence upon the ingroup grow, no matter what the outgroup is. This will foster pressures for conformity and cohesion, unity, and internal solidarity. Outgroup sympathizers such as Communists in the U.S. in the 1950's or leftists in Israel, and even more so, citizens belonging in some tangible way to the outgroup ("hostile minorities" such as Israeli Arabs), are primary targets. Because of the threat to the ingroup's interests or even existence, the identification and mutual dependence on the ingroup is directly related to fear and hostility toward the outgroup. In other words, in situations of conflict, threat increases, ingroup identification strengthens, and also the relationship between the ingroup and outgroup orientations is reinforced.

We rely on these postulates from social identity theory in our exploration of one manifestation of outgroup hate: political tolerance, the willingness to apply political and civil rights to unpopular and disliked groups, individuals and ideas. The specific context is Israel during the Al-Aqsa Intifada, and we compare it to the period of relative quiet before its eruption in September 2000. This latest round of violent confrontations between Israel and the Palestinians followed almost a decade marked by a concentrated effort at peace-making, concurrent with a marked decline in threat perceptions and a growth of conciliatory views among Israelis. Based on three national surveys carried out before and during the Intifada, we study the political tolerance of the Israeli Jewish public, the amount and nature of change therein, and the mechanisms of identity and threat behind it.

Background

The Al-Aqsa Intifada broke out on September 28, 2000 in the territories Israel conquered in 1967—the West Bank (or Judea and Samaria) and the Gaza strip. If the first Intifada (1987-1993) was characterized as a popular uprising, symbolized by youth throwing stones at Israeli soldiers, the second Intifada is distinguished by armed attacks and terrorism, perpetrated by Hamas, Jihad, and Palestinian Authority forces.[13] The number of casualties is also very different and much higher in the second Intifada. Thousands, most of them civilians, have been wounded and killed on both sides.[14] The context of the Intifada is definitely one of acute conflict between two peoples fighting over tangible (territorial) and symbolic (identity) resources, with a high toll in human life and economic damage on both sides.

At the same time the second Intifada erupted and through the first part of October 2000, Israeli Arabs, citizens of Israel, initiated unprecedented violent demonstrations and riots in which thirteen Arabs were killed by police.[15] These October events helped seal in the eyes of the Jewish majority the connection between Israeli Arabs and the Palestinians in the territories. In our January 2001 poll, conducted three months into the Intifada, we asked both Jews and Arabs the reasons for these recent occurrences within Israel. Most of our Jewish respondents (44 percent) thought the main reason was identification of Israeli Arabs with the struggle of the Palestinians in the territories, and 30 percent more attributed it to opposition on a national and religious basis to Jews and the state of Israel. Twenty-five percent thought it was Arabs' sense of discrimination due to their civic status.[16]

Nevertheless, except for these October events, during the current Intifada, just as in the first, Israeli Arabs may be generally characterized as "fans and not as players".[17] The number of Israeli Arabs actually involved in terrorism has grown significantly over these two and a half years, but the absolute numbers are miniscule. Civil and humanitarian support is more prevalent. The discourse of support for the Palestinian cause is more explicit today, to the point where legislation has been initiated to curb it. In the January 2003 elections, there were several attempts to disqualify Arab political parties and candidates from participating on this basis.[18]

Data

The analysis in this paper is based on three national surveys carried out in January 2000, before the Intifada, in January 2001 and in June 2002, three and twenty one months into the Intifada respectively. The interviews were conducted with representative samples of the adult Israeli population, Jews and Arabs, but in this paper we focus on the Jewish respondents only.[19]

To measure political tolerance, we use the standard least-liked group approach.[20] It ensures the necessary element of objection in the measurement of political tolerance, and, in addition, attempts to neutralize or hold constant the content of the group. Respondents are presented with a list of potential target groups and are asked to select the group they like the least or tell the interviewer the name of another group they like even less. Having identified their least-liked group, respondents are asked a series of questions regarding their willingness to extend to the group common political and civil rights. These make up the tolerance measure. The selection of least-liked groups is not only instrumental in the measurement of political tolerance, but also provides indication for the political cleavage structure, for potential targets for intolerance, and for sources of threat in society.

Israel in the Al-Aqsa Intifada

Conflict and Threat

We begin with an examination of the changes in threat perceptions the Al Aqsa Intifada and the concurrent October events have brought about. In the first row of Table 7.1 we see the immediate increase in the focus on Arab target groups with the eruption of the atrocities—clear indication for social categorization along categories germane to the conflict. The number of Jewish respondents who select an Arab political group as their least-liked group jumps from less than a quarter in January 2000 to about a third only three months after the Intifada began, and this percentage grows further to 45 percent in June 2002. The Intifada refocused Israeli Jews on Arab targets—an outcome of the increased salience of the categorization which differentiates between the ingroup and the outgroup in the conflict.

Table 7.1 – Threat perceptions: January 2000, January 2001, and June 2002

	Jan. 2000	Jan. 2001	June 2002
% selecting Arab least-liked groups	23	34	45
Least-liked group threatens:			
Security*	60	68	73
Democracy*	66	62	69
Jewish character of Israel*	53	59	61
Least-liked Arab group threatens:			
Security*	85	80	91
Democracy*	63	51	72
Jewish character of Israel*	76	74	81

* % includes respondents who agree and definitely agree with the statement (on a five-point Likert scale)

Following our least-liked group tolerance questions, we asked whether and to what extent the respondent's least-liked group threatens the security of Israel, democracy in Israel, and the Jewish character of the state. These questions allow us to measure and untangle the nature of the threat.

In the second row of Table 7.1, we can see the increasing threat to security following the outbreak of violence, which is evident right away and continues to grow with the ongoing conflict. Altogether there is an increase of 13 percentage points in the perceived security threat from 60% threatened in January 2000 to 73% in June 2002.

The Jewish character of the state is a core value for most Israeli Jews and embodies, in a way, the essence of Zionist ideology. Following the failed Camp David summit in the summer of 2000 and the outbreak of violence, the "right of return" of the Palestinian refugees to Israel became most salient, bringing this concern to the fore. While this threat is consistently lower than the security threat, here too, the threat to Jewish collective identity increased when conflict erupted, although somewhat less than the security threat: between the first and last observations there is an 8 percentage point increase (see row 4 in Table 7.1).[21]

Where do these changes in least-liked group threat levels stem from? When we distinguish between the threat posed by Arab and Jewish target groups in the three points in time, we find that the overall increase in threat is due much more to changes in threat perceptions from Arab least-liked groups[22] than from Jewish least-liked groups. In addition, the growing focus on Arab rather than Jewish targets contributes to the overall higher threat levels, as Arab groups always present a higher threat than Jewish groups on these two dimensions. The increased threat perception is thus the result of the change in the makeup of the target groups for intolerance and an increased sense of threat mainly from Arab target groups.

Conflict and Collective Identity

In order to examine the effect of the conflict upon the salience and attachment to collective Jewish identity, we use other data from national surveys not analyzed here.[23] The measure was designed for other purposes, but it is useful in the study of the interrelationship between conflict, collective identity, and tolerance. It is a measure of the value conflict existing in Israeli political culture in the context of the Israeli-Arab conflict. Based on a ranking question, it juxtaposes four values, which in an ideal world most Israeli Jews would want to see fulfilled: a Jewish state with a Jewish majority; greater Israel along the post-1967 war boundaries; democracy, defined in the survey as equal political rights to all; and peace, defined as low probability for war. Respondents were asked to rank these values from first to last.

Our interest here lies primarily in the relative ranking of *Jewish majority*. In three surveys conducted in 1999, an average of 26 percent ranked Jewish majority first. In January 2000, 29 percent ranked it first. In January 2001, this figure jumped to 39 percent, and in three additional surveys during 2001, we obtained 37-39 percent. In two surveys in 2002, the figures were 33 and 36 percent. These data thus suggest that the salience of Jewish identity jumped up immediately after the Intifada started and remained at significantly higher levels compared to before the Intifada.

The trend is very similar if we look at the first rankings of *Jewish majority* and *greater Israel* (another relevant dimension of national identity) combined. In the three data points in 1999, an average of 35 percent chose one of these values as their first priority; in January 2000 it was 36 percent. In January 2001, this figure jumped to 52 percent; the four data points in 2001 average 50 percent. Similarly in the two surveys in 2002 an average of 49 percent ranked these two values first. The before-after difference in these indicators for the impact of the conflict upon national identity salience, is thus between 6 and 14 percentage points.

Still another indication of the growing value of national identity following the outbreak of the Al-Aqsa Intifada and the October events is the growth of right-wing political identification by 7 percentage points, and the decline in left identification by 10 percentage points between January 2000 and June 2002.

Conflict and Political Tolerance

We expect growing manifestations of outgroup hate in times of conflict with the primary object of hate being the outgroup. But outgroup hate diffuses also to people and groups who are not part of the outgroup, yet belong to or are connected with it in some way. Citizens linked to the outgroup by ethnicity, religion or national affiliation are primary targets and are often defined as "hostile minorities". Arab citizens of Israel are an obvious case, as are Muslim citizens of the United States following 9/11, and Germans and Japanese in the U.S. during World War II. Even if there are "objective" reasons for suspicion and threat, such as the October riots of Israeli Arabs, and a few instances of members of these groups crossing the line to the enemy, in all of these cases, there is no basis for such distrust with regard to the vast majority of members of this category, and yet it is to be expected. In the next circle of outgroup hate are outgroup sympathizers and more generally political groups which put less emphasis on national identity, and are therefore perceived as being more distanced from the ingroup. Leftist groups in Israel who are considered sympathizers of the Palestinian cause are such groups, as were Communists in the U.S. in the 1950s and civil rights associations in general. Thus we expect the greatest increase in intolerance toward Arab political groups, and to a lesser extent, toward left-wing Jewish groups, followed by other kinds of targets.

The three surveys contained similar batteries of tolerance items referring to the group each respondent selected as least-liked. Respondents were asked to what extent (on a five-point Likert scale) they would extend the group or group members different political and civil rights. The items referred to the right of demonstration, appearance on television, becoming Prime Minister, and phone tapping. We combined these four items into scales, and the tolerance score was computed as the average tolerant response, standardized so as to vary between zero and one hundred. A score of zero indicates intolerance, and a score of one hundred, high tolerance.[24] Table 7.2 presents these tolerance scores for January 2000, January 2001, and June 2002. The items vary much in tandem over time,[25] and the summary scores in Table 7.2 clearly represent the trend.

Political tolerance toward least-liked groups declined between January 2000 and June 2002 by seven points, and the differential pattern for various kinds of least-liked groups corroborates our expectations. Tolerance toward Arab political groups declines by nine points, and tolerance toward left-wing Jewish groups declines by six points. Tolerance toward right-wing and religious groups does not decline, and in June 2002 is even somewhat higher than in January 2000, before the Intifada.

It is worth noting that in all three time points, the lowest tolerance was displayed toward Arab political groups. However, as the conflict unfolded, the difference between tolerance toward Arab and Jewish political groups increased. Also, variation in tolerance toward least-liked groups increases under conflict, indicated by the standard deviations in the table.

Table 7.2 – Political Tolerance: January 2000, January 2001, and June 2002

Target	Jan. 2000	Jan. 2001	June 2002
Least-liked group	55*	57	48
	(20)	(22)	(25)
Least-liked groups			
Arab	44	48	35
	(20)	(21)	(21)
Left (Jewish)	61	64	55
	(18)	(22)	(25)
Right (Jewish)	52	53	55
	(21)	(20)	(21)
Religious (Jewish)	64	67	68
	(16)	(17)	(20)

* average tolerant response on the same four items, standardized so as to vary between zero and one hundred; standard deviation in parentheses.

Threat, Collective Identity and Tolerance: Individual-level Analysis

So far we have seen that since the outbreak of the Al-Aqsa Intifada perceived threat increased, collective identity strengthened, and political tolerance declined. We move now to ascertain and disentangle these relationships on the individual level in the context of conflict and without it.

As proxies for collective identity, or ingroup love, we use one political and one social indicator. Left-right political identification is our first measure, where right-wingers are considered most highly attached to Jewish collective identity. Our second measure is religiosity—respondents' adherence to Jewish tradition and religious practices. The more religious a respondent, the more attached he or she is considered to be to Jewish collective identity.[26]

We begin by looking at the bivariate relationship between identity and threat. Table 7.3 presents correlations between identity and threat indicators in our three surveys. Not surprisingly, there is a significant correlation with threat to the Jewish character of the state in all three points in time. The correlations with threat to security are much weaker or non-significant, the highest ones observed in June 2002. These correlations indicate that greater attachment to the ingroup covaries with higher threat perceptions: right-wingers and religious respondents are more threatened. Threat to democracy does not appear to be related at all to our ingroup love indicators.

Table 7.3 – Correlations between threat and identity indicators

	Jan. 2000	Jan. 2001	June 2002
Left-right identification *with*:			
Group threat to security	.15	.12	.17
Group threat to democracy	(-.04)	(.11)	(-.02)
Group threat to Jewish character	.31	.41	.29
Religiosity *with*:			
Group threat to security	(.03)	(.09)	.20
Group threat to democracy	(-.06)	(-.01)	(.08)
Group threat to Jewish character	.26	.26	.30

All correlations statistically significant (p≤.05) except when in parentheses.

Table 7.4 introduces the correlations between political tolerance and our two identity indicators in the three surveys.

Before the Intifada, and still three months after it broke out, there is no relationship between the two collective identity indicators and tolerance. However in our June 2002 data there is a correlation of .33 between political tolerance and left-right identification and a correlation of .22 with religiosity. Under conflict, amidst the Al-Aqsa Intifada, this relationship emerges.

As can be seen in the lower part of the table, the differences in scores between right and left-wingers were one (non-significant) point in January 2000, and nineteen points in June 2002 (significant). The parallel figures for the differences between the ultra-orthodox and secular categories were three (non-significant) in January 2000, and fourteen (significant) in June 2002.

Following the rows in the lower part of Table 7.4, it is apparent that the decline in political tolerance occurs mainly in the categories which signify high ingroup love or attachment to Jewish collective identity: right-wingers, ultra-orthodox and religious respondents. Conflict seems to have much more impact on right-wingers and the more religious respondents than on the other categories of respondents, less attached to Jewish collective identity.

Table 7.4 - Correlations between political tolerance and identity indicators

	Jan. 2000	Jan. 2001	June 2002
Tolerance toward least-liked group *with*:			
Left-right identification	(.03)	(.06)	.33
Religiosity	(-.00)	(-.02)	.22
Tolerance toward least-liked group*:			
Right	55	56	40
Center	55	60	53
Left	56	59	59
Ultra-orthodox	53	55	43
Religious	60	60	41
Traditional	53	57	47
Secular	56	59	57

All correlations statistically significant ($p \leq .05$) except when in parentheses.
* average tolerant response.

Table 7.5 shows the well-established negative relationship between threat and tolerance.[27] In all three surveys and with all three threat measures, the correlations are negative, indicating that political tolerance declines with increasing threat across individuals. We also note that these correlations are highest in the June 2002 survey, with the most notable increase for the group threat to the Jewish character of Israel. In the first two surveys, the security threat was by far the best predictor of political tolerance toward people's least-liked group. By June 2002, while it is still the most potent correlate, it is not much greater than the threat to the Jewish character of the state.

Table 7.5 – Correlations between political tolerance and threat indicators

	Jan. 2000	Jan. 2001	June 2002
Tolerance toward least-liked group *with*:			
Group threat to security	-.38	-.42	-.49
Group threat to democracy	-.19	-.26	-.30
Group threat to Jewish character	-.20	-.17	-.43

All correlations statistically significant ($p \leq .05$) except when in parentheses.

We move now to examine the multivariate relationship between threat, in-group identity and political tolerance. Figure 7.1 puts together the three constructs in a simple model, which we estimate using structural equation modelling.

Figure 7.1– Tolerance as a function of threat and identity

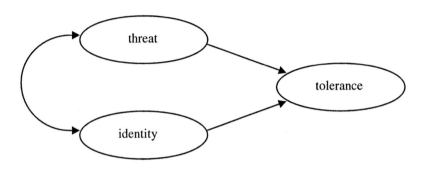

We estimate this model for political tolerance toward least-liked groups at three points in time: January 2000, January 2001, and June 2002 using the same measures in all analyses, so that the unstandardized coefficients can be straightforwardly compared over time. The results are presented in Table 7.6, and allow us to identify the structural effects of threat and identity upon tolerance in each point in time. Table 7.7 reports the measurement models.[28]

Table 7.6– Political tolerance structural equation models

	January 2000		January 2001		June 2002	
	standardized	unstandardized	standardized	unstandardzed	standardized	unstandardized
threat→tolerance	-.53	-.28	-.47	-.39	-.58	-.45
identity→tolerance	(-.03)	(-.03)	(.00)	(.00)	-.33	-.46
threat↔identity	.05	.03	.17	.12	.41	.20
χ^2/d.f.	28.177/21 = 1.342		23.965/18 = 1.331		27.823/19 = 1.46	
RMSEA	0.026		0.028		0.034	
p value of close fit	0.964		0.894		0.834	
GFI	0.988		0.988		0.984	

Entries are standardized and unstandardized structural equation model results obtained with AMOS V. All coefficients are statistically significant ($p \le .05$) except when in parentheses.

All three models obtain acceptable fit indices, as reported in the bottom half of Table 7.6.[29] Threat is the more potent source of tolerance. Identity does not affect tolerance in the first two points in time, before the outbreak of violence, and three months into the Intifada. However by June 2002, well into the Intifada, collective identity becomes an important source of political intolerance. Conflict then seems to activate the relationship between identity and tolerance since the impact of identity on tolerance only appears under conflict.

Table 7.7– Political tolerance structural equation models: measurement model

	January 2000	January 2001	June 2002
Tolerance			
PM	.36	.54	.48
TV	.69	.62	.69
Phone	.39	.49	.59
Demonstration	.65	.70	.59
Threat			
Security	.86	.92	.78
Democracy	.48	.48	.48
Jewish nature	.42	.43	.59
Identity			
Left-right	.64	.80	.61
Religiosity	.55	.49	.51
Threat to Jewish nature	.46	.45	.26

Entries are standardized structural equation model results with AMOS V. All coefficients are statistically significant.

Summary and Conclusions

Our case study focused on Israel in the early 2000's, during the Al-Aqsa Intifada, the latest bloody round of confrontation between Jews and Palestinians, in comparison to previous times of relative quiet and conflict resolution efforts.

Building upon social identity theory, we examine the dynamics of political tolerance. We can point to three kinds of effects of the conflict: through increased threat; through greater salience of and attachment to collective identity; and through the strengthening of the relationship between ingroup identification and political intolerance.

Our data provide support to all three processes based on both temporal aggregate and individual-level covariation. In the first sections of the analysis, we show that since the outbreak of the violence, threat increased, the salience and attachment to Jewish collective identity grew, and political tolerance declined. In the last section we build upon individual-level analysis of the three surveys and their comparison over time. The results demonstrate the strong effect of threat upon political intolerance in all three points in time, and the impact of ingroup identification (ingroup love) upon intolerance (outgroup hate) only under conflict (Tables 7.4 and 7.6).

It is important to note the temporal variation in these processes. The onset of conflict immediately focused social categorization on categories relevant to the conflict, those differentiating between the ingroup and the outgroup in the conflict: Israeli Jews immediately (by January 2001) focused on Arab targets, and this focus rose further through the Intifada (Table 7.1). Also the salience of collective identity and attachment and identification with the ingroup increased right away. However the increase in political intolerance and the process of activation of the relationship between ingroup love and outgroup hate took longer, and we identify them only in our June 2002 survey (Tables 7.2, 7.4 and 7.6).

The increase in political intolerance occurs mainly in the high ingroup love categories. By June 2002, it is primarily the more strongly attached to Jewish collective identity (right-wingers and the more religious) who become less tolerant, rather than those less attached to Jewish collective identity (see the lower part of Table 7.4). They are also more likely to select Arab rather than Jewish target groups, and more so since the Intifada.[30] The more strongly attached to Jewish collective identity were not more intolerant toward their least-liked groups than those with lower ingroup identification before the Intifada. However with the conflict, ingroup love became relevant and induced greater intolerance. The mechanism behind the activation of ingroup identity during the Intifada may be ingroup pressures, but it could also be the result of the changing pattern of target group selection with the priming of the Arab-Jewish social categorization.

Since we have several measures designed to tap different dimensions of threat, we can further dwell upon its meaning. We find that perceptions of security threat are consistently more prevalent than perceptions of threat to Jewish identity in all surveys (see Table 7.1). Furthermore, security threat has higher correlations with political tolerance than threat to Jewish identity; and our structural equation measurement model suggests that security threat is the major component of threat in all points in time (Table 7.7). Nevertheless, by June 2002, well into the Intifada, the weight of these two threat measures becomes very similar in magnitude (see Table 7.5 and Table 7.7). It is then that threat to Jewish identity, combining threat and ingroup attachment, becomes more consequential, together with the activation of the relationship between ingroup love and outgroup hate.

Our study corroborates the contextual variant of social identity theory, and in particular, the effect of the conflict upon the salience of social categorizations and upon the strength of the relationship between ingroup identity and outgroup orientation. The changes we found over changing circumstances on both of these factors were substantial and cannot be ignored. This emphasis on the contextual also carries important implications for theories of tolerance. Our results reveal the changing (contextual) relationship between our identity indicators and political intolerance (Tables 7.4 and 7.6). In studies of tolerance, such variables are usually categorized as social and political factors, and their effect upon tolerance is studied as such. Our study brings to the fore the contextual nature of the impact of such factors upon tolerance. What is usually termed *social* and *political* factors may signify identity (and other) components with different implications for tolerance under distinct circumstances. Our results, based on the study of one country over a short period of time, strongly suggest the contextual interpretation, which must be carried to cross-national and long-term comparisons of single systems.

Our empirical study of the interrelationships between conflict, threat, collective identity, and tolerance is limited to one conflict and one country. Involving a mixture of war and terrorism and the potency of collective identity, this case is not at all unusual among twenty-first century conflicts. The issues we have explored will therefore continue to be on the global agenda for the foreseeable future.

Notes

1. Marilynn Brewer and Rupert Brown, "Intergroup relations," in *The Handbook of Social Psychology*, 4th edition, ed. Daniel T. Gilbert, Susan T. Fiske, and Gardner Lindzey (New York: McGraw-Hill, 1998), 554-94; Miles Hewstone and Katy Greenland, "Intergroup conflict," *International Journal of Psychology* 35, (2000): 136-44.
2. James L Gibson and Amanda Gouws, "Social identities and political intolerance: Linkages within the South African mass public" *American Journal of Political Science* 44 (2000): 272-86; Paul M. Sniderman et. al., *The Outsider – Prejudice and Politics in Italy* (Princeton: Princeton University Press, 2000).
3. Henri Tajfel, *Human Groups and Social Categories* (Cambridge: Cambridge University Press, 1981); Henri Tajfel et. al., "Social categorization and intergroup behavior," *European Journal of Social Psychology* 1 (1971): 149-77.
4. Hewstone and Greenland, "Intergroup conflict," 137-38.
5. John L. Sullivan, James E. Piereson, and George E. Marcus, *Political Tolerance and American Democracy* (Chicago: The University of Chicago Press, 1982); John L. Sullivan et. al., *Political Tolerance in Context: Support for Unpopular Minorities in Israel, New Zealand, and the United States* (Boulder, Colo.: Westview, 1985).
6. Michal Shamir, *The political context of tolerance: Israel in the 1980's and 1990's*, Report to the Israel Science Foundation, 2002.
7. Marilynn Brewer, "The psychology of prejudice: Ingroup love or outgroup hate?" *Journal of Social Issues* 55 (1999): 429-44.
8. Rui J.P. de Figueiredo, Jr. and Zachary Elkins, "Are patriots bigots? An inquiry into the vices of in-group pride," *American Journal of Political Science* 47 (2003): 171-88.
9. See contributions to "Special issue: National identity in Europe," *Political Psychology* 24, 2 (2003).
10. William Graham Sumner, *Folkways: A Study of the Sociological Importance of Usages, Manners, Customs, Mores and Morals* (Boston: Ginn, 1906).
11. E.g. Brewer, "The psychology of prejudice," 429-44.

12. See John Duckitt, "Authoritarianism and group identification: A new view of an old construct," *Political Psychology* 10 (1989): 63-84, and Stanley Feldman and Karen Stenner, "Perceived threat and authoritarianism," *Political Psychology* 18 (1997): 741-70, for interaction between threat and authoritarianism.

13. This is of course a simplified account of the Intifadas, and the overall picture is much more blurred. The first Intifada included terrorist and para-military armed attacks as well, and the second Intifada also has a popular component.

14. The number of casualties is much higher on the Palestinian than on the Israeli side.

15. Twelve of them were Israeli citizens. These events were investigated by an official commission of inquiry, headed by Supreme Court Judge Or, which published its report almost three years later. For clarity of exposition, we refer throughout the paper to the Palestinians in the territories under Israeli occupation as Palestinians, and to Palestinian/Arab citizens of Israel as Israeli Arabs.

16. In contrast, 53 percent of the Arab respondents mentioned discrimination as the main reason, 34 percent—their identification with the struggle of the Palestinians in the territories, and only 9 percent—opposition to Jews and to Israel on a national and religious basis (N=158). There is also a big difference in Jewish and Arab assessment of Arab discrimination in Israel. 84 percent of the Arab sample thought that there is definitely discrimination, compared to 28 percent of the Jews. If we combine the two positive categories, 97 percent of the Arabs think there is discrimination, compared to 64 percent of the Jews

17. Suleiman Shakur, *Yedioth Aharonoth*, 2 Dec. 1988, cited in Sammy Smooha, *Conflicting and shared attitudes in a divided society*, vol. 1 of *Arabs and Jews in Israel* (Boulder, Colo.: Westview, 1989), xvii.

18. Michal Shamir and Keren Weinshall-Margel, "Disqualification of party lists in Israel – Were the 2003 elections unique?" in *The Elections in Israel – 2003*, ed. Asher Arian and Michal Shamir (New Brunswick, N.J.: Transaction, 2005).

19. The data were collected by the B.I. and Lucille Cohen Institute at Tel-Aviv University. All interviews were conducted over the phone. Sample sizes were 536 respondents, (only Jews) in January 2000; 577 (419 Jews and 158 Arabs) in January 2001; 559 (408 Jews and 151 Arabs) in June 2002.

20. Sullivan, Piereson, and Marcus, *Political Tolerance*.

21. There is no such trend in the threat to democracy (row 3 in Table 7.1).

22. Compare rows 2 with 5, and 4 with 7 in Table 7.1.

23. See Shamir, "The political context of tolerance."

24. Alpha coefficients for this scale varied between .59 and .65, with the lowest coefficient obtained in January 2000, and the highest in the June 2002 survey.

25. For the separate items and their trends see Tamy Sagiv-Schifter and Michal Shamir, "Israel as a laboratory for the study of political tolerance," *Deot Baam* 6 (October 2002) (in Hebrew).

26. The correlations in our surveys between these two indicators are between .30 and .42.

27. Samuel A. Stouffer, *Communism, Conformity and Civil Liberties* (New York: Doubleday, 1955); Sullivan, Piereson, and Marcus, *Political Tolerance and American Democracy*.

28. In each model, tolerance was indicated by four items referring to the right of demonstration, appearance on television, becoming Prime Minister, and phone tapping. Threat was indicated by three items referring to respondents' least-liked group threat to security, democracy and the Jewish character of Israel. Since the threat to Jewish identity contains both threat and collective identity components, this last threat indicator was also specified as an indicator of identity, together with left-right political affiliation and religiosity.

29. The Chi square to degrees of freedom ratios are well below two in all models; RMSEA < .05; the GFI's are close to 1.0; only the p value of close fit are not close enough to 1.0. All models incorporate correlated errors between indicators (in the political tolerance toward least-liked group 2000 model—two, in the 2001 mode—four, and in the 2002 model—three). The average absolute value correlation was .20.

30. Sagiv-Schifter and Shamir, "Israel as a laboratory".

Gender and Tolerance
Ewa Golebiowska

Introduction

Women and men hold similar attitudes in most areas and yet persistent gender differences emerge in several issue domains.[1] One area in which women and men have been shown to differ is in their endorsement of citizenship rights for members of disliked political minorities (or in their political tolerance). Generally speaking, women have been shown to exhibit more reluctance than men to extend democratic rights and freedoms to members of unpopular groups (e.g., atheists, racists, or militarists). These gender differences in tolerance have not been large but have been persisting since the beginning of systematic research on the subject in the 1950s.[2] While many studies have noted that women tend to be less tolerant than men, only one published piece of scholarship has made the question of differences in women's and men's political tolerance a centerpiece of its attention.[3] Most studies, in addition, have not identified comprehensive empirical accounts for why women are more reluctant than men to tolerate political unorthodoxy.

While women are more reluctant than men to put up with disliked political minorities' rights, research in other tolerance domains shows that they are not necessarily intolerant across the board. Previous research has consistently shown that women tend to hold more favorable attitudes than men toward racial and ethnic minorities, particularly when their reactions to interpersonal interaction involving minority group members are examined.[4] Generally speaking, women are also more willing than men to express favorable attitudes toward gays and lesbians and this gender difference is particularly pronounced when women's and men's reactions to gay men and lesbians are considered separately.[5] More specifically, while heterosexual women's and men's attitudes toward lesbian women are largely similar, heterosexual women's reactions to gay men are considerably more positive than those of heterosexual men.[6]

In short, research in different tolerance domains suggests a textured relationship between gender and tolerance, although these different research enterprises have not engaged each other directly in an effort to illuminate the rela tionship between gender and tolerance more effectively. In neither tolerance domain, in addition, has the influence of gender on tolerance been accounted for completely. This suggests that scrutiny of the relationship between gender and tolerance broadly conceived might benefit from integrating our knowledge of the dynamics of the gender-tolerance linkage in different tolerance domains. Assuming that different types of tolerance may correspond to a broader tolerance phenomenon, to put it differently, we may illuminate the relationship between gender and tolerance more successfully by "borrowing variables" across different tolerance traditions. This is one of the goals of this chapter. After reviewing extant scholarship on women's and men's support for political minorities' democratic rights, I place gender differences in political tolerance in context by comparing and contrasting what we know about women's and men's attitudes toward political diversity with what we know about their tolerance of racial and ethnic minorities and tolerance of homosexuality. As part of this effort, I empirically examine the relationships between political tolerance, racial and ethnic tolerance, and tolerance homosexuality to establish their hypothesized association and thus to provide a stronger rationale for integrating insights from different models of tolerance. I next seek to demonstrate how women and men differ in their background attributes and psychological and political characteristics that could help to shed light on the sources of gender differences in different tolerance domains. I proceed to an exploration of the linkages between gender and different types of tolerance, considering possible contributions from the models of racial and ethnic tolerance to understanding the sources of gender differences in political tolerance. I conclude the chapter, finally, with suggestions for future research directions in this area.

Importance of Studying the Linkages between Gender and Tolerance

The issue of persistent gender differences in political and racial and ethnic tolerance presents more than an interesting empirical phenomenon. It is important to understand the culprits behind women's attitudes toward political outgroups as well as racial and ethnic minorities in light of the recent disappearance of the gender gap in voting turnout. As voters, women can indirectly shape public policies by electing legislators who are more or less supportive of civil liberties and who may have different ideas bearing on the well-being of different racial and ethnic groups. Because women are beginning to vote as much as or even more than men and constitute a majority of the American population, then, their attitudes have important implications for tolerance of political competition as well as tolerance of racial and ethnic difference in the United States. In a related vein, it is important to understand the underpinnings of women's attitudes toward disliked political minorities and racial and ethnic groups because more and more women have been running for and getting elected to political office. As members of American lawmaking bodies, women can directly influence public policy with implications for the well-being of political, racial, and ethnic minority groups.

Previous Research

Systematic research on gender differences in attitudes toward unpopular political groups (or political tolerance) goes back to a groundbreaking examination of support for civil liberties of communists, socialists, and atheists first published in 1955. In that research, sociologist Samuel Stouffer demonstrated that women were more reluctant than men to extend First Amendment protections to members of those three groups. In his study, Stouffer also commenced an exploration of the etiology of gender differences in tolerance, hypothesizing that they result from gender differences in education, religiosity, personal anxiety, and exposure to diversity (with women being less well-educated, more religious, higher in personal anxiety, and lower in exposure to diversity).[1] Yet, consideration of all these factors did not help Stouffer to account fully for women's lower tolerance, leading him to speculate that gender differences in political socialization (with boys getting more freedom than girls) and men's greater exposure to diversity in the public sphere could be partially to blame.

Many studies since Stouffer's groundbreaking book have noted that men and women differ in their readiness to put up with political unorthodoxy. A replication of Stouffer's study implemented in the early 1970s, for example, showed not only that women continued to be less tolerant than men but also that the gender gap in tolerance of communists, socialists, and atheists grew wider. In their quest for explanations, Nunn and his colleagues mused that gender differences in tolerance reflected "inequality between the sexes in American society . . . [r]epresenting all the ways in which American men have enjoyed dominion, privilege, responsibility and diversity both of expectations and experiences in comparison with women."[8] More recent investigations of tolerance, with one prominent exception,[9] have similarly noted women's greater reluctance to put up with political unorthodoxy.[10]

In one important exception to the weight of scholarly evidence, Sullivan, Piereson, and Marcus argued that gender differences identified in previous studies existed only because of the flaws in the measurement of tolerance.[11] To measure tolerance properly, Sullivan et al. proposed, one must first ensure that respondents dislike the groups about which they are asked. Tolerance is not measured, in contrast, when respondents are asked about groups they evaluate favorably. Previous researchers, Sullivan and his colleagues continued, chose the tolerance targets about which to query their respondents and, in so doing, did not necessarily ask them about groups they disliked. In short, Sullivan, Piereson and Marcus challenged the conclusions of investigations pointing to gender differences in tolerance on the ground that they were "primarily artifactual."[12]

Once women and men were asked to tolerate groups they themselves identified as their least-liked, Sullivan et al. demonstrated that they did not differ in their readiness to put up with the groups' rights.

While most studies noted gender differences in political tolerance, finally, only one placed shedding light on the roots of gender differences in political tolerance at the center of its theoretical and empirical attention. Using measures of tolerance referencing groups disliked by the respondents, this study "confirmed the existence of a small but significant gender gap in the extent and targets of political tolerance."[13] This study concluded, in addition, that women tend to be less tolerant than men because they are less strongly committed to abstract democratic norms, lower in political expertise (or interest in and knowledge about politics), more likely to perceive threat from groups they dislike, and more likely to subscribe to traditional conceptions of morality. While this exploration of the underpinnings of gender differences in tolerance was comprehensive on both theoretical and empirical levels, the explanations it canvassed once again did not fully account for women's lower tolerance (i.e., gender continued to be marginally linked with political tolerance).[14]

Since previous research leaves room for further insights into the sources of gender differences in political tolerance, it might be helpful to place the political tolerance findings into a broader perspective by examining whether and how gender is linked with other forms of tolerance. Although women are less prepared than men to tolerate political unorthodoxy, gender differences in other tolerance domains have been shown to manifest themselves differently. Women are more tolerant than men "in some domains of attitudes toward gay [and lesbian] people."[15] More specifically, women have been shown to support employment protection and adoption rights for gay people more strongly than men and to be willing to extend some form of legal recognition to same-sex couples. Women have also been less likely to endorse stereotypical beliefs about gay people and to exhibit negative affective reactions toward them (although women and men may not differ in their willingness to extend civil liberties to gays and lesbians).[16] Previous research also demonstrates that when heterosexuals' reactions to gay men and lesbian women are scrutinized separately, "heterosexuals tend to express more negative attitudes toward gay people of their same sex," although "this pattern occurs mainly among [heterosexual] men."[17]

Extensive psychological research on stereotyping and prejudice and political science scholarship on racial attitudes have established, finally, that women tend to hold more favorable attitudes toward racial and ethnic minorities, particularly on items tapping interpersonal relations involving different groups (e.g., receptivity to interracial friends, neighbors, or co-workers),[18] otherwise called measures of social distance[19] or social tolerance.[20] Some explanations that have been put forward to account for gender differences in racial prejudice have included gender differences in interracial friendship, religiosity, political beliefs, social dominance orientation, empathy, and orientation toward interpersonal relationships and concern for the well being of others.[21] If women are more likely to have interracial friendships than men, an issue to which previous research does not speak clearly,[22] this may partially explain their more favorable racial attitudes. Similarly women's greater religiosity, typically correlated inversely with racial prejudice,[23] may be one reason for their more positive feelings toward racial minorities as might be their greater tendency to identify with the Democratic party and to place themselves on the liberal end of the political spectrum.[24] Research on the linkages between social dominance orientation (or "the extent to which one desires that one's in-group dominate and be superior to outgroups"[25]) and prejudice shows, in addition, that at least some of the effect of gender on racial prejudice is mediated by social dominance orientation (i.e., women exhibit less prejudice because they score lower on measures of social dominance orientation). Women's greater empathy,[26] negatively correlated with prejudice[27] as well as their greater concern about interpersonal relationships and concern for the well being of others are two other hypothesized causes of their lower prejudice.[28]

In summary, research on the relationship between gender and tolerance suggests a complicated relationship. Women are less likely to embrace civil liberties protections for members of unpopular groups—or be lower in their political tolerance than men. Yet, research in other tolerance domains suggests that women may not necessarily be intolerant in general. In fact, to the extent gender differences in other tolerance domains materialize, women tend to be more approving of homosexuality and more supportive of civil rights protections for gay and lesbian individuals. Women are also more socially tolerant of racial and ethnic minorities—or less likely than men to hold prejudicial attitudes toward racial and ethnic minorities.

Do Different Types of Tolerance Tap the Same Tolerance Dimension?

To provide a rationale for integrating insights from different models of gender and tolerance, I first scrutinize the empirical relationships between political tolerance, racial and ethnic tolerance, and tolerance of homosexuality. To this end, 'I draw on the 2000 General Social Survey, a nationally representative survey of public opinion. To measure political tolerance, I use a set of fifteen questions asking respondents about their willingness to allow members of five generally disliked groups (atheists, communists, homosexuals, racists, and militarists) to engage in three types of activities (making a speech, teaching in public schools, and having book in the public library).[29] These questions have been used in many other examinations of political tolerance, though they have not been devoid of controversy. Because these measures ask respondents about groups that have been pre-selected rather than identified by the respondents as groups they dislike, they have been criticized on the ground that they may not always capture tolerance.[30] These questions only measure tolerance, in other words, if respondents happen to dislike (or at least feel neutral toward) the group(s) about which they are queried. They do not necessarily measure tolerance, on the other hand, when respondents who happen to like the pre-selected group(s) are asked about their willingness to allow the group(s) to practice their democratic freedoms. The limitation of the GSS questions, in short, is that we do not know a priori whether all respondents in fact experience some degree of negative (or at least neutral) affect toward the groups about which they are queried. While these measures are not ideal in a theoretical sense, they have been "useful for identify-ing the proportions of Americans who are tolerant and intolerant."[31] These measures have also fared well in comparison with more theoretically appealing measures (i.e., those that query respondents about groups they themselves iden-tify as disliked) in investigations of the etiology of political tolerance.[32] To par-tially get around the problem of pre-selected targets, finally, I control for some proxy measures of group affect in my multivariate analysis of political tolerance.

Previous research offers less specific guidance on the question of how to measure racial tolerance. In fact, much of the previous research on racial atti-tudes grapples with the question of how to measure racial attitudes most effec-tively, reflecting the challenges of capturing such attitudes in today's socio-political environment characterized by strong normative pressures for public expression of racially egalitarian attitudes.[33] To capture the predicted gender differences in racial and ethnic tolerance, I rely on questions asking respondents about their willingness to reside in racially or ethnically integrated neighbor-hoods. To establish whether and how women and men differ in their tolerance of racial and ethnic groups, more specifically, I employ four questions concerning respondents' feelings about living in a neighborhood that is half Asian, half Black, half Hispanic, or half Jewish. Respondents' answers to the four questions were coded on a five-point scale anchored with "strongly oppose" to "strongly favor" endpoints, with neither oppose nor favor in the middle. These questions clearly do not exhaust a list of possibilities; but, consistent with previous re-search, they can be treated as measures of social tolerance directed at members of minority groups[34] or measures of social distance.[35] I call them measures of racial or ethnic tolerance to capture their reference to members of racial and ethnic minorities.

I use a question concerning respondents' approval of homosexuality as a measure of tolerance of homosexuality. No other measures of attitudes toward gays and lesbians are available in the 2000 GSS (not counting, of course, meas-ures of political tolerance directed at gays and lesbians that I discussed above).

To establish whether the three different types of tolerance are empirically correlated, I first compute scales of political tolerance on the one hand and racial and ethnic tolerance on the other. I add up individual responses to all fifteen indicators of political tolerance into a political tolerance scale. I similarly com-bine individual responses to the four measures of racial and ethnic tolerance into a racial and ethnic tolerance scale. I measure tolerance of homosexuality with a single item concerning respondents' approval or disapproval of homosexuality. In line with my expectations, bivariate correlation analysis demonstrates that all three types of tolerance are correlated, although to differing degrees. Not sur-

prisingly in light of the fact that three of the fifteen indicators of political tolerance refer to homosexuals, the scale of political tolerance and a measure of approval of homosexuality are strongly correlated (r = .39, p < .01). Even when the
scale of political tolerance is re-computed after excluding questions about homosexuals, however, the correlation with attitudes toward homosexuality remains strong (r = .36, p < .01). The extent of political tolerance, whether measured with all fifteen questions or all questions with the exception of those that
ask about homosexuals, is also significantly (although fairly weakly) linked with
racial and ethnic tolerance (r = .13, p < .01 in the former case and r = .11, p <
.01 in the latter case). Racial and ethnic tolerance, finally, is significantly (albeit
weakly) correlated with approval of homosexuality (r = .11, p < .01). In short,
the measures of all three dimensions of tolerance are empirically correlated,
suggesting that they tap a more general dimension of tolerance.

Gender and Tolerance: Bivariate Linkages

In this section, I report the results of an original investigation of the
relationship between gender and political tolerance on the one hand and gender
and racial and ethnic tolerance, and tolerance of homosexuality on the other. I
start by examining bivariate linkages between gender and tolerance in different
domains, proceed to identifying some possible "culprits" responsible for the
relationships between gender and tolerance, and subsequently attempt to shed
greater light on the relationship between gender and political tolerance by borrowing from the models of racial and ethnic tolerance.

Gender and Political Tolerance

Figures 8.1, 8.2, and 8.3 show the percentages of women and men who
would allow a member of each group to speak in their community, teach in public schools, or have a book in the library.[36] The higher bar in each case corresponds to greater tolerance of the group and activity.

With the exception of the three questions tapping tolerance of homosexuals,
more women than men embrace a less tolerant position. Women and men essentially do not differ in their views on allowing a homosexual person to make a
speech; women appear to be more tolerant of a homosexual teacher, on the other
hand, and less tolerant of allowing a book written by a homosexual to be available in public libraries. Bivariate correlation analysis between respondents' sex
and their responses to the fifteen indicators of tolerance establishes that differences in men's and women's attitudes toward all groups and activities—save for
their answers to the three questions concerning homosexuals—are statistically
significant, although weak (ranging from .06 at the lowest end to .12 at the highest). Women are significantly less likely than men to allow atheists, communists,

militarists, and racists to make a speech, teach, and deposit a book in the library. Women and men do not significantly differ, in contrast, in their readiness to put up with homosexuals' exercise of democratic rights.

Figure 8.1: Gender difference in tolerance of speech: 2000 General Social Survey

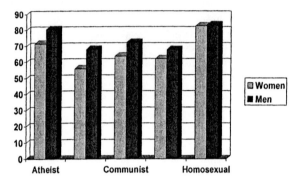

A higher number corresponds to a more tolerant opinion in each case

Figure 8.2: Gender difference in tolerance of teaching: 2000 General Social Survey

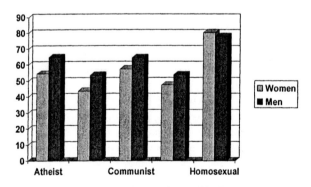

A higher number corresponds to a more tolerant opinion in each case

Figure 8.3: Gender difference in tolerance of book: 2000 General Social Survey

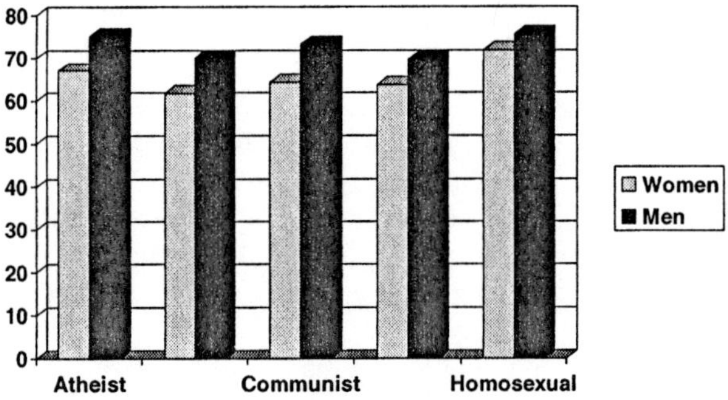

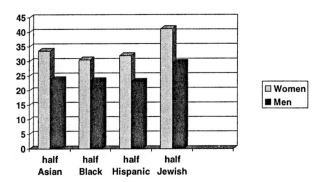

A higher number corresponds to a more tolerant opinion in each case

Figure 8.4: Gender difference in racial and ethnic tolerance of book: 2000 General Social Survey

A higher number corresponds to a more favorable opinion in each case

Gender and Racial and Ethnic Tolerance

Figure 8.4 shows the percentages of racially and ethnically tolerant women and men, or those who strongly favor or favor living in a neighborhood that is half Asian, half Black, half Hispanic, or half Jewish. In each case, as indicated by a higher bar, women express more favorable attitudes.

Bivariate correlation analysis between respondents' gender and their attitudes toward residential integration suggests that women are significantly more likely than men to express enthusiasm about living in a neighborhood that is half Asian, or half Black, or half Hispanic, or half Jewish (though these correlations, once again, are not particularly strong - ranging from .08 to .12).

Gender and Tolerance of Homosexuality

Surprisingly, in light of much previous research on the subject, there are no significant differences in men's and women's approval of homosexuality in the 2000 installation of the General Social Survey ($r = -.02$). In fact, women and men did not differ in their views about homosexuality over the entire span of GSS surveys in which the question about approval of homosexuality was asked (1973 to 2002), although both groups have grown somewhat more tolerant of homosexuality over time (data not shown).

In summary, consistent with previous research, women tend to be somewhat less tolerant than men of generally disliked political groups, with an exception of women's and men's tolerance of homosexuals' civil liberties where gender differences are less pronounced, inconsistent, and statistically insignificant. While women are less politically tolerant than men, women score higher than men on tolerance of racial and ethnic minorities.

Gender and Tolerance: A Closer Look

To show that gender matters in explaining tolerance is not to demonstrate its causal influence. Since women and men differ in background attributes and attitudes relevant to understanding variation in tolerance, to put it differently, we need to control for those attributes and attitudes to determine whether gender is independently linked with tolerance judgments. In this part of the chapter, therefore, I set out to establish whether the relationships between gender and tolerance I reported in the preceding section hold up after controls for a host of alternative explanations. I estimate several multivariate models of tolerance to sort out the influence of gender—in those cases where it was significantly linked with tolerance at the bivariate level.

Before undertaking this multivariate analysis, I seek to establish in what other ways women and men differ that may account for women's greater political intolerance and their lower racial and ethnic intolerance. Based on previous research, albeit constrained by the secondary data I employ, I scrutinize possible demographic (e.g., education, income, and religiosity), psychological (e.g., interpersonal trust, dogmatism, and optimism), and political (e.g., interest in politics and ideological self-identification) differences between men and women that may at least in part help to understand the underpinnings of gender differences in tolerance. In my attempt to account for women's higher racial and ethnic tolerance, in addition, I consider a possibility that women and men may differ in their perceptions of racial and ethnic minorities (or characteristics they ascribe to them) and their experiences with intergroup contact, two important influences on racial and ethnic attitudes in their own right. I borrow these latter two predictors from the model of racial and ethnic tolerance, finally, to determine whether they can shed light on the sources of gender differences in political tolerance.

Gender and Tolerance Predictors

Previous research on political tolerance suggests that women's lower political tolerance may in part be a function of socio-demographic differences between women and men. Most importantly, women's lower education and income and higher religiosity have been shown to contribute to their lower political tolerance—although those factors alone do not explain gender differences in political tolerance completely.[37] Since women tend to be *more* accepting of racial and ethnic diversity, their educational and income deficits cannot explain their greater racial and ethnic tolerance. On the basis of their educational and income deficits, to elaborate, we would expect women to be *less* tolerant of racial and ethnic diversity as well because education and income are inversely correlated with racial prejudice.[38] Women's higher religiosity, in contrast, may in part explain their more favorable attitudes toward racial and ethnic minorities because higher religiosity has been shown to be associated with lower racial prejudice.[39]

Women and men have been shown to differ in their political predispositions, in addition, and those differences may be partially responsible for their differences in tolerance. Women are less likely than men to be interested in and knowledgeable about politics (or lower in political expertise).[40] Differences in political expertise, in turn, have been linked with differences in political tolerance in such a way that individuals lower in political expertise tend to be less tolerant of political unorthodoxy.[41] Women's deficit in political expertise, then, may in part explain their lower political tolerance. Since political experts have been shown to internalize democratic principles more strongly,[42] we would expect them to be more tolerant of racial and ethnic difference as well. Gender differences in political expertise, then, could not account for women's higher racial and ethnic tolerance since women are more likely to be political novices than men. Women have been shown to differ from men, finally, in their partisan and ideological loyalties,[43] although party identification and ideological self-placement have not been consistently linked with political tolerance.[44] Women's preference for the Democratic party and liberal self-placement, in addition, would be of no help in explaining their lower political tolerance because, to the extent that party identification and ideological self-placement matter in political tolerance judgments, Democrats and liberals have been shown to exhibit somewhat more tolerance than their Republican and conservative counterparts. Differences in women's and men's partisan and ideological orientations, in contrast, may be more consequential for understanding women's higher racial and ethnic tolerance because both partisan and ideological self-identification have been linked with racial attitudes.[45] Because Democrats and liberals have been shown to exhibit more favorable racial attitudes, in short, women's tendency to favor the Democratic and liberal identifications may in part account for their greater acceptance of racial and ethnic diversity.

Since women and men may differ in various psychological orientations such as interpersonal trust,[46] dogmatism, or optimism, we may gain greater insight into why they differ in their tolerance as well because all these psychological orientations have been shown to influence the levels of political tolerance[47] and may influence racial and ethnic tolerance as well.[48] Compared to men as a group, women as a group typically score higher on measures of interpersonal trust.[49] Because higher interpersonal trust is linked with higher political tolerance[50] and more positive racial attitudes,[51] it can partially explain women's higher racial tolerance but not their higher political intolerance. It is not clear from previous research whether women and men differ in their dogmatism and optimism but, if they do, perhaps these differences may help explain why they differ in the extent of their political and racial and ethnic tolerance.

Previous scholarship on the etiology of racial attitudes notes the importance of racial stereotypes and intergroup contact in understanding the sources of more or less favorable attitudes toward racial minorities.[52] Generally speaking, individuals who endorse negative racial stereotypes are more likely to exhibit negative racial attitudes than individuals who reject such stereotypes or have more positive images of the group. Under some conditions at least, in addition, those who know members of a minority group subscribe to more positive, less stereotypical views of the group than those who have not had personal or community-level contact with representatives of that minority.[53] In seeking to sort out the bases of gender differences in racial and ethnic tolerance, therefore, we need to take into account possible gender differences in generalized perceptions of minority groups' characteristics and intergroup contact. Individual difference analyses of the roots of stereotype endorsement show that white women are less likely than white men to endorse negative stereotypes of African Americans.[54] Some studies also demonstrate that women are less likely to have interracial contact than men,[55] though this difference disappears "once working outside the home is taken into account."[56] In short, women may be more tolerant of racial and ethnic diversity in part because they should be less likely than men to ascribe negative characteristics to racial and ethnic minorities as a whole.

Table 8.1 contains bivariate correlation coefficients between gender and possible "culprits" for gender differences in tolerance I have discussed above and a few other, control variables I intend to employ in the multivariate analyses to follow. Measures of all concepts are listed in the Appendix.

The data displayed in Table 8.1 suggest that, in line with previous research, women interviewed as part of the 2000 GSS were significantly less well-educated, poorer, and more likely to be religious than men. Women participants in the 2000 GSS were also older than men, more likely to identify with the Democratic party, and more ideologically liberal. Women were less likely to profess, finally, knowing either a Black or a Hispanic person. Women and men did not differ, in contrast, in their tendency to follow news about politics, their interpersonal trust, dogmatism, optimism, their generalized perceptions of Asian, Black, Hispanic, and Jewish Americans' characteristics, or in their familiarity with Asian or Jewish Americans.

Table 8.1: Bivariate correlations between gender and most important tolerance predictors

Education	.06 **
Age	-.06 **
Income	.24 **
Frequency of religious attendance	.10 **
Race	-.07 **
Party identification	-.11 **
Ideological identification	-.05 **
Frequency of following news about politics	.01
Interpersonal trust	-.02
Dogmatism	.04
Optimism	-.01
Perceptions of Asians' characteristics	-.003
Perceptions of Blacks' characteristics	-.04
Perceptions of Hispanics' characteristics	.02
Perceptions of Jews' characteristics	.03
Knowing any Asians	.05
Knowing any Blacks	.08 **
Knowing any Hispanics	.10 **
Knowing any Jews	.05

What the data summarized in Table 8.1 suggest, then, is that women's lower political tolerance may be in part a function of their lower education and income and higher religiosity. Women's higher racial and ethnic tolerance, on the other hand, may in part reflect their more Democratic partisan and liberal ideological views.

Gender and Political Tolerance

To sort out the impact of gender on political tolerance, I estimate a multivariate model of political tolerance with a twelve-item additive scale of tolerance based on respondents' answers to questions about allowing the three types of activities engaged in by atheists, communists, militarists, and racists as the dependent variable.[57] The model includes controls for the standard socio-demographic correlates of tolerance (e.g., education, age, and religion entered as a series of dummy variables), psychological predispositions (e.g., interpersonal trust, dogmatism, and optimism),[58] and political factors (e.g., partisan affiliation, ideological self-identification, and political interest).[59] This model also includes two proxies for group liking: confidence in the military as a proxy for liking for militarists and religiosity as a proxy for liking for atheists.[60] Though reliance on secondary data makes it impossible to control for all theoretically significant predictors of political tolerance, this is not necessarily a damning limitation of the model.

Table 8.2: Multivariate analysis of political tolerance

	b.	s.e.	Beta
Sex	.47	.29	.06 *
Education	.24	.06	.17 ***
Age	-.05	.01	-.24 ***
Income	.04	.03	.06
Frequency of religious attendance	.12	.06	.08 **
Race	-.74	.43	-.07 *
Party identification	-.11	.08	-.05
Frequency of following news	.32	.11	.11 ***
Ideological identification	.07	.11	.02
Protestant dummy	-.27	.62	-.03
Catholic dummy	-.002	.64	.000
Jewish dummy	.07	1.08	.003
No religion dummy	.60	.69	.05 ^{x}
Confidence in army	.07	.21	.01
Interpersonal trust	.19	.07	.11 ***
Dogmatism	.47	.11	.16 ***
Optimism	-.26	.23	-.04
Region of residence	-.35	.30	-.04
R-squared	.26		
F / significance	11.69, p < .00		

*** p < .01
** p < .05
* p < .10
x – "other religion" category left out

To the extent the model does a good job of accounting for gender differences in political tolerance, whether or not it is otherwise fully specified, it serves the goals of my inquiry. If my goal were to explain fully the sources of political tolerance, on the other hand, the model would be more problematic. The results of this estimation are reported in Table 8.2 above.

When controls for a variety of theoretically relevant factors are introduced into the model of political tolerance, the effect of respondents' gender on political tolerance becomes attenuated, although gender continues to be marginally linked with political tolerance ($p < .10$). Consistent with much previous research on political tolerance, education, age, religiosity, interpersonal trust, dogmatism, and political interest emerge as other important influences on political tolerance. The direction of these effects is in line with previous work: respondents who are better educated, younger, less religious, higher in interpersonal trust, higher in political interest and lower in dogmatism are more likely to allow the generally unpopular groups to exercise their democratic rights and freedoms. Given the previously discussed gender differences in tolerance predictors, then, it appears that women are in part less tolerant of unpopular political groups because they are less well-educated, older, and more religious than men. Model fit indicators suggest a good model fit (R-squared = .26, F = 11.69, $p < .000$).

Gender and Racial Tolerance

While women are *less* tolerant of political unorthodoxy, the bivariate results I report above suggest that women tend to be *more* tolerant of racial and ethnic diversity. More specifically, women are more accepting of living in racially or ethnically diverse neighborhoods (or those having a substantial Asian, Black, Hispanic, or Jewish presence). To account for gender differences in racial and ethnic tolerance, I borrow from the model of political tolerance. In addition, based on the prejudice and intergroup contact literatures,[61] I also add measures of perceptions of group characteristics and intergroup contact to the model of respondents' residential preferences—following an expectation that respondents who are more likely to ascribe negative characteristics to a particular group and less likely to know members of that group should be more lukewarm or hostile to living in diverse neighborhoods (see Appendix for measures of perceptions of group characteristics).

While the impact of gender on political tolerance judgments was almost completely accounted for by other factors, gender continues to be significantly linked with attitudes toward residential integration even in the presence of alternative explanations. In particular, women continue to be significantly more likely than men to favor living in residentially diverse neighborhoods. In addition to gender, respondents' residential preferences are affected by a host of other factors. Income partially explains attitudes toward living in residentially diverse neighborhoods, with wealthier respondents less willing to live in such neighborhoods than poorer respondents. Respondents exhibiting higher interpersonal trust are more likely to prefer living in diverse neighborhoods than their counterparts who are lower in interpersonal trust. More dogmatic respondents, on the other hand, are more likely to oppose living in diverse neighborhoods than those who are less dogmatic. Respondents more likely to stereotype Blacks and Hispanics negatively oppose living in diverse neighborhoods to a greater degree than those who stereotype members of those two groups more positively.

Table 8.3: Multivariate analysis of attitudes toward residential integration

	b	s.e.	Beta
Sex	-.67	.26	-.10 ***
Education	.02	.05	.01
Age	-.002	.01	-.01
Income	-.06	.02	-.10 **
Frequency of religious attendance	-.04	.05	-.03
Race	.53	.38	.06
Party identification	.04	.07	.02
Frequency of following news	.10	.10	.04
Ideological identification	.03	.10	.01
Protestant dummy	-.20	.56	-.03
Catholic dummy	-.01	.58	-.001
Jewish dummy	-.16	.97	-.01
No religion dummy	-.12	.63	-.01[x]
Interpersonal trust	.15	.06	.10 **
Dogmatism	.23	.10	.10 **
Optimism	-.02	.21	-.004
Region of residence	.29	.27	.04
Perceptions of Asians and Jews	.002	.02	.003
Perceptions of Blacks and Hispanics	.17	.03	.26 ***
Intergroup contact with Asians, Blacks, and Hispanics [xx]	.24	.15	.07 *

R-squared	.15
F / significance	5.39 / .00

*** p < .01   x – "other religion" category left out
** p < .05   xx – I exclude contact with Jews from this measure because, due to a small
* p < .10   number of cases, the more comprehensive contact variable gets "bumped out"
                 from the model

Finally, intergroup contact is marginally linked with attitudes toward living in residentially diverse neighborhoods. The direction of this effect is such that those with less contact with Blacks, Hispanics, or Asians are more likely to feel lukewarm or opposed to living in diverse neighborhoods.

Table 8.4: Multivariate analysis of political tolerance, including controls for perceptions of racial and ethnic groups' characteristics and familiarity with racial and ethnic groups

	b	s.e.	Beta
Sex	.40	.31	.05
Education	.15	.06	.11 ***
Age	-.04	.01	-.18 ***
Income	.03	.03	.04
Frequency of religious attendance	.11	.06	.07 *
Race	-1.06	.45	-.10 **
Party identification	-.10	.09	-.05
Frequency of following news	.35	.12	.12 ***
Ideological identification	.000	.12	.000
Protestant dummy	-.09	.66	-.01
Catholic dummy	.25	.69	.03
Jewish dummy	.004	1.16	.000
No religion dummy	.84	.75	.07^x
Confidence in army	.08	.23	.01
Interpersonal trust	.19	.07	.10 ***
Dogmatism	.43	.12	.15 ***
Optimism	-.39	.25	-.06
Region of residence	-.34	.32	-.04
Perceptions of Asians and Jews	.04	.03	.06 *
Perceptions of Blacks and Hispanics	.08	.03	.10 ***
Intergroup contact with Asians,Blacks, and Hispanics ^{xx}	.69	.17	.17 ***

R-squared   .29

F / significance   10.50 / .000

*** p < .01   x – "other religion" category left out
** p < .05   xx – I exclude contact with Jews from this measure because, due to a small
* p < .10   number of cases, the more comprehensive contact variable gets "bumped out"
                     from the model

As for the reasons why women are more accepting of living in diverse neighborhoods, then, it could be partially a function of their lower incomes (since lower income is in this case conducive to more tolerant attitudes). None of the other predictors can help to account for why women are more tolerant of residential diversity than men. Model fit indicators suggest a poorer (R-squared = .15) though significant model fit ($F = 5.14$, $p < .000$).

At the final step in my analysis, I re-estimate the model of political tolerance after adding three predictors borrowed from the model of attitudes toward residential integration: perceptions of Jews' and Asians' characteristics, perceptions of Blacks' and Hispanics' characteristics, and a measure of intergroup contact with Asians, Blacks, and Hispanics.[62] The results of this estimation are depicted in Table 8.4 below.

The influence of respondents' sex is no longer significant in this new model (or, to put it differently, it is now completely accounted for by the model). Of great interest in this table are the coefficients shedding light on the predicted relationship between political tolerance and the three measures borrowed from the model of racial and ethnic tolerance. All three turn out to be important influences on tolerance of political nonconformity, although respondents' beliefs about Asians' and Jews' characteristics are linked with political tolerance at a marginal level only. The direction of these effects is such that respondents who perceive members of the four racial and ethnic minorities more negatively are also less likely to endorse civil liberties protections for members of political minorities. Those who have had less contact with racial and ethnic minorities, similarly, are less likely to tolerate political nonconformity. These are remarkable findings given that the effects of racial and ethnic group perceptions and intergroup contact hold up in the face of controls for many competing explanations. The influence of remaining factors remains largely the same with the exception that respondents' race is now significantly (rather than marginally significantly) linked with political tolerance.

The direction of this effect is such that black respondents are less tolerant of political nonconformity than their white counterparts. Examination of standardized regression coefficients demonstrates that intergroup contact with racial and ethnic minorities, important in a model of racial and ethnic tolerance, is also one of the strongest predictors of political tolerance. The percentage of variance explained by this expanded model improves somewhat (R-squared = .29; $F = 10.50$, $p < .000$). Given that women are less likely to report knowing members of different racial and ethnic minorities, then, this model suggests that their less significant contact with racial and ethnic minorities in part accounts for their lower political tolerance.

Concluding Thoughts

The research I have reviewed and conducted for this chapter demonstrates that there are small, albeit diachronically consistent, gender differences in tolerance. When women's and men's attitudes toward civil liberties of political outgroups are compared and contrasted, women turn out consistently less tolerant than men. Yet, women's reluctance to put up with political diversity does not extend to other tolerance domains. Women and men as groups largely resemble each other in their tolerance of homosexuality. When compared to men, in addition, women are more tolerant of racial and ethnic diversity than men.

My initial search for the sources of gender differences in political tolerance, inspired by much previous work on political tolerance, led to a partial solution for the existence of gender differences in political tolerance. Even though my modeling was constrained by the secondary data at my disposal, the multivariate analysis I conducted largely accounted for gender differences in political tolerance (gender lost much of its predictive capacity, although it continued to be a marginally significant source of attitudes toward political diversity). My efforts to shed light on the underpinnings of gender differences in tolerance of racial and ethnic diversity were less successful in the sense that gender continued to be significantly linked with this type of tolerance even in the presence of compelling alternative explanations. More interestingly, my subsequent expansion of the political tolerance model using several theoretical predictors of tolerance of racial and ethnic difference provided additional clues about the sources of gender differences in political tolerance. Specifically, their lesser familiarity with diversity, racial and ethnic, appears to be one reason why women tend to be less tolerant of political diversity. In fact, contact with racial and ethnic minorities is the second, most powerful predictor of attitudes toward political minorities, rivaled in its influence only by respondents' age. This is a particularly striking finding because familiarity with racial and ethnic diversity might not seem on its face relevant to understanding the sources of attitudes toward political diversity. Yet, this finding is not entirely inconsistent with early work on political tolerance which suggested that one reason for women's lower tolerance is that they are less likely than men to have contact with diversity.[63] While they do not help to account for gender differences in political tolerance, in addition, differences in perceptions of racial and ethnic minorities' characteristics significantly contribute to differences in political tolerance. All else being equal, individuals who endorse more negative characterizations of Blacks and Hispanics are significantly less tolerant of political minorities than those whose images of Blacks and Hispanics are more positive. To a marginally significant extent, those with more negative perceptions of Jews and Asians are similarly less willing to put up with political unorthodoxy than their counterparts with more positive perceptions of those two groups. "Transplanting" these three predictors of racial and ethnic tolerance into a model of political tolerance completely eliminates the influence of gender on political tolerance.

My analysis of the sources of gender differences in tolerance has a number of important implications for tolerance of diversity in the United States in the twenty-first century. Given my complete success in accounting for gender differences in political tolerance, and some recent changes in the relationship between gender and important predictors of political tolerance, women's greater reluctance to extend First Amendment rights to political outgroups is likely to diminish even further. Because women have been recently enrolling in colleges and universities in greater numbers than men, their educational deficit should disappear over time and this should dampen or even eliminate gender differences in political tolerance. To the extent that education is associated with greater likelihood of intergroup contact (data not shown), in addition, men's advantage in this regard should diminish over time as well and lead to an eventual disappearance of the gender gap in political tolerance (or perhaps its reversal, with women becoming more tolerant than men). All this bodes well for the future of tolerance of political diversity because women have been outparticipating men as voters in the last quarter century or so and have been running for political office and getting elected in greater numbers as well. Both in their capacities as voters and elected officials, as I have suggested above, women can shape public policies with implications for tolerance of political diversity.

Since I was less successful in identifying the sources of gender differences in racial and ethnic tolerance, it is more difficult to talk about the implications of these differences for tolerance in the twenty-first century. Men, in this case, harbor less tolerant views and the analysis I have conducted suggests this is in part a function of their higher incomes. To the extent that gender differences in income narrow over time, this should in turn lead to a shrinking of the gender gap in racial and ethnic tolerance. Because the influence of gender in the model I estimated to explain gender differences in racial and ethnic tolerance held up, however, more work is necessary to identify other reasons for why women and men differ in this regard.

Appendix

Measures and Coding of All Variables

Sex: 1 = female, 2 = male

Education: R's highest year of school completed, ranging from "0" to "20"

Age: R's age in years, ranging from "18" to "89"

<u>Income</u>: R's income, ranging from "low" to "high"

<u>Frequency of religious attendance</u>: ranging from "0" (very frequently) to "8" (never)

<u>Race</u>: 1 = white, 2 = black

<u>Party identification</u>: 0 = strong Republican, 1 = not strong Republican, 2 = Independent, near Republican, 3 = Independent, 4 = Independent, near Democrat, 5 = not strong Democrat, 6 = strong Democrat

<u>Ideological identification</u>: 1 = extremely conservative, 2 = conservative, 3 = slightly conservative, 4 = moderate, 5 = slightly liberal, 6 = liberal, 7 = extremely liberal

<u>Frequency of following news about politics</u>: How often do you read the newspaper? 1 = never, 2 = less than once a week, 3 = once a week, 4 = few times a week, 5 = every day

<u>Religion</u>: A set of dummy variables representing respondents' religious affiliation (Protestant, Catholic, Jewish, No religion, Other religion)

<u>Interpersonal trust</u>: a three-item scale based on the following questions: 1) do you think most people would take advantage of you if they got a chance, or would they try to be fair; 2) generally speaking, would you say that most people can be trusted or that you can't be too careful in life; and 3) would you say that most of the time people try to be helpful, or that they are mostly looking out for themselves? Lower score on the scale = lower interpersonal trust

<u>Dogmatism</u>: Which thing is most important for the child to learn to prepare him or her for life? To obey – 1 = most important, 2 = 2nd most important, 3 = 3rd most important, 4 = 4th most important, 5 = least important; lower score = higher dogmatism

<u>Optimism</u>: Measured with a proxy indicator of happiness, correlated with optimism – 1 = not too happy, 2 = pretty happy, 3 = very happy

<u>Region</u>: 1 = South, 2 = Non-South

<u>Perceptions of Asians, Blacks, Hispanics, and Jews:</u> I measure group evaluations using a set of four seven-point rating scales on which respondents were asked to place the four groups: unintelligent/intelligent, violent/non-violent, poor-rich, and lazy-hardworking. Based on factor analysis and reliability analysis, I com-

bine the ratings of Asians and Jews into one additive scale of <u>perceptions of Asians and Jews</u> and those of Blacks and Hispanics into a <u>perceptions of Blacks and Hispanics</u> scale.

<u>Intergroup contact with Asians, Blacks, Hispanics, and Jews:</u> Four questions asking whether respondents personally know any Asians, Blacks, Hispanics, or Jews – coded 1 = no, 2 = yes. I combine the first three into an intergroup contact scale.

Notes

1. Robert Y. Shapiro and H. Mahajan, "Gender differences in policy preferences: A summary of trends from the 1960s to the 1980s," *Public Opinion Quarterly* 50, no. 1 (1986): 42-61.
2. E.g. Samuel A. Stouffer, *Communism, Conformity and Civil Liberties* (New York: Doubleday, 1955).
3. Ewa A. Golebiowska, "Gender gap in political tolerance," *Political Behavior* 21, no. 1 (1999): 43-66.
4. E.g. Monica Kirkpatrick Johnson and Margaret Mooney Marini, "Bridging the racial divide in the United States: The effect of gender," *Social Psychology Quarterly* 61, no. 3 (1998): 247-58.
5. E.g. Gregory M. Herek, "Gender gaps in public opinion about lesbians and gay men," *Public Opinion Quarterly* 66, no. 1 (2002): 40-66.
6. Herek, "Gender gaps in public opinion," 40-66.
7. Stouffer, *Communism, Conformity and Civil Liberties.*
8. Clyde Z. Nunn, Harry J. Crockett, and J.A. Williams, *Tolerance for Nonconformity* (San Francisco: Jossey-Bass, 1978), 119.
9. John L. Sullivan, James E. Piereson, and George E. Marcus, *Political Tolerance and American Democracy* (Chicago: The University of Chicago Press, 1982).
10. E.g. James L. Gibson, "Alternative measures of political tolerance: Must tolerance be 'least-liked'?" *American Journal of Political Science* 36, no. 2 (1992): 560-77; Ewa A. Golebiowska, "Individual value priorities, education, and political tolerance," *Political Behavior* 17, no. 1 (1995): 23-48; Golebiowska, "Gender gap in political tolerance."
11. Sullivan, Piereson, and Marcus, *Political Tolerance and American Democracy.*
12. Sullivan, Piereson, and Marcus, *Political Tolerance and American Democracy*, 129.
13. Golebiowska, "Gender gap in political tolerance," 58.
14. Golebiowska, "Gender gap in political tolerance."
15. Gregory M. Herek and John P. Capitanio, "Some of my best friends: Intergroup contact, concealable stigma, and heterosexuals' attitudes toward gay men and lesbians," *Personality and Social Psychology Bulletin* 22, no. 4 (1996): 412-24; Herek, "Gender gaps in public opinion," 41.
16. Gregory M. Herek and Eric K. Glunt, "Interpersonal contact and heterosexuals' attitudes toward gay men: Results from a national survey," *The Journal of Sex Research* 30, no. 3 (1993): 239-44; Herek and Capitanio, "Some of my best friends"; Mary E. Kite and Bernard E. Whitley, Jr., "Sex differences in attitudes toward homosexual persons, behav-

ior, and civil rights: A meta-analysis," *Personality and Social Psychology Bulletin* 22, no. 4 (1996): 336-53; Herek, "Gender gaps in public opinion."

17. Herek, "Gender gaps in public opinion," 58.

18. B. Altemeyer, "The other 'authoritarian personality.'" *Advances in Experimental Social Psychology* 30 (1998): 47-92; A.L. Hoxter and D. Lester, "Gender differences in prejudice," *Perception and Motor Skills* 79 (1994): 1666; J. W. Moore, W. E. Hauck, and T. C. Denne, "Racial prejudice, interracial contact, and personality variables," *Journal of Experimental Education* 52 (1984): 168–73; R.C. Quails, M.B. Cox, and T.L. Schehr, "Racial attitudes on campus: Are there gender differences?" *Journal of College Student Development* 33 (1992): 524-30; J. Sidanius and F. Pratto, *Social dominance: An intergroup theory of social hierarchy and oppression* (New York: Cambridge University Press, 1999); Watts 1996; Bernard E. Whitley, "Right-wing authoritarianism, social dominance orientation, and prejudice," *Journal of Personality and Social Psychology* 77, no. 1 (1999): 126-34.

19. Emory S. Bogardus, "Measuring Social Distances," *Journal of Applied Sociology* (1925): 299-308.

20. Sullivan, Piereson, and Marcus, *Political Tolerance and American Democracy.*

21. E.g. Kirkpatrick Johnson and Mooney Marini, "Bridging the racial divide"; Whitley, "Right-wing authoritarianism."

22. Christopher G. Ellison and Daniel A. Powers, "The Contact Hypothesis and Racial Attitudes Among Black Americans," *Social Science Quarterly* 75 (1994): 385-400; Hallinan and Texeira 1987; H. A. Sagar, J.W. Schofield, and H. N. Snyder, "Race and gender barriers: Preadolescent peer behaviour in academic classrooms," *Child Development* 54 (1983): 1032–40.

23. Kirkpatrick 1993.

24. Frankovic 1982.

25. Felicia Pratto et. al., "Social dominance orientation: A personality variable predicting social and political attitudes," *Journal of Personality and Social Psychology* 67, no. 4 (1994): 741-763.

26. S. A. Basow, *Gender: Stereotypes and roles*, 3rd ed. (Pacific Grove, Calif.: Brooks/Cole, 1992).

27. M. E. Johnson, C. Brems, and P. Alford-Keating, "Personality correlates of homophobia," *Journal of Homosexuality* 34 (1997): 57-69.

28. Kirkpatrick Johnson and Mooney Marini, "Bridging the racial divide"; Whitley, "Right-wing authoritarianism."

29. Questions asking about a book in the library are phrased differently from the questions about speaking and teaching. In particular, these questions ask whether the respondent favors or opposes removing a book written by a member of one of the groups from the public library. A question about a communist's teaching does not follow the allow/not allow format either. This question asks whether the respondent favors or opposes firing a communist teacher. In all the analyses reported in this chapter, all tolerance indicators have been recoded such that a low response to the question indicates an intolerant response (would not allow an activity or favors removing a book or favors firing a communist teacher) and a high response indicates a tolerant response (would allow an activity or opposes removing a book or opposes firing a communist teacher).

30. E.g. Sullivan, Piereson, and Marcus, *Political Tolerance and American Democracy.*

31. Jeffery J. Mondak and Mitchell S. Sanders, "Tolerance and intolerance, 1976-1998," *American Journal of Political Science* 47, no. 3 (2003): 492-502.

32. Gibson, "Alternative measures of political tolerance."

33. Tali Mendelberg, *The Race Card: Campaign Strategy, Implicit Messages and the Norm of Equality* (Princeton: Princeton University Press, 2001).

34. Sullivan, Piereson, and Marcus, *Political Tolerance and American Democracy.*

35. Bogardus, "Measuring Social Distances."

36. I have re-coded each book question so that a response of "1" on the question means the respondent would not remove a book from the library and a response of "2"means the respondent would favor removing the book.

37. E.g. Stouffer, *Communism, Conformity and Civil Liberties*; Sullivan, Piereson, and Marcus, *Political Tolerance and American Democracy*; Golebiowska, "Gender gap in political tolerance."

38. Paul M. Sniderman and Michael Hagen, *Race and Inequality: A Study in American Values* (Chatham, N.J.: Chatham House, 1985); James R. Kluegel and Eliot R. Smith *Beliefs about Equality: Americans' Views of What Is and What Ought to Be* (New York: Aldine De Gruyter, 1986); Lee Sigelman and Susan Welch *Black Americans' Views of Racial Inequality* (New York: Cambridge University Press, 1991).

39. Kirkpatrick 1993; c.f. S. Welch et. al., *Race & place: Race relations in an American city* (Cambridge: Cambridge University Press, 2001).

40. Sidney Verba, Nancy Burns, and Kay Schlozman, "Knowing and caring about politics: Gender and political engagement," *Journal of Politics* 59, no. 4 (1997): 1051-72.

41. E.g. George E. Marcus et. al., *With Malice to Some: How People Make Civil Liberties Judgment* (Cambridge: Cambridge University Press, 1995); Golebiowska, "Gender gap in political tolerance."

42. Herbert McClosky and Alida Brill *Dimensions of Tolerance* (New York: Sage, 1983); H. McClosky and J. Zaller, *The American ethos: Public attitudes toward capitalism and democracy* (Cambridge, Mass.: Harvard University Press, 1984).

43. Felicia Pratto, Lisa M. Stallworth, and Jim Sidanius, "The gender gap: Differences in political attitudes and social dominance orientation," *British Journal of Social Psychology* 36 (1997): 49-68; Barbara Norrander and Clyde Wilcox, eds., *Understanding Public Opinion* (Washington, D.C.: CQ Press, 2002).

44. Sullivan, Piereson, and Marcus, *Political Tolerance and American Democracy*; c.f. Lawrence Bobo and Frederick C. Licari, "Education and political tolerance: Testing the effects of cognitive sophistication and target group affect," *Public Opinion Quarterly* 53 (1989): 285-308; Golebiowska, "Individual value priorities."

45. Paul M. Sniderman and Thomas Piazza, *The Scar of Race* (Cambridge, Mass.: Harvard University Press, 1993).

46. A. Feingold, "Gender differences in personality: A meta-analysis." *Psychological Bulletin* 116 (1994): 429-56.

47. Sullivan, Piereson, and Marcus, *Political Tolerance and American Democracy*; Marcus et. al., *With Malice to Some.*

48. Minako K. Maykovich, "Correlates of racial prejudice," *Journal of Personality and Social Psychology* 32, no. 6 (1975): 1014-20.

49. Feingold, "Gender differences in personality."

50. Marcus et. al., *With Malice to Some.*

51. C.H. Persell, A. Green, and L. Gurevich, "Civil society, economic distress, and social tolerance," *Sociological Forum* 16, no. 2 (2001): 203-30.

52. E.g. Mark Peffley, Jonathan Hurwitz, and Paul M. Sniderman, "Racial stereotypes and whites' political views of blacks in the context of welfare and crime," *American Journal of Political Science* 41, no. 1 (1997): 30-60.

53. Thomas F. Pettigrew, "Intergroup contact theory," *Annual Review of Psychology* 49 (1998): 65-85; Welch, et. al., *Race & place.*

54. Welch et. al., *Race & place.*

55. J. Blackwell and P. Hart, *Cities, suburbs, and blacks: A study of concerns, distrust, and alienation* (Bayside, N.Y.: General Hall, 1982); Welch et. al., *Race & place.*

56. Welch, et. al., *Race & place,* 65.

57. I do not include here questions about tolerance of homosexuals because there were no gender differences on these measures of tolerance.

58. E.g. Sullivan, Piereson, and Marcus, *Political Tolerance and American Democracy.*

59. E.g. Golebiowska, "Gender gap in political tolerance"; Marcus et. al., *With Malice to Some.*

60. No proxies for liking for communists and racists were available in the 2000 GSS.

61. Peffley, Hurwitz, and Sniderman, "Racial stereotypes"; Pettigrew, "Intergroup contact theory."

62. I exclude a question about familiarity with Jews from the overall measure of intergroup contact because this question was asked of very few respondents. As a consequence, the measure of intergroup contact is "bumped out" of the model when it is in part based on a question about familiarity with Jews.

63. For example, Stouffer, *Communism, Conformity and Civil Liberties.*

Youth, Schooling, and the Development of Political Tolerance
Pat Avery

There has been far less research on political tolerance among children and adolescents than among adults. National surveys of adult levels of political tolerance extend back to the 1950s,[1] and much of the significant work that has been done refining the conceptualization and measurement of political tolerance comes from scholars studying tolerance among adults.[2] Studies of tolerance among youth are more sporadic, generally less sophisticated, and often sidebars within broad studies of civic education and political socialization.

The relative lack of attention to youth is unfortunate. If we had a better understanding of the dimensions and development of political tolerance among young people, precollegiate educational institutions might better be able to identify their role in promoting or inhibiting young people's tolerant stances. I am particularly concerned with the role of elementary and secondary schooling in promoting tolerance, in part because almost all young people in the United States participate in precollegiate schooling, and in part because the increasing ethnic, racial, linguistic, and cultural diversity among our school-age youth presents challenges and opportunities for addressing tolerance issues within the classroom and school setting.

In this chapter, I briefly examine the nature of political tolerance, and then summarize the research related to political tolerance among children and youth. I argue that precollegiate schools are particularly important institutions for developing our young people's understanding of tolerance and its relationship to the democratic ideals of freedom of expression and minority rights. I am, however, poignantly aware of the obstacles to developing political tolerance in precollegiate school settings, and conclude with a discussion of those barriers and how they might be addressed.

Most scholars today agree that political tolerance involves the willingness to extend basic rights and civil liberties to those groups with whom you disagree. For example, consider the classic type of scenario: the Aryan Nation, a group whose views are disliked by the majority of Americans, is distributing pamphlets espousing its views in your neighborhood. Should this be allowed? There are many ways one might arrive at a tolerant stance given this situation, but it is likely that the tolerant stance is grounded in the recognition that a democratic principle, freedom of expression, is involved, and that this principle is a fundamental right accorded all citizens. Note that three abilities or understandings are important: the ability to link an abstract principle to a concrete situation, a belief in individual freedoms and rights, and an understanding that these rights are embedded in the U.S. Constitutional framework and accorded (in principle) to all.

An even more sophisticated tolerant stance would be further grounded in an understanding of the role of diverse beliefs in a democracy. Democracy is predicated on the belief that the people as a whole—not the elite, a monarch, or a religious leader—can govern themselves. "The people" is composed of individuals and groups with widely diverse beliefs, and some of those beliefs reflect profound disagreements about social and political issues. John Stuart Mill, of course, argued in *On Liberty* that the open exchange of those conflicting viewpoints was essential in the pursuit of truth: "Since the general or prevailing opinion on any subject is rarely or never the whole truth, it is only by the collision of adverse opinion that the remainder of the truth has any chance of being supplied."[3] Conflict of ideas, then, is not to be avoided, but to be embraced in a democratic society. Return to the example of the Aryan Nation's distribution of leaflets. However abhorrent their views may be, the Aryan Nation's ideas are part of that democratic process of exchanging, refuting, clarifying, and refining positions in the search for truth. The robust tolerant stance differentiates between the Aryan Nation's right to express their beliefs and the actions and behaviors the group advocates. According to the tolerant stance, the suppression of those beliefs is a greater threat to democracy than is their expression.

Tolerance for diversity of belief, then, involves the recognition of basic rights and civil liberties, and how they are part of our constitutional framework. A deep appreciation of tolerance also entails an understanding of how conflict is an integral part of a democratic society. What do we know about young people's understanding of concepts central to tolerance, such as rights, conflict, political groups, and democracy? What role do schools play in developing our youth's understanding?

Young People and Political Tolerance

In the early elementary grades, children demonstrate an emerging notion of the principles of freedom of speech and religion. In interviews conducted by Helwig, six-year-olds were likely to support a story character's right to talk about rock music or to say a particular prayer in the presence of disapproving adults.[4] Young children understand that people have different beliefs, and they support the expression of those beliefs when related to conventions like etiquette or taste. In a study by Wainryb, Shaw, Langeley, Cottam and Lewis, five-year-olds understood that others have different tastes and different beliefs about "facts," and did not evaluate these others negatively.[5] However, most children said it was unacceptable for someone to express different moral beliefs (e.g., it's alright to hit someone). Children's willingness to tolerate or allow the expression of diverse moral beliefs increased with age (6 percent of five-year-olds versus 22 percent of nine-year-olds), perhaps indicating the ability to distinguish between *expressing beliefs* (it's okay to hit someone) and *engaging in specific behaviors* (hitting someone). Similar to adolescents and adults, children who found diverse moral beliefs unacceptable expressed concern for the potential consequences of those beliefs.

The classic studies of young people's developing understandings of rights, conflict, and democratic values were conducted by Joseph Adelson.[6] Approximately 450 American, British, and West German young people between the ages of eleven and eighteen were interviewed about concepts such as individual rights, dissent, and the public good. Young people's thinking and reasoning processes were examined as they confronted issues such as "Should a dissenting religious group be vaccinated?" and "Should people without children pay taxes?" A subtle shift in the quality of thought could be detected at about the age of fourteen. Young people between fourteen and eighteen, in contrast to their younger counterparts, were beginning to recognize the potential conflict between individual rights and the public good, to connect specific examples of rights with abstract principles, and to consider the long-term consequences of given actions on individuals and communities. Adelson noted that "the older adolescent . . . can move from the concrete to the abstract and back again. Having stated a principle, he illuminates it by a concrete instance, or having mentioned specific examples, he seeks and finds the abstract category that binds them."[7] The movement from specific situations to democratic principles is prerequisite to the development and sustenance of political tolerance. Individuals must be able to see the relationship between a protest by the National Gay and Lesbian Task Force, for example, and the principles of freedom of speech and assembly.

Young people profess strong support for democratic principles, such as freedom of expression and freedom of assembly. In a recent international study, 90 percent of U.S. fourteen-year-olds said that it was "somewhat good" or "very good" for democracy when "everyone has the right to express their opinions freely."[8] They also seem to recognize, at least at a surface level, that it is good to hear different opinions. Nearly three-fourths of the U.S. students surveyed said that it would be "bad" or "very bad" for democracy if all television stations present the same opinion about politics. Support for dissent was moderately strong: 78 percent of students felt that it is "somewhat good" or "very good" for democracy when people peacefully protest against a law they believe to be unjust.

Similar to adults, however, youth support for democratic principles decreases when applied to specific situations and groups, particularly those groups that are disliked.[9] Together with colleagues, I have interviewed adolescents about civil liberties issues, and tried to probe their understanding of selected democratic principles.[10] In general, we find that tolerant and intolerant students approach civil liberties issues differently. For example, tolerant students' conceptualizations of conflict and "out-groups" differ from those of their intolerant peers. When presented with situations involving the civil liberties of a group that espouses views they dislike, tolerant students envision a conflict that could be negotiated through words, whereas intolerant students are more likely to foresee a conflict that results in physical violence. Tolerant students are cognizant of the *potential* for physical conflict, but intolerant students tend to be *certain* that physical violence will ensue. This is consistent with social psychological theories of intergroup relations which suggest that the [intolerant person's] perception of a "zero-sum game" between two groups, in which one group wins everything, is likely to result in overt conflict. On the other hand, when the relationship between two groups is not viewed in such competitive, absolutist terms, members of one group are more likely to be able to make accommodations to coexist with the other group.[11]

The language used by tolerant and intolerant students reflects their conceptualization of civil liberties issues. Tolerant students are likely to use the language of rights when confronted with civil liberties issues (e.g., "it's their right," "it's in the Constitution," "people have the right to express themselves"), whereas intolerant students tend to focus on the specifics of a situation and fail to make connections to underlying abstract principles (e.g., "I don't want to hear their opinions. I already know what they are about."). Tolerant students are more likely to see members of their least-liked group as having been influenced by outside forces, such as family socialization or peer group pressure. Intolerant students, on the other hand, are more likely to attribute members of their least-liked group's attitudes to some innate quality or characteristic (e.g., "He's just a bad person"). The different ways in which the tolerant and intolerant students view the groups reflects, in part, their view of humanity. Importantly, the negative outside influences tolerant students mention can be changed to positive outside influences, but the innate characteristics intolerant students attribute to members of their least-liked group are unlikely to change.

Similar to the more sophisticated students interviewed by Adelson in the early 1970s, tolerant students tend to display an understanding of the broader context of dissent, to think in terms of possibilities and probabilities instead of absolutes, and to link abstract democratic principles to concrete situations. There is reason to believe, however, that the tolerant students' responses are rarely grounded in an in-depth understanding of democratic principles. For example, although the tolerant students are more likely to invoke the principle of minority rights than are their peers with intolerant stances, their conception of minority rights is still fragile and tenuous. When pressed to explain why freedom of expression is so important in a democracy, few of the tolerant students can provide more than simplistic, tautological reasons (e.g., "because it's one of our rights in a democracy"). And perhaps more disturbing, tolerant students are unlikely to protest if the right to assemble, for example, is denied their least-liked group, but intolerant students are quite likely to say they would protest if their least-liked group were *allowed* to gather for a rally. In other words, tolerant students are unlikely to take action to support the rights of disliked groups, but intolerant students are likely to protest when their disliked groups are accorded civil liberties.

Intolerance is more likely to be our natural state than is tolerance.[12] That is, we are not born tolerant, but must learn to be tolerant. Intolerance is cognitively easier because we tend to categorize groups as *ingroups* (our groups) and *outgroups* (the other groups). In a revealing study by Devine, the first response of individuals, regardless of whether they perceive themselves to hold prejudices against other groups, is to adopt the negative stereotypes they acquired through socialization.[13] People need to actively work to override their natural impulse toward intolerance. Educational institutions could thus play a very important role in helping people to develop more tolerant orientations.

The Schools and the Development of Political Tolerance

One of the most powerful predictors of political tolerance among youth and adults is education. Research consistently shows that the higher the level of education, the higher the level of political tolerance; however, post-secondary experiences appear to have a far greater impact than elementary and secondary education. Studies have been less successful in uncovering the aspects of educational experiences that contribute to the development of political tolerance. In most college and university settings, people are likely to come into contact with persons whose views and experiences differ from their own. The classic liberal arts education thrives on challenging students' worldviews and widening their perspectives. Elementary and secondary schooling, on the other hand, is narrowly focused on achieving basic literacy goals. Additionally, the current emphasis on standards and testing is inimical to the development of higher order thinking and deep understanding. Student knowledge of names, dates, and facts is easier to measure than is their ability to engage in thoughtful discussions about public issues.

It is impossible to separate what young people learn about civil liberties, conflict, and democracy in school from what they learn from other sources. The early political socialization research identified the agents of political socialization as school, family, media, and peers, as if these were discrete spheres of influence. They are not only interactive, but how individual students interpret these influences is profoundly shaped by their experiences and beliefs. With this caveat in mind, what is the "typical" schooling experience likely to convey to our youth about concepts relate to political tolerance?

There are two primary ways in which students may learn about concepts related to political tolerance in schools: the curriculum and classroom experiences. There is some evidence that the curriculum and classroom experiences can have an impact on students' levels of tolerance, as will be described later. These avenues are equally important and mutually reinforcing. That is, students might learn about the legal protections for our civil rights and liberties through textbooks, and experience classroom discussions in which dissenting perspectives are encouraged and supported. One might think of these as the *textbook version* and the *classroom experience*. If the textbook version is in place without the classroom experience, then civil liberties remain an abstraction for students; more importantly, students are not likely to see how sharing divergent perspectives can enhance the quality of thinking about issues. However, the classroom experience without the textbook version doesn't allow students to understand how civil liberties are embedded within our Constitutional framework. But the classroom experience and textbook version must each have depth and substance, without which young people are likely to be "lip-synching to the tune of democracy," a phrase my colleagues and I used to describe adolescents' responses to interviews we conducted with them about civil liberties issues.[14]

The Textbook Version

Studies indicate that young people are likely to learn about the Constitutional protections of individual rights in their civics and history classes. Analyses of textbooks and national standards documents reveal a strong emphasis on rights. In an analysis of three of the most widely used eighth grade American history textbooks, Simmons and I found that the European settlement in America is depicted as a search for personal liberties and religious freedom. In civics textbooks, typically used at the ninth grade level, individual rights are a major theme.[15] General references to rights, First Amendment freedoms, and the right to vote are those most frequently mentioned in texts. U.S. history and civics textbooks devote attention to "minority rights," but it is almost always in the context of the Civil Rights Movement, and in relation to persons of color. Students are unlikely to learn that respect for minority rights refers as well to groups whose ideas the dominant group may find abhorrent.

Deep and substantive attention to political tolerance as a democratic value would require textbooks to present historical and contemporary instances in which the rights of dissidents have been abrogated. But even with regard to the Civil Rights Movement, a topic to which texts devote a fair amount of space, historian James Loewen found secondary U.S. history textbooks silent on the dark side of U.S. history, such as the FBI's attempts to thwart the movement. In his examination of 12 U.S. history textbooks, he found:

The stories that history textbooks tell are predictable; every problem has already been solved or is about to be solved. Textbooks exclude conflict or real suspense. They leave out anything that might reflect badly upon our national character. When they try for drama, they achieve only melodrama, because readers know that everything will turn out fine in the end.[16]

Examinations of civics textbooks reveal a similar avoidance of controversial issues.[17]

Curricula specifically designed to teach young people about the role of tolerance in a democracy can impact levels of tolerance. An early study by Goldenson examined the effects of a three-week civil liberties unit on high school students' level of tolerance.[18] As part of the unit, students conducted in-depth investigations of the way in which the abstract "slogans of democracy" are applied in concrete situations. Students interviewed community members such as police, court officials, and staff at the local American Civil Liberties Union to gain a sense of the complexity of civil liberties issues as well as the range of perspectives on such issues. Students who took part in the unit demonstrated greater levels of tolerance at the end of the unit as compared to a control group. Goldenson also found that students' perception of the teacher's credibility affected the degree to which tolerance scores improved as a result of the unit. Students who saw their teacher as more credible (e.g., fair, knowledgeable) showed greater increases than those who perceived the teacher as less credible.

In 1993, political scientist Richard Brody examined the effects of the high school level *We the People* program *With Liberty and Justice for All,* on students' level of political tolerance. Teachers using the program were randomly selected from across the country, and asked to survey their students upon completion of the program. A comparison group was randomly drawn from a list of National Council for the Social Studies teachers; high school teachers who were teaching classes in American History or Government, but not using the *We the People* materials, were asked to administer the survey to their students. Students were asked to respond to items that measured their support for freedom of speech and assembly, due-process laws, and freedom of the press. Students were presented with various scenarios in which they were asked whether they would support civil liberties for a range of traditional outgroups such as atheists, Gay Liberation Organizations, American Nazis, and advocates of the violent overthrow of the government. Items also measured the degree to which students thought criminals should be accorded rights such as the right to a public trial and the right to be treated humanely by law enforcement officials. Brody compared students' responses with responses collected in a previous study from the general public. Overall, the high school students (both those using and *not* using the *We the People* material) demonstrated higher levels of tolerance than the mass public, and students who were using the *We the People* materials demonstrated greater levels of tolerance than did students not using the materials. For example, when students were asked whether a community should allow its civic auditorium to be used by atheists who want to preach against God and religion, 40 percent of the *We the People* students and 30 percent of the comparison group responded affirmatively. (Only 18 percent of the general public responded affirmatively.) When asked the same question about members of the Gay Liberation Movement, 53 percent of the *We the People* students, 46 percent of their peers, and 26 percent of the general public gave a tolerant response. Brody attributed the impact of the *We the People* material to its combined emphasis on constitutional principles, the norms of democracy, and the contemporary relevance of the U.S. Constitution and the Bill of Rights.

In the early 1990s, my colleagues and I conducted two studies of the impact of a four-week curriculum unit, *Tolerance for Diversity of Beliefs*,[19] on ninth graders' level of political tolerance.[20] We designed the unit to reflect the research on political tolerance, pedagogy, and developmental psychology. For example, the research on political tolerance suggests that many people do not make the connection between the abstract principles of democracy, such as freedom of expression, and concrete situations of violations of civil liberties. Thus, the curriculum includes many historical and contemporary case studies of civil liberties issues.

To evaluate the effectiveness of the curriculum, students completed a pretest, the four-week curriculum, and a posttest. The measure of political tolerance required students to identify their least-liked social or political group, and then to respond to six standard questions used in the literature on a five-point scale ranging from "strongly agree" to "strongly disagree" (e.g., "Members of the [student's least-liked group] should be allowed to make a public speech.").

We gathered information on other factors, most of which had been shown to be related to tolerance in previous studies: support for democratic norms, perceived threat, authoritarianism, self-esteem, knowledge of curriculum content, attitude toward the curriculum, race/ethnicity, gender, and achievement level. Appropriate control groups and a delayed posttest, to see if any effects endured, were part of the research design.

Findings indicated that the students who studied the curriculum developed significantly higher levels of tolerance at the conclusion of the unit in comparison to the control groups, and that the effects diminished only slightly after one month. Good predictors of a high level of political tolerance included perceived threat (low), authoritarianism (low), support for democratic norms (high), self esteem (high), knowledge of the curriculum (high); gender, academic grades, and enjoyment of the curriculum did not predict levels of tolerance.

Both tolerant and intolerant individuals felt threatened by their least-liked group. Why did these two groups of students choose different responses? When we asked students to explain their choices, tolerant students were likely to make frequent references to the U.S. Constitution, the Bill of Rights, and values such as freedom of expression. Conversely, when intolerant students were asked to explain their views, they were likely to describe expectations of violence, such as "The [least-liked group] would hurt, torture and kill many people in their demonstration. There would be a lot of deaths or arrests." Tolerant students were more likely to believe that democratic institutions could withstand the challenges associated with diverse—and sometimes hateful—viewpoints, whereas intolerant students' concern for violence guided their thinking.

We also found, however, that tolerant students' commitment to democratic principles is limited. When asked whether they would take action to support their least-liked group if it were denied freedom of expression, the majority said no. The majority of intolerant students, however, reported that they would take action if their least-liked group were allowed certain civil liberties. Demonstrating tolerance in the face of a disliked group is difficult enough for most people. Taking action to defend the rights of that group against the majority of the public requires a firm commitment to democratic principles.

This set of curriculum studies suggests that when education texts are specifically designed to engage students in issues related to tolerance, they can influence students' orientations toward tolerance dilemmas. The traditional civics or U.S. history curriculum, however, is unlikely to have such an impact.

Classroom Experiences

There is some evidence to suggest that students' level of political tolerance is related to their classroom experiences, more specifically, students' participating in the discussion of controversial public issues in an open and supportive classroom climate.[21] The link makes sense intuitively. First, teachers who actively create an open classroom climate demonstrate that they value divergent viewpoints. Second, when students practice listening to different perspectives they may come to appreciate the complexity of public issues and how such discussions may increase their understanding of issues. They are less likely to categorize issues as *good* or *bad*, *pro* or *con*. Finally, when students regularly engage in discussions about controversial issues, they are less likely to feel threatened by views that are opposed to their own.

In the IEA study of civic knowledge and engagement among fourteen-year-olds from twenty-eight countries, students from the United States generally reported experiencing class discussions in positive classroom environments. Students indicated that:

- they are encouraged to make up their own minds about issues (85 percent);
- they are free to express their opinions (78 percent);
- they are free to disagree with teachers about social and political issues (73 percent);
- their teachers encourage them to discuss political and social issues about which people have different opinions (69 percent);

- teachers respect their opinions (79 percent)
- teachers present several sides of an issue (79 percent)[22]

In comparison to students from other countries, U.S. students scored above the international mean on the measure of classroom climate.

Other findings suggest that the picture is more complicated. Students (and teachers) often confuse student participation with class discussion; researchers often find that a "discussion" is much more akin to a recitation in which students respond to teachers' factually-oriented questions.[23] Thoughtful class discussions about significant public issues in which students engage in substantive conversation, challenge one another's thinking, and build a collective understanding of issues are rare.[24]

Why are secondary social studies classrooms *not* likely to be places in which young people grapple with complex social and political issues, explore competing values and perspectives, and practice tolerance for diversity of beliefs? These are areas in which many teachers feel uncomfortable, and for good reason. Political scientist Paul Vogt describes the precollegiate context as follows:

> Schools have little incentive to go beyond sloganeering. Because tolerance involves not repressing "subversive" ideas, "disgusting" practices, and "evil" people, teaching tolerance is usually controversial. Educators are unlikely to enhance their careers by courting controversy and discussing the rights of unpopular minorities, to say nothing of advocating those rights. Prior to university-level studies, public education is usually too vulnerable to popular pressure to handle the conflict of values that can ensure from any serious attempt to deal directly with political tolerance.[25]

Additionally, many history and civics teachers feel pressure—real, imagined, or both—to cover material, and coverage is inimical to in-depth discussions of issues related to tolerance.

Linda McNeil's excellent ethnographic study of four Midwestern high schools suggests that teachers fear losing control of their classrooms if they engage in discussions of controversial issues.[26] And, indeed, facilitating in-depth discussions about controversial social and political issues requires complex skills that many educators have not developed.[27] Teachers' images of discussions that spill into chaos are particularly associated with lower-socioeconomic-status and lower-achieving students. Several studies indicate that these students are least likely to experience issues-centered discussions and inquiry.[28]

But resistance to discussing controversial issues comes from a somewhat unexpected source as well—students. Studies suggest that students recoil from expressing viewpoints that differ from their classmates for fear of embarrassment or losing face.[29] The peer culture is particularly important in shaping how young people feel about participating in class discussions, and that culture is likely to silence dissenting views.[30]

Teacher and student reluctance to engage in controversial public issues discussions must also be placed within the broader societal context. Americans in general do not like to discuss opposing political viewpoints.[31] Merelman argues that the degree of political conflict within a society affects the way in which conflict is perceived.[32] Citizens of relatively uncontested or stable democracies, such as the United States, tend to have a low tolerance for conflict of beliefs and overestimate the degree to which violence is a part of political conflict. Taken together, neither teachers, students, nor the broader society emerge as strong advocates for deep and thoughtful discussions of controversial public issues in secondary classrooms.

Concluding Thoughts

A strong conceptualization of tolerance goes beyond the recognition of basic rights and civil liberties and how they are part of our constitutional framework. It encompasses an understanding of how diverse beliefs and the ensuing conflict of ideas is fundamental to the sustenance of a democratic society. In our highly individualistic, rights-oriented culture, the school curriculum reinforces the message that to be an American is to have "freedom of expression" and "the right to believe as I choose." But the message is often taught at the superficial level of a political sound bite. Most students support freedom of speech and religion, for example, and recognize that those rights are guaranteed all citizens through the Constitution. But they (along with adults) are far less likely to apply those principles in concrete situations or to recognize that the concept of minority rights extends beyond the Civil Rights Movement.

Schools are not the panacea, but they could be doing far more than they currently do in promoting young people's understanding of the role of conflict and dissent in a society. Secondary curricula in particular should acquaint students with historical and contemporary examples of the abrogation of basic rights and civil liberties. Students should regularly participate in class discussions in which public issues are examined from multiple perspectives, conflicting viewpoints are interrogated and the value of diverse beliefs is affirmed. Hibbing and Theiss-Morse note:

> Students will not become good citizens by memorizing lists of what a good citizen does but rather by recognizing that ordinary people have refreshingly different interests, that these interests must be addressed even when they appear tangential, that each issue has an array of possible solutions, and that finding the most appropriate solution requires time, effort, and conflict.[33]

Conover and Searing explain the connection between discussion and support for democratic ideals in terms of social capital theory.[34] Participation in regular class discussions strengthens students' skills in articulating their viewpoints, listening to others, and analyzing issues—all valuable skills (i.e., social capital) in the formal political sphere. The education literature offers several research-based pedagogical methods for classroom discussion of controversial issues.[35]

If young people are *not* to learn about historical and current government abrogations of civil liberties in their pre-collegiate classrooms, from where should they learn it? If they are *not* to experience and practice in their pre-collegiate classrooms discussions of controversial public issues in which they purposefully interrogate diverse perspectives, where will they experience it? We are not prone to seeking out information and perspectives that differ from our own. True, many of our young people will go on to gain such knowledge and experiences in postsecondary institutions, but many will not. And those who will not are precisely those who are least empowered in society.

Secondary schools in particular are well situated to developing our young people's understanding of tolerance and its relationship to the democratic ideals of freedom of expression and minority rights. Adolescents are capable of linking abstract principles to concrete situations, and with practice, are likely to make those connections on a regular basis. And as they experience controversial public issues discussion in open, supportive classroom climates, they are likely to see the value of sharing multiple perspectives. It will not be easy, but then, democracy has never been an easy proposition.

Notes

1. Samuel A. Stouffer, *Communism, Conformity and Civil Liberties* (New York: Doubleday, 1955).
2. See, for example, D. Chong, "How people think, reason, and feel about rights and liberties," *American Journal of Political Science* 37, no. 3 (1993): 867-99; James L. Gibson, "Alternative measures of political tolerance: Must tolerance be 'least-liked'?" *American Journal of Political Science* 36, no. 2 (1992): 560-77; J.J. Mondak and J. Hurwitz, "Values, acts, and actors: Distinguishing generic and discriminatory intolerance," *Political Behavior* 20, no. 4 (1998): 313-39; John L. Sullivan, James Pierson, and George E. Marcus, *Political Tolerance and American Democracy* (Chicago: University of Chicago Press, 1982).
3. J.S. Mill, *On liberty* (Orchard Park, NY: Boardview Press, 1869/1999), 116.
4. C. C. Helwig, "The role of agent and social context in judgments of freedom of speech and religion," *Child Development* 68, no. 3 (1997): 484-95.
5. Cecilia Wainryb et. al., "Children's thinking about diversity of belief in the early school years: Judgments of relativism, tolerance, and disagreeing persons," *Child Development* 75, no. 3 (2004): 687-703.
6. J. Adelson, "The political imagination of the young adolescent," *Daedalus* 100 (1971): 1013-50.
7. Adelson, "The political imagination," 1015.
8. S. Baldi et. al., *What democracy means to ninth-graders: U.S. results from the international IEA Civic Education Study (NCES 2001-096)*, U.S. Department of Education, Na-

tional Center for Education Statistics (Washington, D.C.: U.S. Government Printing Office, 2001).

9. P.J. Conover and D.D. Searing, "A political socialization perspective," in *Rediscovering the Democratic Purposes of Education* ed. L.M. McDonnell, P.M. Timpane, and R. Benjamin (Lawrence, Kans.: University of Kansas Press, 2000), 91-124; D. Owen and J. Dennis, "Preadult development of political tolerance," *Political Psychology* 8 (1987): 547-61; K. Thalhammer et. al., "Adolescents and political tolerance: Lip-synching to the tune of democracy," *Review of Education, Pedagogy, and Cultural Studies* 16 (1994): 325-47.

10. P. G. Avery, "Political tolerance: How adolescents deal with dissenting groups," in *The development of political understanding* ed. H. Haste & J. Torney-Purta (San Francisco: Jossey-Bass, 1992), 39–51; Thalhammer et. al., "Adolescents and political tolerance."

11. J.F. Dovidio, G. Maruyama, and M.G. Alexander, "A social psychology of national and international group relations," *Journal of Social Issues* 54, no. 4 (1998): 831-46.

12. F. Aboud, *Children and prejudice* (Oxford, U.K.: Blackwell, 1988); K. Kawakami, J.F. Dovidio et. al., "Just say no (to stereotyping): Effects of training in the negation of stereotypic associations on stereotype activation," *Journal of Personality and Social Psychology* 78, no. 5 (2000): 871-88.

13. P.G. Devine, "Stereotypes and prejudice: Their automatic and controlled components," *Journal of Personality and Social Psychology* 56, no. 1 (1989): 5-18.

14. Thalhammer et. al., "Adolescents and political tolerance."

15. P.G. Avery and A.M. Simmons, "Civic life as conveyed in U.S. civics and history textbooks," *International Journal of Social Education* 15, no. 2 (Fall 2000/Winter 2001): 105-30; M.H. Gonzales et. al., "Variations of citizenship education: a content analysis of rights, obligations, and participation concepts in high school civic textbooks," *Theory and Research in Social Education* 32, no. 3 (2004): 301-25.

16. J.W. Loewen, *Lies my teacher told me: Everything your American history textbook got wrong* (New York: Touchstone, 1995), 13.

17. J. Carroll et. al., *We the people: A review of U.S. government and civics textbooks* (Washington, D.C.: People for the American Way, 1987).

18. D.R. Goldenson, "An alternative view about the role of the secondary school in political socialization: A field-experimental study of the development of civil liberties attitudes," *Theory and Research in Social Education* 6 (1978): 44-72.

19. P.G. Avery et. al., *Tolerance for diversity of beliefs: A secondary curriculum unit* (Boulder, Colo.: Social Science Education Consortium, 1993).

20. P.G. Avery et. al., "Exploring political tolerance with adolescents: Do all of the people have all of the rights all of the time?" *Theory and Research in Social Education* 20, no. 4 (1992): 386-420; K. Bird et. al., "Not just lip-synching anymore: Education and tolerance revisited," *The review of Education/Pedagogy/Cultural Studies* 16, nos. 3-4 (1994): 373-86.

21. L.H. Ehman, "The American school in the political socialization process," *Review of Educational Research* 50, no. 1 (1980): 99-119; C. L. Hahn, *Becoming political: Comparative perspectives on citizenship education* (Albany, N.Y.: SUNY Press, 1998); J.V. Torney, A. N. Oppenheim, and R. F. Farnen, *Civic education in ten countries: An empirical study* (New York: John Wiley and Sons, 1975).

22. Baldi et. al., *What democracy means*, 34.

23. D. Alvermann, D. O'Brien, and D. Dillon, "What teachers do when they're having discussions of content area reading assignments: A qualitative analysis." *Reading Research Quarterly* 24 (1990): 296-322; B.E. Larson and W.C. Parker, (1996) "What is classroom discussion? A look at teachers' conceptions." *Journal of Curriculum and Supervision* 11, no. 2 : 110-26; F.M. Newmann, "Qualities of thoughtful social studies classes: An empirical profile," *Journal of Curriculum Studies* 22, no. 3 (1990): 253-75.

24. C. Cornbleth, "Images of America: What youth do know about the United States," *American Educational Research Journal* 29, no. 2 (2002): 519-52; J. Kahne et. al., "Developing citizens for democracy? Assessing opportunities to learn in Chicago's social studies classrooms," *Theory and Research in Social Education* 28, no. 3 (2000): 311-38; F.M. Newmann and Associates, *Authentic achievement: Restructuring schools for intellectual quality* (San Francisco: Jossey-Bass Publishers, 1996).

25. W. P. Vogt, *Tolerance and education: Learning to live with diversity and difference* (Thousand Oaks, Calif.: SAGE Publications, 1997), 179.

26. L.M. McNeil, *Contradictions of control: School structure and school knowledge* (New York: Routledge, 1986).

27. D. Hess, "Controversies about controversial issues in democratic education," *PS: Politics and Society* 37, no. 2 (2004): 257-61; W.C. Parker, "Classroom discussion: Models for leading seminars and deliberations," *Social Education* 65, no. 2 (2001): 111-15.

28. Baldi et. al., *What democracy means*; Conover and Searing, "A political socialization perspective"; L.M. McNeil, *Contradictions of control*; R. Page, *Lower-track classrooms: A curricular and cultural perspective* (New York: Teachers College Press, 1991).

29. K. Bickmore, "Learning inclusion/inclusion in learning: Citizenship education for a pluralistic society," *Theory and Research in Social Education* 21. no. 4 (1993): 341-84; L. Delpit, *Other people's children: Cultural conflict in the classroom* (New York: New York Press, 1995).

30. D. Hess and J. Posselt, "How high school students experience and learn from the discussion of controversial public issues," *Journal of Curriculum & Supervision* 17, no. 4 (2002): 283-314.

31. J.R. Hibbing and E. Theiss-Morse, *Stealth democracy: Americans' beliefs about how government should work* (Cambridge: Cambridge University Press, 2002).

32. R. Merelman, "The role of conflict in children's political learning," in *Political socialization, citizenship education, and democracy*, ed. O. Ichilov (New York: Teachers College Press, 1990), 47-65.

33. Hibbing and Theiss-Morse, *Stealth democracy*, 225-26.

34. Conover and Searing, "A political socialization perspective."

35. See P.G. Avery et. al., "Teaching an understanding of war and peace through structured academic controversies," in *How children understand war and peace*, ed. A. Raviv, L. Oppenheimer, & D. Bar-Tal (San Francisco: Jossey-Bass, 1999), 260-80; W.C. Parker and D. Hess, "Teaching with and for discussion," *Teaching and Teacher Education* 17 (2001): 273-89.

Political Tolerance and Civic Education in Developing Democracies[1]

Steven E. Finkel

Introduction

Political tolerance, or the willingness to extend procedural liberties such as free speech and association to unpopular or disliked individuals or groups, has long been viewed as essential for the stability of democratic regimes.[2] Much research in the new democracies of Eastern Europe, the former Soviet Union, Latin America, and South Africa, however, has documented the generally low levels of tolerance and support for minority rights after the emergence of democratic institutions.[3] Though there is also a limited willingness to extend civil liberties to unpopular groups in established democracies, the abysmally low levels of tolerance and support for what Gibson and Duch term "minoritarian" principles in developing contexts may pose a significant danger to the future stability and effectiveness of these democratic systems.[4] Indeed, Gibson's finding that individuals who embraced democratic principles were more likely to resist the attempted coup staged in Moscow in 1991 suggests that increasing tolerance can be instrumental in the consolidation of fledgling democratic regimes.[5] Given the powerful racial, ethnic, and political animosities that characterize many developing democracies, as well as the strains placed on these systems by poor economic and political performance, raising the levels of support for the exercise of democratic political liberties and "the rules of the democratic game" is an especially urgent task.

To this end, the United States and many West European countries have devoted considerable resources over the past several decades to funding various kinds of democracy assistance programs in emerging democracies around the world.[6] Some of these activities center around the training of lawyers, journalists, and other social elites in the rule of law, in assisting constitutional reform, and in strengthening democratic political parties, non-governmental organizations, and other elements of a country's newly-emerging civil society. Some of the activities, though, are directed explicitly at promoting support for democratic

153

norms and values among ordinary citizens. These efforts constitute "civic education programs," and range from the adoption of new curricula in primary and
secondary schools to teach young people about democracy, to programs that
provide instruction about the social and political rights of women, to voter education programs, to neighborhood problem-solving programs that bring individuals in contact with local authorities for purposes of promoting collective
action to benefit local communities.

In this chapter, I examine the effect of adult civic education programs on the
core value of tolerance in two developing democracies, the Dominican Republic
and South Africa. The inquiry has, of course, important practical implications
for democracy assistance programming and implementation. Moreover, the investigation seeks to add to the growing empirical literature on the ways that
civic education can affect democratic attitudes and participation among youth
and adults in new democracies.[7] Finally, the exploration of civic education's
effects on tolerance affords an important real-world test of recent experimental
findings that individual levels of tolerance may change considerably in response
to argumentation and efforts at political persuasion.[8] As opposed to the notion
that individuals have fixed, long-standing attitudes toward tolerance, this line of
research views tolerance as the product of *judgments* made by individuals, depending on the considerations they bring to bear at the time, their prior store of
political information, attachment to democratic norms, and psychological openness to change. Civic education programs are institutionalized attempts at attitude change. They aim to change tolerance judgments by imparting new information to individuals, information that promotes the linkage of tolerance to
more abstract democratic values, to prior political and psychological dispositions, and to more general positive outcomes associated with democratic systems. Hence an examination of the effects of civic education can provide important theoretical insights into how values may change in response to efforts at
persuasion outside the laboratory setting, and increase our understanding of the
conditions under which value change is likely to occur.

Civic Education and the Development of Political Tolerance: Theoretical Perspectives

How much effect on a value such as political tolerance are civic education programs likely to have? The voluminous literature on the determinants of political
tolerance would suggest a very limited impact. Many of the most important predictors of tolerance would appear to be well beyond the ability and scope of
even the most intensive short-term civic education program. For example, individuals who are more dogmatic, mistrustful, inflexible, and "psychologically
insecure" are less willing to extend procedural liberties to individuals or groups
with whom they disagree, and these kinds of deeply-rooted personality charac-

teristics are likely to be relatively impervious to change.[9] Similarly, political and religious conservatism have also been linked consistently to levels of political tolerance, as have attitudes towards out-groups and the potential threats that they may represent.[10] Only for attitudes about groups and threat perceptions would civic education appear to have a chance for success, but, as Sullivan and Transue note, threat perceptions contain a large "chronic, dispositional role" as well.[11] And attitudes about racial outgroups, for example those forged in contemporary South Africa, are likely to be deeply rooted in the experiences of living under the apartheid regime, making it difficult to undo a lifetime of socialization in a series of democracy workshops.

Recent developments in the literature, however, suggest that democratic values, and political tolerance in particular, may be more malleable than previously thought. First, a steady stream of findings over the past several decades has shown that more immediate variables such as the individual's perceptions of current economic conditions, assessments of governmental competence, and political and social participation can affect orientations such as the individual's "normative commitment to democracy," and the internalization of democratic values, social and institutional trust, and political efficacy.[12] The widespread demonstration of such effects has led many to conclude that, although early socialization and social-structural factors play a role in determining democratic attitudes, these factors must be augmented by variables related to adult political experiences.

Second, a related stream of recent research has challenged the notion that tolerance is a stable or fixed individual-level attitude, arguing instead that individual judgments are highly responsive to political argumentation and efforts at persuasion.[13] Using a variety of innovative experimental and quasi-experimental research designs, these studies have shown that tolerance can be quite pliable, changing in predictable ways according to the nature of the information presented to respondents. Kuklinski et al., for example, showed that tolerance responses could differ substantially, depending on whether respondents were encouraged to view a situation through an "emotional" or "cognitive" frame.[14] Similarly, Nelson et al. showed that experimentally emphasizing the frame of "rights of free speech" or the "need for public order" in a given tolerance situation had a significant effect on whether individuals' attitudes on those dimensions would be brought to bear in formulating their responses.[15] And Gibson, Marcus et al., and Sniderman et al. have used the "counterargument technique" to great effect, showing that tolerance changes considerably after respondents are presented with reasons why they might reconsider their initial view.[16] This work has called into question much of the received wisdom in the field; most importantly, it has shown that, at least in the laboratory or in experimental survey situations, substantial change in tolerance through political persuasion is possible.

The recent linkage of the tolerance literature to persuasion and attitude change research is an important one, one with clear implications for the analysis of the impact of civic education. Civic education is properly viewed as *an insti-*

tutionalized mechanism for attempted attitude and value change in newly democratizing societies.[17] Through means of workshops, community problem-solving activities, voter education drives, and the like, it is hoped that individuals will be persuaded by the messages conveyed to convert towards tolerance and the internalization of other democratic orientations. As such, it may be expected that the conditions that facilitate attitude change in general should facilitate attitude change via the mechanism of civic education.

The vast literature on attitude change in psychology and political psychology contains a number of theories specifying alternative routes to persuasion. There is, however, unanimity on one fundamental point with direct relevance for the analysis here: attitude change does not occur uniformly across populations upon exposure to persuasive messages. That is, we should expect to see *conditional* effects of exposure to messages on the likelihood of change, as certain kinds of messages are more likely to bring about change, and certain kinds of individuals are more receptive to change than others. For example, McGuire's well-known "reception-acceptance" model of attitude change, adapted and extended into political psychology by Zaller, asserts that the *reception* of messages varies directly with the individual's level of interest, motivation, and political awareness, while the individual's *acceptance* of messages varies inversely with those same variables, as highly aware individuals are less likely to accept messages that run counter to their prior attitudes and predispositions.[18] Thus attitude change is most likely to occur among individuals who are moderately aware and interested: less interested and aware individuals are unlikely to receive messages and more engaged individuals are unlikely to accept them.

Other models of attitude change stress the characteristics of the message,[19] the degree of trust placed in the source of the message,[20] the intensity of the previously-held attitude,[21] the degree to which the attitude is embedded in a more complex associative network,[22] and many others.[23] All of these variables operate as mediating factors, establishing firmly the observation that attitude change occurs only under certain conditions for certain kinds of individuals.

What factors are likely to condition whether individuals receive and accept tolerance messages in the real-world context of civic education? Attitude change depends first on the individual's *reception* of a particular message. In the civic education context, the reception of a tolerance message should depend directly on the individual's frequency of attending civic education sessions: the more exposures to civic education, the greater the likelihood that political tolerance will have been discussed in enough detail to constitute a "message" for purposes of persuasion. More importantly, tolerance messages are difficult ones to accept in general. The notion that individuals ought to extend civil liberties to hated and potentially dangerous groups is not only "unnatural" in many ways, but also rooted in fairly abstract conceptions about due process, democratic procedures, reciprocity, and political competition. Thus frequent exposures may be needed before tolerance messages begin to be understood. If this is the case, then there may not be monotonic increases in political tolerance as individuals attend more civic education sessions; rather there may be *threshold* effects, such that no change is observed until individuals are exposed repeatedly to pro-tolerance messages.[24]

We also expect a series of conditional relationships between civic education, tolerance, and certain attitudes and attributes of the individual. Following Zaller, civic education messages will be accepted to the extent that the individual's psychological and political dispositions are otherwise favorable towards tolerance, *and* the individual is able to make linkages between the messages received in civic education and those prior dispositions.[25] That is, individuals who are able to "contextualize" or integrate the tolerance messages into a supportive system of democratic orientations are more likely to change than individuals whose prior attitudes and values are either anti-democratic or too compartmentalized to allow links from a persuasive message to other pro-democracy attitudes and values.[26] This suggests that the individual's prior political awareness and motivation should be critical in the attitude change process, as should the extent to which the individual's prior orientations are more or less favorable towards democracy in general.

Political *information* and *interest* are likely to be important conditioning variables in attitude change for several reasons. First, these factors make it more likely that individuals will receive messages from civic education, as more interested and informed individuals may be likely to attend civic education in the first place and continue to attend after an initial experience. Second, politically aware and knowledgeable individuals will likely have the cognitive skills to *understand* the message from civic education to which they are exposed; even repeated exposures for individuals who lack the cognitive abilities to process them may not be enough to bring about attitude change. And third, politically aware individuals are best equipped to make the necessary associations between the tolerance messages and other supportive values. That is, higher levels of information and interest are likely to lead to greater contextualization of civic education messages, and hence greater acceptance, when individuals' other attitudes incline them to be more tolerant.

As noted above, however, awareness and interest may have curvilinear effects on the likelihood of attitude change. At the highest levels of awareness, individuals who are predisposed to be democratic may already be relatively tolerant, and individuals who are predisposed against tolerance should possess enough countervailing information to resist the new information. Thus we may expect change to be concentrated among individuals with enough prior information and cognitive skills to receive and comprehend tolerance messages, but not enough countervailing information to resist them.

Finally, several attitudes, perceptions, and values should predispose individuals to either accept or reject the tolerance messages in civic education. First, as the discussion thus far has made clear, the individual's prior adherence to other democratic values represents important predispositions to change. If individuals are more democratic in their orientations to begin with—that is, they accept principles such as the rule of law and the need for political liberty over social order, and believe that individuals can influence the political process— then they should be less likely to resist tolerance messages and more able to see the connections between those messages and their other supportive democratic beliefs.

Second, personality factors such as dogmatism or close-mindedness were found by Gibson to impede efforts at persuasion.[27] In Zaller's terms, dogmatic individuals will be more likely to resist messages that promote tolerance; their inflexible belief system is unlikely to change generally, and also unlikely to change towards a value which they are predisposed to oppose in the first place.

Further, it may be hypothesized that perceptions related to the immediate political and economic situation of the country will join longer standing predispositions to affect the likelihood of accepting tolerance messages. In situations where individuals have little other experience with democratic institutions and governance, the associations that are made with tolerance messages are likely to be based on individuals' overall satisfaction with the economic and political performance of the democratic system itself. Hence when messages promoting the applied democratic value of tolerance are received, individuals may naturally be more likely to accept or reject those messages based on other associations they currently have with the political system. In the absence of long-standing experiences with democracy, performance ratings are all that many individuals have— especially those with lower levels of prior political information. For this reason perceptions about the system's economic and political performance may represent a powerful conditioning factor that determines the individual's susceptibility to persuasive messages via civic education.

Research Design

The study examines these processes by analyzing the effects of civic education on individuals trained in four U.S. Agency for International Development (USAID) civic education programs conducted in the Dominican Republic in the mid to late 1990s and three programs conducted in South Africa between 1998 and 1999. USAID's Center for Democracy and Governance initiated the evaluation of civic education efforts in the Dominican Republic in 1996-97, with South Africa added in mid-1998. The Dominican Republic was selected for several reasons, notably the scope of its civic education efforts since the early 1990s and the relative ease of data collection due to the small size of the country. Equally important, the country was coming out of a period of semi-authoritarianism and afforded an excellent opportunity to assess the effects of civic education during a particular kind of political transition.[28]

South Africa was included in the study in 1998 because USAID had long targeted the country for democracy assistance, and there were a significant number of ongoing civic education programs over the past year in preparation for the June 1999 elections. In addition, the USAID mission in Pretoria took particular interest in the project in order to obtain information about how better to implement civic education and other programs in the future.

Dominican Republic

The first of the programs studied was conducted by a national elections oriented non-governmental organization, *Participación Ciudadana (PC)*. For the 1996 presidential elections, PC created another group, called *La Red de los Observadores Electorales*, to organize and train youth and adults to serve as election observers in 1996 and to conduct a quick count of the vote. The program ran from 1995 to mid-1996, although PC activities continued into 1997, still focused on elections. Of those in the sample 14 percent of the respondents were exposed to PC and Red training sessions but did not eventually work as election observers.

The second program was conducted by a newly formed non-governmental organization, *Grupo Accion por la Democracia (GAD)*. The program was conducted in two phases, with the first phase dedicated to a general educational program concerning basic political rights and obligations in a democracy, primarily through a lecture format. The second phase brought these people together to hold a series of national and local issues forums to discuss problems and solutions in specific policy areas, such as justice, health, and education. Local government authorities attended these forums as well. The two phases were intended to create a national NGO with a network of local branches outside of Santo Domingo and to mobilize citizens to participate in these new structures. The program ran from November 1995 to October 1996.

The third program was part of a larger community finance and small business development program for women conducted through women's small business NGO, *Asociación Dominicana para el Desarrollo de la Mujer (ADOPEM)*. The program trained women community leaders in women's rights, democratic values, democracy in the family, and self-esteem, using a classroom/workshop format, and ran from January 1996 to January 1997.

The fourth program studied was conducted by a local NGO affiliated with a local radio station in La Vega, *Radio Santa María (RSM)*. The project trained intermediaries (typically leaders of rural towns) who then conducted civic education in their local communities. The subject matter focused on civic knowledge and values, such as rights and duties in a democracy, the importance of participation, and democracy in the family. RSM ran two consecutive projects, from 1994 to 1995 and from 1995 to December 1996.

In all of the programs in the Dominican Republic except Radio Santa Maria, treatment samples were drawn from lists of participants provided by the implementing organizations. For the Radio Santa Maria program, only lists of the "leaders" or first-stage participants were maintained, and we obtained names of ordinary participants through "snowball" sampling methods from interviewers with the first-stage participants. The number of individuals interviewed from the four programs totaled 1018.

The strategy for obtaining appropriate control samples was to select non-participants at random in each of the regions where the programs were conducted. The sampling began with a national stratified random sample of fifty municipalities, as the PC program operated nation-wide, and GAD operated in all areas except for Santo Domingo, the country's capital. Individuals were selected for inclusion in the sample in proportion to the population of the selected municipality. This control sample was then supplemented with an oversample of individuals in La Vega, where the Radio Santa Maria program operated, and an oversample of women in the four areas where ADOPEM conducted its training. The number of individuals interviewed for the control groups was 1017. Table 10.5, in Appendix A, summarizes the participant and control samples for each of the four Dominican programs.

The in-country survey was conducted by the *Instituto de Estudios de Población y Desarrollo* (IEPD), the statistical office affiliated with PROFAMILIA. Data were collected from February to April 1998. The response rate for the survey was an excellent 90.5 percent, with 98 percent response for the participant sample and 83.7 percent response for the control group. Due to the lack of appropriate Census-type data, it is impossible to assess definitively the representativeness of the sample, but the age, educational level, and marital status of our control sample closely resemble the levels seen in the 1993 DEMOS survey conducted on behalf of USAID, which at the time represented the last official survey of political values of the Dominican Republic population before the current study.

South Africa

The South African study included three programs that conducted civic education among black and coloured adults. The first was run by the National Institute for Public Interest Law and Research (NIPILAR). NIPILAR is the lead organization of an NGO consortium operating in the fields of rights education and public interest law. One of the main civic education programs conducted by *NIPILAR* during the period under study was its Women's Rights program, designed to promote awareness of the United Nations Women and Children's Rights Convention. One of the main civic education programs conducted by NIPILAR over the past several years was its Women's Rights program, designed to promote awareness of the United Nations Women and Children's Rights Convention.

The second program was operated through the Community Law Centre-Durban (CLC). CLC is part of the Consortium described above, and thus has many of the same goals and activities as NIPILAR. CLC, however, operates almost exclusively within the province of KwaZulu Natal, where NIPILAR does not operate. Its primary activities are to coordinate approximately thirty rural legal advice offices in the province. The advice offices provide assistance to community members on legal and human rights issues. Democracy and civic education workshops are also conducted through the advice centers.

The third South Africa program was conducted by Lawyers for Human Rights (LHR). LHR is a national organization aiming to increase the awareness of human and democratic rights in South Africa. The organization holds an extensive series of workshops yearly on democracy and human rights issues, with different aspects of democracy receiving particular emphasis in different years. Workshops in the last two years have emphasized the Constitution and the Bill of Rights, and participation in politics, respectively.

The first two groups were selected primarily because of the support that USAID-South Africa has provided for their civic education efforts. LHR was included in the study in order to examine a non-USAID-funded group, and because it is a well-known NGO promoting democracy and human rights in South Africa. LHR also conducted civic education in eight of the nine provinces of South Africa; NIPILAR was also more or less national in focus, while CLC-Durban's area of operation was mainly within one province, KwaZulu Natal.

The three NGOS operate in generally similar fashion with regard to their civic education activities. Representatives from the central offices train a core group of individuals, called "paralegals," in democracy and human rights instruction. These activities, generally known as Training of Trainers (ToT), consume a considerable amount of the group's time and resources. The paralegals then go on to operate offices in villages and towns across country, from which they provide a number of services for individual residents. Some of these services have nothing to do with civic education, for example providing advice on economic development or labor law. However, the paralegals are also expected to conduct community workshops on different aspects of democratic governance and human rights, and these activities are the focus of our study. According to interviews with the groups' staff conducted by members of our research team, the number of workshops throughout the country are claimed to be in the hundreds yearly by LHR and NIPILAR, reaching many thousands of ordinary citizens.

As in the Dominican Republic, the treatment group interviews were obtained through sampling lists of civic education participants provided by the three NGOs (either national representatives or the facilitators or paralegals who ran the civic education programs in each of the areas). Participants were selected systematically from the lists whenever addresses and contact information was provided. In regions where no lists of names and addresses existed, the facilitators or paralegals themselves located the requisite number of participants and provided contact information to the South African survey organization, Markinor, which collected the data. The sample of participants is shown in Appendix A, Table 10.6.

The control group of non-participants in South Africa was designed slightly differently than in the Dominican Republic. Instead of aiming to produce a random sample of the South African black or coloured population, we attempted to introduce more rigorous experimental control at the outset by "mirroring" the participant sample on a number of important demographic dimensions. Interviewers were instructed to conduct an interview with a civic education participant selected according to the procedures just described, and then to conduct an identical interview in the same area with a person who had not participated in civic education. The control group respondent was to be the same race, gender, and age group as the participant. Interviewers were instructed to make a systematic selection of houses, beginning with the third house from the civic education participant who had been interviewed, in order to find an appropriate non-participant for inclusion.

These sampling procedures produced a total of 1550 interviews for the study, with the final data collection conducted between 10 May and 1 June 1999. The questionnaires were translated into Zulu, Xhosa, Tswana, Northern Sotho, Southern Sotho, and Afrikaans so that respondents could be interviewed in the language with which they felt most comfortable. The result was a final sample of 475 adult participants in civic education and 475 adult non-participants who were matched on race, gender, and age. Ten individuals from the treatment group were eliminated from the analysis because it became unclear in the course of the interview how many workshops they had attended, or whether they had been exposed to civic education "treatment" at all.

Measurement of the Dependent Variable: Political Tolerance

The studies followed the basic GSS format for tolerance questions (as opposed to Sullivan's "least-liked" group method) by testing the respondent's willingness to extend freedoms of association, participation, and speech to individuals from different political groups designated by the researcher. The groups in the Dominican Republic were atheists, communists, and militarists ("those who would suspend elections and install the military into power"), while the groups in South Africa were atheists, racists ("those who assert that blacks are genetically inferior"), and sexists ("those who believe that women are genetically inferior"). The "sexist" group has not regularly been part of the standard tolerance repertoire, but was included in South Africa because of the focus on NIPILAR's gender awareness program.

For each group, respondents were asked whether such a person should be allowed to speak publicly in your locality, to vote, and to organize peaceful demonstrations to express his/her point of view. Answers to all questions were on a four-point agree/disagree scale, and an overall scale was created by averaging the responses. In the Dominican Republic, the nine items generated a well-defined scale of tolerance, with the reliability (alpha) being .78. In South Africa, factor analysis of the tolerance items showed that the questions regarding "voting" comprised a separate dimension from tolerance for speaking in public and organizing a peaceful demonstration. I therefore created a tolerance scale from the six non-voting questions (two questions for the three unpopular groups) by averaging the six scores. The reliability of the resulting scale was high (alpha=.87).

Independent Variables

A series of independent variables were included as predictors of political tolerance aside from the individual's experience with civic education. Unfortunately, the surveys did not include direct questions related to either personal dogmatism or perceived threat of the target groups, two factors that have been shown to be strongly associated with tolerance in previous literature.[29] As partial surrogates for these variables, I used questions related to *openness to compromise* and *support for paternalism (authoritarian leaders)* in the Dominican Republic, and questions related to *openness to other cultures* and *affect for racial out-groups* in South Africa. More details on these questions can be found in Appendix A.

I also included variables that measured other democratic orientations aside from tolerance, including factual *political knowledge*, *political efficacy*, and *support for the value of liberty*.[30] Evaluations pertaining to the current *economic* situation were included in both countries, and in South Africa additional items were included that related to assessments of the *political performance* of the incumbent authorities, and the individual's *satisfaction with political freedoms* in the current system. Details on these questions can also be found in the Appendix.

I also included a series of demographic and political control variables, including educational attainment, age, income, gender, race, size of community, religiosity (church attendance), political ideology, interest, media exposure, and the number of voluntary organizations to which the individual belongs. Details on these items are also found in the Appendix.

Statistical Methods

After presenting the simple bivariate relationships, I estimate several models that attempt to isolate the effect of civic education on political tolerance, controlling for other known determinants of tolerance, as well as controlling for the selection biases that are inherent in the civic education programs examined in the two countries. The fundamental problem in assessing the effect of civic education on tolerance or other democratic orientations is that, in the absence of a pre-test and/or randomized assignment of individuals to civic education "treatments," we cannot rule out with absolute certainty the possibility that individuals who were trained in civic education workshops already possessed those attributes that correlate with tolerance, or that pre-disposed them to developing greater levels of tolerance in the absence of any "treatment" whatsoever. Indeed those attributes, such as education, group memberships, political interest, and the like, are exactly the factors that may lead individuals to attend civic education workshops in the first place. Thus any observed difference between civic education participants and the control group on tolerance may be due to the pre-existing differences on these other variables.

The most basic approach for dealing with these selection biases is to include all other variables that are known to be related to both civic education exposure and political tolerance into the statistical model. These variables are entered along with the treatment variables in an OLS multiple regression analysis, or through analysis of covariance methods, which estimate the mean difference in tolerance for the treatment and control groups, after taking into account the differences between the two groups' mean values on the control variables, and the estimated effect of the control variables on tolerance. Thus the treatment effect in these models represents the estimate of how much civic education affects tolerance, over and above the effects of all the observed control variables. I present these estimates below under the label "Regression Model—OLS."

As many scholars have shown, however, the OLS approach fails to account for an additional, and potentially important, source of bias in the estimation of treatment effects. As Achen, Barnow et al., Heckman and Robb, and others suggest, there may be differences between the treatment and control group on relevant *unmeasured* variables that influence both the decision to attend a treatment program as well as the program's desired outcome.[31] For example, individuals who decide to attend civic education workshops may differ from other individuals not only in terms of observed characteristics such as group memberships, educational attainment, and political interest, but also in terms of unobserved variables such as their intrinsic predisposition toward democracy, their motivation to succeed in a democratic society, their need for sociability, and the like. If these factors related to self-selection are also positively (or negatively) related to political tolerance, then estimates of the treatment effect of civic education will be biased, as the estimated regression coefficient for attending civic education would include some of the effect of these unmeasured variables as well.

More technically, the problem exists because of the potential for a correlation between the error terms in the *selection equation* (i.e. the decision to attend a civic education workshop) and the *outcome equation* (the prediction of political tolerance), due to unmeasured factors or to random perturbations that influence both the decision to participate and the outcome in question.[32] To correct this problem, which biases estimates of coefficients in the outcome equation,

Heckman has proposed the following two-step procedure,[33] also discussed at length in Greene, Vella, and Winship and Morgan.[34]

In the first step, the decision to participate in the treatment program is modeled via probit analysis, with individuals who were exposed to the treatment **T** coded as "1" and the control group coded as "0." Thus

$$(1) \; T_i = \gamma_k \, \mathbf{w}_i + \upsilon_i$$

where the **w** represent all independent variables that predict whether individuals attend civic education workshops or not, the γ_k are their respective regression coefficients, and the υ_i are assumed to be normally distributed. The "generalized probit residuals"[35] from this equation are then calculated as

$$(2) \; \lambda_i = \phi(\gamma_k \, \mathbf{w}_i)/\Phi(\gamma_k \, \mathbf{w}_i)$$

for the civic education participants (**T** = 1) and

$$(3) \; \lambda_i = -\phi(\gamma_k \, \mathbf{w}_i)/(1 - \Phi(\gamma_k \, \mathbf{w}_i))$$

for the control group (**T** = 0) , where $\phi(\gamma_k \, \mathbf{w}_i)$ represents the height of the normal distribution (the probability density) at the point $\gamma_k \, \mathbf{w}_i$, and $\Phi(\gamma_k \, \mathbf{w}_i)$ represents the cumulative probability at the same point.[36]

The second step in the process is to use those residualized estimates as an additional independent variable in the outcome equation, as in:

$$(4) \; y_i = \beta_k \mathbf{x}_i + \beta_t T + \beta_\lambda \lambda_i + \varepsilon_i$$

where the **x** represent all independent variables that affect the outcome in question, **T** represents the treatment, and the β are respective regression coefficients.[37] It can then be shown that the regression coefficient for the generalized residual term, β_λ, is an estimate of *Rho* (ρ), the correlation between the errors in the selection and outcome equations, multiplied by the outcome equation's standard error of estimate ($\rho\sigma_\varepsilon$). Alternatively, the regression coefficients for the selection and outcome equations, *Rho* and σ_ε can all be estimated simultaneously (and more efficiently) though maximum likelihood methods.[38] If *Rho* is positive, this means that, other things being equal, the estimated "true" effect of civic education on tolerance will be smaller than in an OLS formulation.[39] If *Rho* is negative, the estimate of the "true" effect of civic education on tolerance will be correspondingly larger than the estimated obtained in OLS. If *Rho* is statistically indistinguishable from zero, then the unmeasured factors that lead individuals to participate in civic education programs, over and above the variables that are included in the participation equation, are irrelevant for the prediction of political tolerance. In that case the results from what I will refer to as the "Self-Selection Model" and the OLS regression model will be substantively equivalent. The models were estimated using LIMDEP 7.0.

Table 10.1: Tolerance by Frequency of Civic Education—Dominican Republic and South Africa

	Control Group[a]	Civic Education: 1-2x[a]	Civic Education: 3x or more[a]	Strength of Association[b]
Dominican Republic				
Would allow an **atheist** to. . .				
Speak in Public	42.9	46.5	52.4	.14**
Vote	52.4	61.5	62.7	.17**
Organize a Peaceful Demonstration	52.5	52.7	60.0	.10**
Would allow a **militarist** to. . .				
Speak in Public	39.3	37.6	43.4	.05
Vote	41.0	33.8	46.5	.09*
Organize a Peaceful Demonstration	48.6	47.0	54.5	.08*
Would allow a **communist** to. . .				
Speak in Public	51.0	52.7	68.9	.28**
Vote	58.5	59.7	75.0	.24**
Organize a Peaceful Demonstration	54.9	58.6	68.4	.28**
Tolerance Scale Score	2.43[c]	2.50[c]	2.70[c]	.16**[d]
Number of Cases	1019	407	611	
South Africa				
Would allow an **atheist** to. . .				
Speak in Public	38.0	37.7	45.3	.04*
Organize a Peaceful Demonstration	43.9	42.2	52.0	.05*
Would allow a **racist** to. . .				
Speak in Public	32.7	38.8	47.4	.18**
Organize a Peaceful Demonstration	41.9	40.3	50.8	.06**
Would allow a **sexist** to. . .				
Speak in Public	41.1	37.7	44.5	.00
Organize a Peaceful Demonstration	39.6	40.3	52.0	.11**
Tolerance Scale Score	2.28[c]	2.29[c]	2.50[c]	.09**[d]
Number of Cases	475	331	134	

Notes
[a] Column entries are percent "Agreeing" or "Strongly Agreeing" with tolerant statement
[b] Column entries are gamma coefficients unless otherwise noted **p<.05 *p,.10
[c] Rox entries are scale means (1+least tolerant, 4+most tolerant)
[d] Cell entry is eta coefficient

Results

Bivariate Findings

The first step in assessing the effect of civic education's effects on tolerance in the Dominican Republic and South Africa is simply to compare the responses for civic education participants with the control group in both countries. Table 10.1 displays the simple percentage differences in tolerant responses between individuals who were exposed to varying amounts of civic education. The percentages for individuals who received no civic education (the control group) are displayed in the first column of results, followed by the percentages for individuals who attended only one or two civic education sessions, and then percentages for those who attended civic education more frequently. A "tolerant" response was indicated when individuals "strongly agreed" or "agreed" that an atheist, militarist, communist, racist, or sexist should be allowed to speak in public or organize peaceful demonstrations. As discussed earlier, the "vote" questions were not included in the South African tolerance scale, and hence only the Dominican Republic results for those questions are reported here.

As can be seen in the top half of Table 10.1, the raw differences between tolerant responses for the three civic education groups are moderate in magnitude in the Dominican Republic. Differences of approximately ten percentage points exist between the tolerant responses of the control group and those with the highest frequency of exposure to civic education. The largest differences are provoked by questions related to communists (fourteen to eighteen percentage points), with smaller differences on responses towards atheists (eight to ten points) and militarists (four to seven points). The gamma statistic in the last column confirms that there is a relatively large association between civic education exposure and tolerance toward communists, with associations of smaller magnitude between civic education and tolerance towards militarists and atheists. Individuals in the frequent civic education group are significantly more tolerant on the overall scale than individuals in the control group (2.70 versus 2.43), with a corresponding Eta value of .16.

The bottom half of the table shows that civic education significantly influences tolerance in South Africa as well, though the patterns are less pronounced than in the Dominican Republic. The differences between the control group and those exposed frequently to civic education varies from four percentage points (allowing a sexist to speak) to fourteen percentage points (allowing a racist to speak), with the overall average difference being about nine points. There are few remarkable differences in the tolerance accorded atheists as opposed to racists or sexists, nor does tolerance depend on whether the question concerns speaking in public or organizing peaceful demonstrations. The gammas in South

Africa, ranging from zero to .18, confirm the slightly smaller differences between the civic education groups than in the Dominican Republic.

Interestingly, the results from both countries show that there is very little difference in the tolerant responses between individuals in the control group and individuals who attended only one or two civic education workshops. That is, differences in tolerance emerge only between the control group and individuals who attended three or more civic education sessions. This pattern is confirmed through further analysis, as simple t-tests between the control group and the infrequent civic education group show few significant differences. This provides initial support for our hypothesis earlier that there may be *threshold effects* for civic education on political tolerance: attending one or two workshops may simply not be enough to effect value change, and repeated exposures to democratic civic instruction may be necessary for any effect whatsoever to occur.

The threshold pattern seen for the Dominican Republic, whereby infrequent exposure to civic education has little effect on tolerance responses, is even more pronounced in South Africa. On most items, there is absolutely no difference between the control group and those who attended only one or two civic education workshops. This pattern was confirmed in further analyses: simple t-tests of the differences between the control group and *all* civic education recipients in South Africa show no statistically significant results, and the simple correlations (a linear measure) between the number of workshops the individual attended and tolerant responses similarly showed few significant relationships. Similarly, the overall tolerance scale mean is nearly identical for the control group (2.28) and the infrequent exposure group (2.29). This figure rises to 2.50 for those in the highest exposure group. Thus there is strong preliminary support for the notion that civic education can have some effect on tolerance in both the Dominican Republic and South Africa, but that effects are seen only after individuals are exposed repeatedly to democratic messages.

Multivariate Analysis and Controls for Selection Effects

Tables 10.2 and 10.3 present the results of multivariate analysis of the effects of political tolerance in the Dominican Republic and South Africa, respectively. In order to allow for the possibility of threshold effects, as suggested in Table 10.1, two dummy variables were constructed to signify whether the respondent had attended one or two civic education workshops, or three or more sessions. In model (1) in both tables, the effects of these civic education dummies are shown, controlling for a series of demographic, psychological, and political variables that may relate to both political tolerance and to the likelihood of exposure to civic education. Model (2) displays the effects of the same independent variables in the context of the self-selection model, which introduces an added control for unobserved factors that may influence both the probability of exposure to civic education and political tolerance.

Table 10.2: The Effect of Civic Education on Political Tolerance—Dominican Republic

	Regression Model—OLS			Self-Selection Model	
	B	**S.E.**	**Beta**	**B**	**S.E.**
Frequency of Civic Education					
One or Two Sessions	.02	.05	.01	.02	.05
Three or More Sessions	.11**	.04	.06	.11**	.04
Dem. Values and Civic Competence					
Support for Liberty	-.01	.02	-.02	-.01	.02
Political Efficacy	.13**	.02	.12	.13**	.02
Political Knowledge	.02	.02	.04	.02	.02
Economic Evaluations					
Low Concern about Economy	.01	.07	-.01	.01	.08
Psychological Predispositions					
Open to Compromise	.15**	.02	.13	.15**	.02
Low Paternalism	.001	.001	.04	.001	.001
Demographic and Political Controls					
Age	.09	.06	.14	.10	.07
Age Squared	-.01	.01	-.12	-.01	.01
Black Respondent	.05	.04	.03	.06	.04
White Respondent	.08*	.05	.03	.08*	.05
Gender (1=Male)	-.04	.04	-.03	-.04	.04
Education	.08**	.01	.17	.08**	.01
Income	.01	.02	.01	.01	.02
Church Attendance	-.02**	.01	-.04	-.02**	.01
Santo Domingo Resident	.13**	.05	.07	.13**	.05
Other Urban District	.09**	.04	.06	.09**	.04
Group memberships	.05	.13	.01	.04	.14
Political Ideology (Right-wing)	-.04**	.01	-.06	-.04**	.01
Political Interest	-.03	.02	-.03	-.03	.02
Media Use	.06**	.02	.08	.06**	.02
Rho	----	----		-.03	.06
Constant	1.44**	.24		1.45**	.24
R-Squared	.18			.18	
Standard Error of Estimate	.69			.69	
N=2037 (both Models)					

The results of these analyses indicate that civic education has significant effects on political tolerance in both countries, controlling for other variables and controlling for potential biases due to self-selection into the civic education "treatment." But as in Table 10.1, these effects exist *only when individuals are exposed to three or more civic education sessions.* In model (1) in Table 10.1, it can be seen that individuals who were exposed to only one or two sessions in the Dominican Republic were no more likely to report tolerant responses than the control group, once other variables in the model are taken into account. By contrast, individuals who attended three or more sessions were, on average, .11 units higher on the tolerance scale than individuals who received no civic education.

Table 10.3: The Effect of Civic Education on Political Tolerance—South Africa

	Regression Model—OLS			Self-Selection Model	
	B	**S.E.**	**Beta**	**B**	**S.E.**
Frequency of Civic Education					
One or Two Workshops	.03	.06	.02	.04	.06
Three or More Workshops	.17**	.07	.07	.15*	.08
Dem. Values and Civic Competence					
Support for Liberty	.09**	.02	.10	.10**	.03
Political Efficacy	.06	.04	.05	.06	.04
Political Knowledge	.07**	.03	.09	.07**	.03
Economic Evaluations					
Perceived Government Performance	-.06	.04	-.05	-.05	.04
Perceived Personal Economic Situation	-.01	.03	-.01	-.01	.03
Perceived National Economic Situation	-.05	.03	-.06	-.04	.03
Psychological Predispositions					
Open to Other Cultures	.11**	.06	.06	.11*	.06
Positive Affect towards Racial Out-groups	.01	.01	.01	.01	.01
Demographic and Political Controls					
Age	.19**	.11	.26	.19*	.11
Age Squared	-.03	.02	-.23	-.03	.02
Race (1=Colored)	.46**	.09	.17	.45**	.11
Gender (1=Male)	.02	.06	.01	.03	.06
Education	.03	.03	.05	.03	.03
Income	-.05	.03	-.01	-.01	-.03
Church Attendance	.01	.02	.01	.01	.03
City Resident	.04	.07	.02	.03	.07
Group memberships	-.21*	.13	-.06	-.24*	.14
Political Interest	-.05	.04	-.04	-.05	-.05
Media Use	.04	.05	.04	.04	.05
Rho				-.29**	.14
Constant	2.02	.28		2.19	.31
R-Squared	.08			.08	
Standard Error of Estimate	.82			.84	
N=940 (both Models)					

The effect of civic education on tolerance can also be expressed in terms of the "effect coefficient" or Cohen's "d," commonly used in experimental and quasi-experimental research.[40] In the multiple regression context, d is equal to the unstandardized regression coefficient divided by the standard error of estimate, which conveys a sense of how much of an effect a treatment has *in (adjusted) standard deviation terms* on the dependent variable, once the effects of all other control variables are taken into account. Thus the .11 coefficient for the effect of civic education indicates that a three or more session "treatment" of civic education in the Dominican Republic is associated with a .16 (.11 divided by .69) standard deviation increase in tolerance.

Model (1) also shows significant effects from many variables found in previous research to influence tolerance as well, notably educational attainment, urban residence, ideology, religiosity, media exposure, and psychological openness to compromise. As many of these variables are also associated with the probability of exposure to civic education, it is evident that some of the initial difference in tolerance between civic education groups observed in Table 10.1 was attributable to the background characteristics of civic education participants rather than the programs themselves. Substantively, the effect coefficient of .16 (and the standardized coefficient of .06) ranks civic education exposure at approximately the same magnitude of importance as urban compared to rural residence, or moving from center-left to right wing in political ideology. This is evidence of a relatively small but substantively meaningful effect of civics instruction on Dominicans' level of political tolerance.[41]

The significant effect of multiple exposures to civic education also persists after controlling for potential biases due to self-selection in Model (2). As discussed above, the first stage in the self-selection process is to model explicitly the decision to attend civic education workshops, and to produce an estimated residual from this equation for both civic education participants and the control group which is introduced into the model predicting political tolerance. In Appendix B, Table 10.7, I show the results of the probit model predicting civic education participation, indicating that a series of demographic (age, race, education, gender, employment status, rural residence) and political factors (interest, group memberships, prior voting behavior, media exposure) are associated with civic education participation. But as can be seen in Model (2) in Table 10.2, the estimate of *Rho*, the correlation between the error terms in the civic education treatment and tolerance equations, is insignificant, indicating that there is no residual correlation between treatment and tolerance once the observed variables are taken into account. For this reason the estimated coefficients in the multiple regression model (1) and the self-selection model (2) are nearly identical.

Table 10.3 shows similar outcomes for the South African sample. Model (1) shows that, controlling for a series of demographic and political factors, the effect of civic education remains significant, and follows the same threshold pattern seen in model (1) in the Dominican Republic. There are no differences in tolerance between the control group and individuals who attended only one or two workshops, whereas individuals who were exposed to civics workshops more frequently showed significant increases in tolerance over the control group. The average tolerance score for individuals who attended three or more workshops was .17 units higher than the score for individuals in the control group, controlling for all other variables in the model. This translates into an effect coefficient of .24, meaning that a three workshop "treatment" of civic education is associated with a nearly one-quarter (adjusted) standard deviation change in political tolerance. This is an even larger net effect than seen in the Dominican Republic, and one of the largest effects in the South African model overall.

The self-selection model (2) in the table shows a similar set of results, as civic education has a significant effect on tolerance, provided the individual attends at least three workshops. The model also shows an interesting kind of selection bias that was not captured in model (1): individuals who selected themselves into civic education workshops were *less* likely to be tolerant, controlling for the observed factors that relate to both civic education participation and tolerance. This can be seen from the significant coefficient estimate of -.29 for *Rho*, the correlation between the error terms of the selection and outcome equations.

Substantively, this result may appear at first to be puzzling, as the more obvious hypothesis is that individuals who were already predisposed toward tolerance (i.e., more "democratically-oriented") would choose to participate in civic education workshops. A closer examination of the selection process, however, shows that civic education in South Africa appears to attract individuals who possess attributes that predispose them toward *intolerance*. Appendix B presents evidence that poorer and less well-educated respondents are more likely to attend civic education workshops, and individuals who have less positive affect toward racial out-groups are more likely to attend as well. At the same time, individuals who are politically interested and active in secondary groups are also more likely to be exposed to civic education. Yet, as Table 10.3 shows, political interest and secondary group memberships are *negatively* related to tolerance, with the effect of group memberships being statistically significant. This indicates that civic education is attracting individuals who generally possess characteristics that are negatively related to tolerance in the South African context, and the negative value for *Rho* in the self-selection model suggests that unmeasured factors in the selection process also reinforce this tendency. The effect is not large enough to produce important substantive differences between the OLS and self-selection models; nevertheless it shows that predispositions to tolerance are not necessarily higher among the types of individuals who are more frequent participants in democracy training sessions, and this makes successful civic education that much more difficult to achieve in the South African context.

The "Persuasability" of Tolerance: The Role of Individual Awareness, Values, and Attitudes

According to the theories of attitude change discussed previously, persuasion is most likely to occur under certain conditions related to the frequency and nature of the individual's exposure to pro-tolerance messages, and conditions related to attitudes and prior attitudes of the individual. The results thus far reinforce the conditional relationship between civic education and political tolerance. Civic education's influence on tolerance depends on the frequency of exposure to tolerance messages; three or more sessions are necessary for any effect of civic education to occur.

I also hypothesized that, aside from the frequency of exposure and the nature of the methodologies utilized in the civic education instruction, certain attributes of the individual would condition the likelihood of attitude change. Specifically, individuals require some cognitive sophistication, political awareness, and interest in order to understand tolerance messages at all. Further, individuals who are less psychologically dogmatic, and those who are more supportive of democratic values in general, will be more likely to accept tolerance messages in civic education than individuals who are more close-minded and anti-democratic to begin with. Finally, the more immediate influence of economic and political performance evaluations should also condition the extent of attitude change, as individuals will be more likely to accept democratic messages to the extent that they perceive the democratic system to be delivering important economic and political goods.

I test the hypotheses for democratic orientations and performance evaluations by dividing the sample in each country into separate groups corresponding to "high" and "low" values on each of these variables and re-estimating a model predicting tolerance from all significant variables from Tables 10.2 and 10.3. In South Africa I included an additional performance variable, assessing the extent to which individuals report that they are satisfied with the political freedoms that they have now compared with the apartheid system.[42] Thus three different performance measures were available for the South African analysis, measuring economic performance, the actions of the incumbent authorities in handling important problems, and the performance of the system as a whole in guaranteeing individual political freedoms. Unfortunately only one performance measure regarding the economy was available for use in the Dominican Republic data set.

In both countries I use education as a surrogate for the individual's level of prior political awareness, though the results are identical if I substitute factual political knowledge instead. For both education and political interest, I divided the sample into three categories in order to test the potential for a non-monotonic relationship between political awareness and change in tolerance, as predicted by the reception-acceptance model of attitude change discussed above.[43] I divide the sample into those who did not graduate from high school, those who graduated high school, and those who have some additional education beyond the high school degree. For political interest, I chose cutpoints that divided the sample nearly into thirds. I show the results of all of these analyses in Table 10.4, including the unstandardized coefficient for the effect of attending "three or more" workshops or civic education sessions for each subgroup, as well as the corresponding effect coefficient, Cohen's *d*. Because the OLS and self-selection models yielded nearly identical results in the earlier analyses, I use OLS regression to estimate these models.

Table 10.4: The Effects of Civic Education by Awareness, Psychological Predispositions, and Perceptions of Economic and Political Performance

	Dominican Republic		South Africa	
	Unstandardized[a]	Effect Coefficient (*d*)	Unstandardized[a]	Effect Coefficient (*d*)
Education				
No High School	.04	.06	.13	.17
High School	.18**	.25	.21	.25
Beyond High School	.12	.18	.10	.11
Political Interest				
Low	.05	.08	-.24	-.20
Medium	.17**	.24	.17	.22
High	.03	.04	.39**	.43
Openness to Compromise (DR)/				
Other Cultures (SA)				
Low	.08	.11	.03	.04
High	.15**	.23	.21*	.25
Political Efficacy				
Low	.05	.07	.13	.16
High	.13**	.19	.20**	.24
Support for Liberty				
Low	.04	.05	.21	.25
High	.15**	.23	.10	.12
Economic Perceptions				
Poor	.09**	.13	.10	.12
Good	.36**	.55	.20*	.25
Government Performance				
Poor	----		.09	.11
Good	----		.21*	.25
Satisfaction with Freedoms				
Low	----		.05	.06
High	----		.17*	.20

Note: [a] Column entries are unstandardized OLS regression coefficients *p<.10 **p<.05

The results reflect slightly different patterns for the Dominican Republic and South Africa, but demonstrate clear support for the conditional attitude change hypotheses. The tests for education and interest are shown in the top rows of Table 10.4. In both the Dominican Republic and South Africa, there is no effect of civic education among individuals with low levels of education or political interest. Regardless of how often the individual is exposed to civic education, without a certain level of prior awareness, ability, or motivation to accept democratic messages, no change in tolerance is likely to occur. In both countries, moreover, the effects of civic education are concentrated among individuals at medium levels of education, with smaller effects among those who have more than a high school education. This indicates that attitude change conforms exactly to the non-monotonic relationship with awareness postulated by the reception-acceptance model; at high levels of education, individuals are more likely to resist accepting messages than individuals with moderate levels of prior information.

This non-monotonic pattern, however, emerges for political interest only in the Dominican Republic. In South Africa, civic education exerts a steadily increasing effect on tolerance as individuals become more interested in politics; the effect of civic education on tolerance among highly interested South Africans is nearly double the overall effect in the sample, reaching a relatively large d value of .43. There is no clear explanation for the difference in South Africa from the Dominican Republic, though it is the case that, due to the nature of the programs that were included in the study, there are more political elites among highly interested Dominicans who received civic education than there are than among the treatment group of highly interested South Africans. Thus in the Dominican Republic there may have been more individuals at high levels of interest whose tolerance judgments were relatively fixed.

There is also substantial evidence in Table 10.4 for the importance of prior democratic dispositions in facilitating the individual's acceptance of tolerance messages. Individuals who were more open to compromise in the Dominican Republic were more likely to be influenced by civic education than others; similarly in South Africa, individuals who were more open to other cultures showed substantially greater effects from civic education than more ethnocentric individuals. The effects of political efficacy are nearly identical, as are the effects for support for liberty in the Dominican Republic. In all of these cases, three or more exposures to civic education affected individuals who were more democratically inclined than individuals whose predispositions were less democratically oriented. The sole piece of evidence disconfirming the predisposing effects of prior orientations regards the value of liberty in South Africa, where the effects were more concentrated on individuals with less supportive democratic attitudes.

For the performance evaluations in the last three rows of Table 10.4, the results are clear and unequivocal: civic education has much stronger effects among individuals with more positive evaluations of the economy, the performance of incumbents, and the political system. Among the (few) Dominican Republic respondents who are less concerned about inflation and unemployment, the effect of civic education is four times greater than when economic evaluations are more negative. Among these favorably-disposed individuals, three exposures to civic education brings about a .55 standard deviation change in tolerance, the largest single effect in the study. The corresponding value is .25 in South Africa, and reaches approximately that level for individuals who rate the government's performance highly on handling important problems, and among those more satisfied with the level of political freedom in the country. Individuals with negative performance evaluations, by contrast, show much weaker effects from civic education, with *d* values ranging from .06 to .12. This is strong evidence that individuals are likely to accept pro-tolerance messages when they perceive the system as delivering on important economic and political goods.

Interestingly, these same variables did not exert a *direct* effect on tolerance in either the Dominican Republic or South Africa in earlier analyses. That is, tolerance does not depend directly on the individual's evaluations of economic and political performance. What the results in Table 10.4 suggest, instead, is that individuals with higher evaluations of the actual performance of a democratic system are more receptive to internalizing new messages about the values that inhere in that system. When such individuals are exposed to tolerance messages, they are able to relate those messages to other favorable associations with democratic institutions or incumbents, and hence more likely to integrate the value of tolerance into their otherwise favorable evaluation of the democratic system. This, of course, is not necessarily an unconditionally positive result for democratic development, as the facilitative effect of *positive* performance means that the system must deliver on important political and economic goods in order for civic education to "work"; in the very common situation of a newly-emerging democracy that is struggling to generate favorable economic and political outputs, civic education is likely to have less success at instilling democratic values.

Conclusion

This study of the impact of adult civic education on political tolerance in two developing democracies, the Dominican Republic and South Africa, showed that democracy training significantly affected tolerance judgments in both countries. This effect remained significant in multivariate models, and in models that attempted to control for the self-selection processes that are inherent in the implementation of civic education programs. Equally important, the effects of civic education on tolerance in both countries were conditional, depending on the levels of other variables in ways that are consistent with predictions from theories of attitude change and political persuasion. Differences in tolerance judgments between the civic education participants and non-participants were greatest when individuals were exposed to frequent training, Civic education also had a greater influence on tolerance among individuals with sufficient cognitive skills and prior political awareness to understand and contextualize tolerance messages, and among those whose prior values and personal dispositions, such as political efficacy and openness to compromise, were more favorable towards democracy. Finally, individuals with higher evaluations of the current economic and political performance of the system were more likely to accept tolerance messages as well; such individuals appeared to link messages concerning the values inherent in democracy with other positive associations about the political system. In short, tolerance can be taught through civic education in newly-democratizing societies, but the learning takes place only under certain conditions for certain kinds of individuals.

The findings have important theoretical implications for our understanding of the development of tolerance and democratic political culture, as well as practical implications for the implementation of civic education programs in emerging democracies. First, they lend additional credence to the growing claim that democratic values can change significantly in response to short-term stimuli. As suggested by the "lifetime learning model," democratic orientations—even those thought by many to be relatively impervious to change— may be altered under the right conditions.[44] Within the category of short-term influences on tolerance, in fact, exposure to civic education was found in both the Dominican Republic and South Africa to have a more sizeable *direct* effect than economic judgments or perceptions of current political performance. The findings thus provide an interesting twist to Dalton's assertion in the East German context that "democratic norms are not learned through formal education and indoctrination but through experience with the democratic process."[45] Civic education, perhaps by mixing "formal indoctrination" with direct experience with the new democratic regime, has the potential to effect short-term change in even "difficult" democratic norms like tolerance.

At the same time, the conditional nature of the effects of civic education suggests that important limits still exist on the amount of change that is possible in the short term. Not only must individuals be somewhat predisposed towards democratic values in order for civic education to effect changes in tolerance, they must also possess sufficient cognitive skills and political information to understand tolerance messages and associate them with their predispositions. The pool of individuals who are most susceptible to change—those who are moderate to highly aware and equipped with favorable personality and attitudinal attributes—is likely to be relatively small in many contexts.

Moreover, the facilitative effects of immediate economic and political performance evaluations also mean that civic education's influence on tolerance is contingent to a considerable degree on the achievements of new democratic systems. Civic education may not always succeed in promoting unconditional or intrinsic support for democratic norms. Put another way, the interaction effects between civic education, tolerance, and performance evaluations observed here imply that civic education acts to "prime" the role of performance judgments on tolerance. Among individuals who did not experience civic education, perform-

ance ratings are irrelevant for political tolerance while such evaluations exert a
more substantial effect on tolerance among those exposed to multiple civic education treatments. Civic education, whether intentionally or not, appears to be
promoting tolerance judgments that are more "instrumentally-based," that is,
contingent on positive outcomes from the political system.

One finding that mitigates this worry, however, is the effect associated with
perceived freedoms seen in the South African data, where civic education served
to heighten the respondent's linkage between political liberties in the post-
apartheid era and the general value of tolerance. This increase in tolerance,
though "instrumentally-based" in the sense of being associated with the delivery
of a *political* good by the system, accords more with the spirit of civic education
as promoting democracy because of its provision of intrinsically desirable liberties and freedoms.[46] Further research is clearly needed to determine whether
these same kinds of effects are present for other democratic orientations and
values, and whether the "intrinsic" versus "instrumental" aspects of civic education can be more thoroughly disentangled.

The results regarding the frequency of civic education training also have
important practical consequences. I have shown that when individuals are
trained frequently *and* are trained with active, participatory methodologies,
changes in tolerance can be at least of moderate magnitude. But in most cases
only a small portion of individuals who receive civic education instruction are
exposed to these beneficial pedagogical conditions. For example, only one-third
of all civic education recipients in South Africa attended three or more workshops, meaning that two-thirds of the recipients did not cross the initial "threshold" for civic education effects to be seen. The more intensive programs in the
Dominican Republic were more clearly designed to deliver frequent exposure,
yet even in that context, just over half of civic education recipients were trained
three times or more times. The results thus illuminate the difference between the
potential effect of civic education on changing tolerance and the *actual* effects
witnessed in these democratizing contexts. The severe barriers to the implementation of civic education, ranging from financial constraints, logistical difficulties in reaching potential respondents, and political turmoil in certain areas, raise
serious issues for policy makers regarding the feasibility of utilizing civic education as part of a democratization program in many instances.[47]

Finally, the results shed additional light on the burgeoning literature on the
"persuasability of tolerance."[48] I have shown that a real-world example of attempted attitude change conforms with many of the same processes that have
been modeled in the laboratory or via combined survey and experimental methods. That is, tolerance judgments can be affected via persuasive argumentation
when the messages are understood and the individual is able to link them with
"collateral democratic values."[49] The list of collateral values, however, must be
expanded to include the individual's evaluation of the current performance of
the political system. Tolerance judgments in the real world do not necessarily

depend *directly* on such evaluations, but positive economic and political evaluations do facilitate the acceptance of tolerance messages in civic education. For better or worse, tolerance is more "persuadable" when it is in line with the individual's transitory judgments regarding the outcomes produced by the political system.

Appendix A—Measurement of Control Variables and Sample Information

Psychological Predispositions

Openness to Compromise (Dominican Republic only). Respondents were asked two questions, each measured on a four point agree-disagree scale: whether "it is dangerous to compromise with one's enemies," and "groups that tolerate differences of opinion tend not to survive long."

Support for Paternalism (Dominican Republic only). Respondents were asked two questions, each measured on a four point agree-disagree scale: "A good president should be like a father – someone to whom you should look to solve your problems," and "A president needs to maintain order and stability, even if it means ignoring or breaking some laws."

Openness to Other Cultures (South Africa only). Respondents were asked four questions regarding their views of other cultures, each measured on a four point agree-disagree scale, including "It is easy for you to like people who have different views to your own," and "you can usually accept people from other cultures, even when they are very different to you." The four questions were averaged to create a single scale.

Affect towards Racial Out-Groups (South Africa only). Respondents were asked whether they had a favorable or unfavorable opinion of "whites," "blacks," and "coloured" groups on a 0-10 scale. I averaged the favorability ratings for "whites" and "coloured" to create the out-group affect measure for black South Africans, and averaged the ratings for "whites" and "blacks" to create the measure for coloured respondents.

Democratic Orientations

Political Knowledge. In the Dominican Republic, I added the number of correct answers out of four questions concerning knowledge of incumbents and the electoral process (i.e., "When are the next presidential elections?" "Who is the mayor of this municipality?"). In South Africa I added the number of correct answers out of four questions concerning knowledge of the institutional structure of the government (i.e., "How long is the President's term in office?" "Who has the power to decide whether a law is constitutional?").

Political Efficacy. Respondents in the Dominican Republic were asked three questions on efficacy, all asking the respondent to agree or disagree on a four-point scale to a series of questions concerning their views of their influence on the political system. The three questions were: (1) Sometimes politics and government are so complicated that people like me can't understand what is going on; (2) People like me have no say in what the government does; and (3) There is no point in getting involved in politics because I would have no influence anyway. In South Africa, the first two questions were supplemented with: (1) I feel well prepared for participating in political life; and (2) If I wanted to discuss my political views, I would know where and how to contact elected officials.

Support for the Value of Liberty. Following Gibson et al. (1992), respondents were asked their support for the value of liberty versus social order on a four point agree-disagree scale with the following statement: "It is better to live in an orderly society than to allow people so much freedom that they can be disruptive."

Economic and Political Performance Evaluations

Perceptions of Economic Performance. In the Dominican Republic, there were no direct questions regarding economic performance. I created a surrogate by asking respondents the degree to which they were "concerned" with inflation and the cost of living and "concerned" with unemployment, reasoning that high levels of concern would likely be associated with more negative perceptions. In South Africa, the performance questions were more direct. Respondents were asked to rate their *personal* economic situation now and compared to what it was under apartheid on a 5-point scale. They were then asked the same questions regarding the *national* economy.

Perceptions of Government Performance (South Africa only). Respondents were asked to rate "how satisfied," on a four point scale, with "what the government is doing to prevent crime in your community," with "what the government is doing to improve healthcare in your community," and "with the quality of services, such as water and electricity, provided by the municipal government."

Satisfaction with Political Freedoms (South Africa only). Respondents were asked to "think about the amount of freedom that you now have, like freedom of

speech and freedom to join political groups," and to rate how much more freedom they had than they had under apartheid on a four point scale.

Demographic and other Control Variables

Education. Seven categories ranging from no education to profession training
beyond a university degree.

Age. Five categories, grouped from 18-24, 25-34,35-49,50-64, and 65 and older.

Income. Seven grouped categories in the Dominican Republic, fifteen grouped
categories in South Africa.

Church Attendance. Frequency of attending religious services on a 0-5 scale, 0
being "no religion" to 5 for "every day."

Dummy variables were created to signify: gender, race, urban residence, and
residence of Santo Domingo (the Dominican Republic's national capital).

Political Ideology (Dominican Republic only). Five-point self-placement question ranging from "left," "left-center," "center" "center-right" to "right." The
question was asked in South Africa but few respondents placed themselves on
the scale, and those that did placed themselves largely in the center.

Political Interest. In the Dominican Republic, I averaged two questions measuring local and national political interest on a four-point scale from "none" to
"much" interest. In South Africa, a question on interest in the "current election
campaign" was added, and in that country the response categories ranged from
"very little" to "a great deal" of interest on a three-point scale.

Media Exposure. In the Dominican Republic, I averaged two questions on a
four-point scale measuring the respondent's attentiveness to information about
politics on "television and radio" and then in "newspapers" ("never" to "every
day or almost every day"). In South Africa the radio and television questions
were separated, resulting in a three-question scale for attentiveness, with each
measured on the same four-point scale as in the Dominican Republic.

Table 10.5: Characteristics of Civic Education and Control Group Samples—Dominican Republic.

Location	Civic Education Program					Control Group
	Participación Ciudadana	GAD	ADOPEM	Radio Santa Maria (direct)[7]	Radio Santa Maria (indirect)	
National						
Sampling Method	Random, From lists	Random, From lists[8]				Random Stratified
N	250	247				695
La Vega						
Sampling Method			Random, From lists	Random, From lists	Snowball from RSM—Direct participants	
N			201[9]	152	153	189
San Pedro de Macoris						
Sampling Method						Random
N						50
San Cristobal						
Sampling Method						Random
N						50
Herrera						
Sampling Method						Random
N						50
Sabana Perdida						
Sampling Method						Random
N						50
TOTALS	250	247	201	152	153	2084

[1] The Radio Santa Maria project was a training of trainers activity. The implementing organization only maintained lists of the "direct" participants or trainers that it trained. After interviewing the "direct" participants, the interiewers would ask for names of "indirect" participants they had trained who would then be interviewed. This second set constitutes the "indirect" respondents.
[2] The national sample for the GAD program excluded Santo Domingo.
[3] The total N of 201 for the ADOPEM program was drawn from San Pedro de Maois, San Cristobal, Herrera, and Sabana Perdida as well as from La Vega.

Table 10.6: Characteristics of Civic Education and Matched Control Group Samples—South Africa

PROVICE	AREA		Civic Education Program			Control Group
		Total N	CLG-Durban 100	NIPILAR 150	LHR 225	475
Eastern Cape	Mt. Fletcher				14	14
	Qumbu				11	11
					25	25
Free State	Bethlehem				10	10
	Bloemfontein				8	8
	Botshabelo				7	7
	Phuthaditja/Witsieshoek			30		30
				30	25	55
Gauteng	Bronkhorstspruit				5	5
	Johannesburg					
	KwaMhlanga/Bronkhorstsp Ruit			20		20
	Pretoria				5	5
	Soweto			10		10
	Vaal Area				5	5
	West Rand (Johannesburg)				10	10
				30	25	55
KwaZulu-Natal	Cornfields		25			25
	Durban					
	Eshowe				13	13
	Muden		25			25
	Pinetown				12	12
	River View		25			25
	Sankotshe		25			25
			100		25	125
Mpumalanga	Bosbokrand				10	10
	Dennilton			15		15
	Graskop			15		15
	Leandra				5	5
	Siyabuswa				10	10
				30	25	55
Northern Province	Lebowakgomo			10	8	18
	Nebo			10		10
	Nebo/Sekhukhune				8	8
	Pietersburg			10		10
	Warmbaths				9	9
				30	25	55

Table 10.7: Probit Models Predicting Civic Education Participation

	Dominican Republic		South Africa	
	B	S.E.	B	S.E.
Psychological Predispositions				
Open to Compromise/Other Cultures	-.002	.04	.15*	.08
Low Paternalism/Affect for Racial Out-Groups	-.003	.002	-.04**	.02
Demographic and Political Controls				
Age	-.10**	.03	----	----
Black Respondent	.22**	.09	----	----
White Respondent	-.13	.10	----	----
Gender (1=Male)	-.59**	.07	----	----
Education	.10**	.02	-.08**	.04
Income	.02	.04	-.08*	.04
Church Attendance	.11**	.02	.03	.04
Santo Domingo Resident	-.71**	.10	----	----
Other Urban District	-.29**	.08	----	----
Group Memberships	3.80**	.18	.92**	.19
Political Ideology (Right-Wing)	-.03	.03	----	----
Political Interest	.37**	.05	.18**	.07
Media Use	-.01	.04	.10	.07
Previous Voting Behavior	.21**	.11	.15	.11
Employed	.13*	.08	.28**	.09
Constant	-2.39**	.36	-1.31**	.33
Pseudo-R-squared	.26		.07	
Number of Cases	2037		940	

Notes

1. This study was conducted as part of a larger project commissioned by the United States Agency for International Development and implemented by the Washington, D.C.–based consulting company Management Systems International. I thank Gary Hansen of USAID, Gwen Bevis, Sheryl Stumbras, Dawn Emling and Roberta Warren, all currently or formerly of MSI, and Chris Sabatini, Robert Mattes and Michael Bratton for their roles in getting the project started and completed. I thank Raymond Duch, James Gibson, and Hans-Dieter Klingemann for helpful comments on an earlier draft of the chapter.

2. See John Sullivan and John Transue, "The Psychological Underpinnings of Democracy: A Selective Review of Research on Political Tolerance, Interpersonal Trust, and Social Capita," *Annual Review of Psychology* (1999): 625-xxx; and Steven E. Finkel, Lee Sigelman, and Stan Humphries, "Democratic Values and Political Tolerance," chap. 5 in *Measures of Political Attitudes*, ed. John P.Robinson, Philip R. Shaver, and Lawrence S. Wrightman (San Diego: Academic Press, 1999), 203-96, for recent reviews

3. Russell Dalton, "Communists and Democrats: Democratic Attitudes in the Two Germanies," *British Journal of Political Science* 24, (1994): 469-93; James L. Gibson, Ray-

mond Duch, and Kent Tedin, "Democratic Values and the Transformation of the Soviet Union," *Journal of Politics* 54 (1992): 329-71; James L. Gibson and Raymond Duch, "Political Intolerance in the USSR: The Distribution and Etiology of Mass Opinion," *Comparative Political Studies* 26 (1993): 286-329; James L. Gibson and Amanda Gouws, *Overcoming Intolerance in South Africa: Experiments in Democratic Persuasion* (Cambridge: Cambridge University Press, 2003); Amanda Gouws, "Political Tolerance and Civil Society: The Case of South Africa," *Politikon* 20 (1993): 15-31; F. D. Weil, "The Development of Democratic Attitudes in Eastern and Western Germany in a Comparative Perspective," *Research on Democracy and Society* 1 (1993): 195-225.; see also Mitchell Seligson and John Booth, "Political Culture and Regime Type: Evidence from Nicaragua and Costa Rica," *Journal of Politics* 55 (1993): 777-92.

4. Gibson and Duch, "Political Intolerance."

5. James L. Gibson, "Mass Opposition to the Soviet Putsch of August 1991: Collective Action, Rational Choice and Democratic Values in the Former Soviet Union," *American Political Science Review* 91 (1997): 671-84.

6. See Thomas Carothers, *Assessing Democracy Assistance: The Case of Romania* (Washington, D.C.: Carnegie Endowment for International Peace, 1996); Thomas Carothers, *Aiding Democracy Abroad: The Learning Curve* (Washington, D.C.: Carnegie Endowment for International Peace, 1999); Larry Diamond, *Promoting Democracy in the 1990s: Actors and Instruments, Issues and Imperatives* (New York: Carnegie Corporation of New York, 1995); Kevin F. F. Quigley, "Political scientists and assisting democracy: too tenuous links," *PS: Political Science & Politics* 30 (1997): 564-68.

7. Michael Bratton et al., "The Effects of Civic Education on Political Culture: Evidence from Zambia," *World Development* 27 (1999): 807-24; Steven E. Finkel, "Civic Education and the Mobilization of Political Participation in Developing Democracies," *Journal of Politics* 64 (2002): 994-1020; Steven E. Finkel, "Can Democracy Be Taught? Adult Civic Education, Civil Society, and the Development of Democratic Political Culture," *Journal of Democracy* 14 (2003); Steven E. Finkel and Howard A. Ernst, "Civic Education in Post-Apartheid South Africa: Alternative Paths to the Development of Political Knowledge and Democratic Value," *Political Psychology* 26 (2005): 333-64; Steven E. Finkel, Christopher A. Sabatini, and Gwendolyn G. Bevis, "Civic Education, Civil Society, and Political Mistrust in a Developing Democracy: The Case of the Dominican Republic," *World Development* 28 (2000): 1851-74; K. M. Slomczynski and G. Shabad, "Can Support for Democracy and the Market Be Learned in School? A Natural Experiment in Post-Communist Poland," *Political Psychology* 19 (1998): 749-79; Judith Torney-Purta et al., *Citizenship and Education in Twenty-Eight Countries: Civic Knowledge and Engagement at Age Fourteen* (Amsterdam: IEA, 2001).

8. James L. Gibson, "A Sober Second Thought: An Experiment in Persuading Russians to Tolerate" *American Journal of Political Science* 42 (1998): 819-50; Gibson and Gouws, *Overcoming Intolerance*; Paul Sniderman et al., *The Clash of Rights* (New Haven: Yale University Press, 1996); George Marcus et al., *With Malice Toward Some: How People Make Civil Liberties Judgments* (New York: Cambridge University Press, 1995).

9. John Sullivan, J. E. Piereson, and G. E. Marcus, *Political Tolerance and American Democracy* (Chicago: University of Chicago Press, 1982); Herbert McClosky and A. Brill, *Dimensions of Tolerance: What Americans Believe About Civil Liberties* (New York: Russell Sage, 1983)

10. Sullivan, Piereson, and Marcus, *Political Tolerance*; James L. Gibson and Raymond Duch, "Putting Up with Fascists in Western Europe: A Comparative Cross-Level Analysis of Political Tolerance," *Western Political Quarterly* 45 (1992): 237-73, Gibson and Duch, "Political Intolerance"; Marcus et al., *With Malice Toward Some.*

11. Sullivan and Transue, "The Psychological Underpinnings," 5.

12. E.g. William Mishler and Richard Rose, "Trust, Distrust, and Skepticism: Popular Evaluations of Civil and Political Institutions in Post-Communist Societies," *Journal of Politics* 59 (1997): 418-51; Richard Rose and William Mishler, "Mass Reaction to Regime Change in Eastern Europe: Polarization or Leaders and Laggards?" *British Journal of Political Science* 24 (1994): 159-82; John Booth and Patricia Richards, "Civil Society, Social Capital and Democratization in Central America," *Journal of Politics* 60 (1998): 780-801; Dalton, "Communists and Democrats"; G. Evans and S. Whitefield, "The Politics and Economics of Democratic Commitment: Support for Democracy in Transitional Societies," *British Journal of Political Science* 25 (1995): 485-514; Robert Mattes and Hermann Thiel, "Consolidation and Public Opinion in South Africa," *Journal of Democracy* 9, no. 1 (1998): 95-110.

13. Sullivan and Transue, "The Psychological Underpinnings"; Marcus et al., *With Malice Toward Some*; J. Kuklinski et al., "The Cognitive and Affective Bases of Political Tolerance Judgments," *American Journal of Political Science* 35 (1991): 1-27; Gibson, "A Sober Second Thought."

14. Kuklinski et al., "The Cognitive and Affective Bases."

15. Thomas Nelson, R. A. Clawson, and Z. M. Oxley, "Media Framing of a Civil Liberties Conflict and its Effects on Tolerance," *American Political Science Review* 88 (1997): 635-52.

16. Gibson, "A Sober Second Thought"; Marcus et al., *With Malice Toward Some*, and Sniderman et al., *The Clash of Rights*.

17. Finkel, "Civic Education"; Finkel, "Can Democracy Be Taught?"

18. John R. Zaller, *The Nature and Origins of Mass Opinion* (New York: Cambridge University Press, 1992)

19. J. Kuklinski and N. Hurley, "It's a Matter of Interpretation," chap. 5 in *Political Persuasion and Attitude Change*, ed. D. Mutz, D. P. Sniderman, and R. Brody (Ann Arbor: University of Michigan Press, 1996), 125-44.

20. R. E. Petty and J. T. Cacioppo, "Source Factors and the Elaboration Likelihood Model of Persuasion," *Advances in Consumer Research* 11 (1984): 668-72.

21. J. Krosnick and R. Petty, "Attitude Strength: An Overview," in *Attitude Strength: Antecedents and Consequences*, ed. R. Petty and J. Krosnick (Mahwah, N. J.: Erlbaum Press, 1995), 1-24.

22. S. Chaiken, E. Pomerantz, and R. Giner-Sorolla, "Structural Consistency and Attitude Strength," in *Attitude Strength: Antecedents and Consequences*, ed. R. Petty and J. Krosnick (Mahwah, N. J., Erlbaum, 1995), 387-412; Paul Sniderman, R. Brody, and P. E. Tetlock, *Reasoning and Choice: Explorations in Political Psychology* (New York: Cambridge University Press, 1991).

23. A. H. Eagly and S. Chaiken, *The Psychology of Attitudes* (Ft. Worth, Tex.: Harcourt, Brace, Jovanovich, 1993)

24. It is also the case that more frequent exposures to civic education will likely be associated with more participatory teaching methodologies and with greater satisfaction with instruction. These factors may also stimulate greater acceptance of the tolerance messages, though I do not examine their independent effects here.

25. Zaller, *The Nature and Origins of Mass Opinion*

26. See also Gibson, "A Sober Second Thought," 833-34.

27. Gibson, "A Sober Second Thought."

28. See J. Hartlyn, *The Struggle for Democratic Politics in the Dominican Republic* (Chapel Hill: University of North Carolina Press, 1998); R. Espinal, "The Dominican Republic: An Ambiguous Democracy," in *Constructing Democratic Governance: Mexico, Central America and the Caribbean in the 1990s*, ed. J. Dominguez and A. Lowenthal (Baltimore: Johns Hopkins University Press, 1996)

29. Sullivan and Transue, "The Psychological Underpinnings."

30. Following Gibson, Duch, and Tedin, "Democratic Values."

31. Christopher H. Achen, *The Statistical Analsis of Quasi-Experiments* (Berkeley: University of California Press, 1986); Burt Barnow, Glen Cain, and Arthur Goldberger, "Issues in the Analysis of Selectivity Bias," in *Evaluation Studies Review Annual*, vol. 5, ed. E. Stromsdorfer and G. Farkas (Beverly Hills, Calif.: Sage Publications, 1980); James J. Heckman and Richard Robb, "Alternative Methods for Evaluating the Impact of Interventions," in *Longitudinal Analysis of Labor Market Data*, ed. James J. Heckman and Burton Singer (Cambridge: Cambridge University Press, 1985), 156-245.

32. Richard A. Berk and Subhash C. Ray, "Selection Biases in Sociological Data," *Social ScienceResearch* 11 (1982): 352-98; Richard Breen, *Regression Models: Censored, Sample-Selected, or Truncated Data* (Thousand Oaks, Calif..: Sage Publications, 1996)

33. E.g. James J. Heckman, "Selection Bias and Self-Selection," in *The New Palgrave Econometrics*, ed. John Eatwell, Murrary Milgate, and Peter Newman (London: MacMillan, 1992), 201-24.

34. William Greene, *Econometric Analysis* (New York: Prentice Hall, 1993), 713-74; Francis Vella, "Estimating Models with Sample Selection Bias: A Survey," *The Journal of Human Resources* 33 (1998): 135-38; Winship Christopher Winship and Stephen L. Morgan, "The Estimation of Causal Effects from Observational Data," *Annual Review of Sociology* 25 (1999): 669-87

35. Vella, "Estimating Models," 136.

36. This expression is also often referred to as the Inverse Mills Ratio (IMR). The IMR decreases monotonically for the treatment group as the probability that $T = 1$ increases, and decreases monotonically for the control group as the probability that $T = 0$ increases.

37. Though it is not absolutely necessary for model identification, it is recommended that variables be included in x that are not also included in w, that is, variables that affect the selection equation and not the outcome equation; see Breen, *Regression Models*; and Winship and Morgan, "The Estimation of Causal Effects". In this case I included the individual's employment status and their self-reported voting behavior in previous national elections. I assume that these factors affect tolerance only via their impact on other variables specified in the models below.

38. Greene, *Econometric Analysis*

39. Intuitively, a positive *Rho* means that individuals who are treated tend to have larger error terms in the outcome equation than individuals in the control group. OLS ignores this fact and produces an exaggerated impact of the treatment on the outcome. A negative *Rho* indicates the reverse; smaller error terms in the outcome equation for treated individuals and, consequently, an underestimation by OLS of the "true" causal impact of the treatment.

40. Harold O. Kiess, *Statistical Concepts for the Behavioral Sciences* (Boston: Allyn and Bacon, 1989); Charles Judd and David Kenny, *Estimating the Effects of Social Interventions* (New York: Cambridge University Press, 1981)

41. It is also the case that civic education may exert *indirect* effects on tolerance, through its effect on the other democratic orientations in Table 1.2 such as support for liberty, efficacy, and knowledge. Civic education does appear to influence both efficacy and

knowledge in the Dominican Republic, see Finkel, Sabatini, and Bevis, "Civic Education," but overall the indirect effects of civic education on tolerance are relatively small.

42. The satisfaction with freedom variable has an insignificant effect on tolerance if entered into the model of Table 1.3 and does not alter the effects of other variables in the model.

43. Zaller, *The Nature and Origins of Mass Opinion*

44. Mishler and Rose, "Trust, Distrust, and Skepticism."

45. Dalton, "Communists and Democrats," 490.

46. Michael Bratton and Robert Mattes, "Support for Democracy in Africa: Intrinsic or Instrumental?" *British Journal of Political Science* 31 (2001): 447-74; Evans and Whitefield, "The Politics and Economics of Democratic Commitment."

47. Carothers, *Aiding Democracy Abroad*

48. Gibson, "A Sober Second Thought"; Nelson, Clawson, and Oxley, "Media Framing"; Sniderman et al., *The Clash of Rights*

49. See Gibson and Gouws, *Overcoming Intolerance.*

Tolerance as a Criterion for Just War
Henrik Syse[1]

Introduction

The idea that there can be just wars has met criticism on two flanks: from pacifists who claim that the use of violent force can never be morally sanctioned, and from political realists who hold that warfare should not be judged by moral standards, but rather, has to be understood on its own terms as an outgrowth of national and personal self-interest.[2]

In spite of such criticism, the idea of just war has stood its ground and has even gained increasing currency over the last half-century, not the least due to debates over US involvement in Vietnam and the development of massive nuclear arsenals. Such situations seemed to demand a moral—even existential—debate about war. The just war tradition has provided many of the actual ideas and much of the terminology for this debate. These ideas make it possible to distinguish morally between different wars as well as judge means of warfare in ethical terms, thus avoiding the extremes: either wholesale condemnation or passive approval of all wars.[3]

I will argue that tolerance, both as a political idea and as a moral virtue, constitutes an essential part of the just war idea.[4] The definition of tolerance that I take as my point of departure is relatively simple: the acceptance of or willingness to live peacefully with lifestyles, cultures, or beliefs that conflict with one's own.[5] I aim to show that tolerance constitutes an essential part of the restraint that the just war tradition has tried to impose on warfare.

Brief Historical Background

Just war is an idea dating back at least to the Church Fathers Ambrose and Augustine in the fourth and fifth centuries.[6] While holding that the basic Christian attitude in and to the world should be one of love and peacefulness, these thinkers also emphasized that keeping peace and opposing evil sometimes make recourse to armed force not only a possibility, but a duty.[7]

The just war ideas of Ambrose and Augustine were not strictly organized and did not develop into a full-fledged teaching until the development of Canon Law in the twelfth century and Thomas Aquinas's discussion of war and sedition in the thirteenth. In the latter era, other influences became visible as well, especially the chivalric and knightly traditions, which formulated rules and ideals concerning the actual execution of war. Thus developed a two-fold teaching which a later age organized under the headings of *ius ad bellum* (right recourse to war) and *ius in bello* (right conduct in war). The latter aspect had been addressed indirectly even by Augustine and the jurists and theologians following his lead, but a more detailed list of restrictions on the actual conduct of war was not worked out in a scholarly fashion until writers addressing the chivalric codes such as John of Legnano, Honoré Bouvet, and Christine de Pizan did so in the fourteenth and fifteenth centuries.[8]

With the creation of the nation state in the seventeenth century, and the subsequent development of international law, just war ideas took a back seat to reason of state (*raison d'état*) as the ruling ideology, especially within the realm of *ius ad bellum*. However, just war ideas lived on among several jurists and philosophers, and the basic attitude that war can and should be judged not only legally, but morally, gained new acceptance after the World Wars of the twentieth century. Today, international law and just war exist as two separate, but often overlapping and complementary, sources of moral discourse on armed force, and much of what is written and said about the ethics of war takes its cue from the just war tradition.[9] Writers such as Paul Ramsey, Jean Bethke Elshtain, Michael Walzer, and James Turner Johnson have all contributed to a significant revival of the tradition, the latter two also bringing it into dialogue with Jewish and Islamic sources.

Tolerance and war

The preceding brief overview catches little of the contents of the just war idea. We need to concentrate on the dramatic and horrific subject matter of the tradition if we are to understand the role of tolerance and restraint within it.

War, after all, involves violence and lethal force normally directed against people who, in their individual capacities, have done nothing wrong against the killer(s). For that reason alone, war is hard to reconcile with religious and political ideas of harmony, justice, charity, or goodness. On the other hand, political communities often come to be threatened in a way that seemingly leaves no choice: one is forced to resort to lethal force in order to survive, either culturally or physically. War is thus made against the *intolerable*. Had one reasonably been able to tolerate the evil of the other side with no significant harm to oneself, war would have been unnecessary and indeed, immoral.

There have actually been those who have held war to be a positive good that strengthens morale and community, thus making the unavoidable deaths of war a necessary expense in the self-contained pursuit of the good.[10] Others have held war to be a legitimate means of spreading culture and religion without any prior attack or concrete evil-doing necessarily having taken place.[11] But these are not the mainstream views of what we today call the just war tradition. Just war thinkers have mostly followed St. Augustine in holding that war is regrettable and to be avoided whenever possible, even if its conduct may involve acts of great courage and valor.[12]

According to the view outlined so far, a war can be just only if one party to the war has committed some wrong that needs to be rectified—a wrong that can be rectified solely by resort to armed force. If no one has committed such a wrong, use of military force cannot be justified since there is nothing legitimately to react against. This constitutes the gist of the *justa causa* (just cause) idea within the just war tradition: war should be used to restrain and punish wrongdoing; it is not an instrument for subduing others or for gaining more power and riches for oneself.

However, not every kind of wrongdoing in the international arena justifies a resort to armed force. Cities, states, and nations have to be able to live with differences and disagreements without outbreak of war; otherwise international politics would be reduced to incessant fighting and large-scale destruction.

Actions that are considered wrong, yet not subject to reaction by armed force constitute a special class of "tolerated" actions in the international sphere. One of the most important tasks of just war theorizing always has been to answer what kinds of actions and situations should belong within this class, i.e., should be "tolerated" in the international arena in the sense that they should not to be reacted against with the use of armed force.

The situation one faces could be deemed tolerable for at least three reasons: (1) the wrong or evil the other party represents or has perpetuated is of such a kind that one ought to be able to live with it; (2) going to war would lead to such destruction and suffering that it is better to find other ways of living with the situation in question; or (3) one can and should do something about the wrong or evil faced, but there are other situations even more pressing where one should use one's forces and resources.[13] Let us call these "tolerance 1, 2, and 3," and treat each in turn.

Tolerance 1

"Tolerance 1" comes the closest to what we normally associate with tolerance, namely, the idea that one should learn to live with differences amicably, both in order to avoid unnecessary violence, and because of the limits of human reason—no human being has, after all, been given the gift of unerring knowledge of right and wrong.

Most cultural and many political differences would normally fall under this latter heading according to the last five hundred years of just war theorizing in the West. The fallibility of human reason has been invoked powerfully by several recent thinkers such as Richard Miller, who has listed "relative justice" as one criterion of *ius ad bellum*. The criterion points out that no party can be certain of having all justice on its side, not least because many differences between peoples and cultures have reasons and roots that should not lead to moral condemnation from one side against the other. This leads to the conclusion that restraint and care should be exercised in the use of armed force.[14] James Turner Johnson has traced a similar idea, which he calls "simultaneous ostensible justice," back to the Dominican theologian Francisco de Vitoria in the sixteenth century, who claimed that the religious and (what we today would broadly call) cultural differences between the Old and the New World called for restraint in the use of force and a better understanding of ways of life that may seem strange or savage at first glance.[15] Johnson's (and Vitoria's) point is that what seems perfectly just to one side may appear very different to the other, and what seems evil to one side may be part of deeply held cultural convictions to the other—convictions that one cannot reasonably expect the other party to understand as wrong.

In Vitoria's view, the so-called Indians of South America could not reasonably understand or accept most of the Christian, European claims made on behalf of papal rights and trade privileges. Even if some of the latter claims were just *per se*, one could not necessarily expect the American Indians to find them so. Therefore, a policy of (what we would call) tolerance was in fact a morally more acceptable policy than war. One should have accepted, however grudgingly, that land and resources on the other side of the Atlantic would for a large part remain inaccessible to European claims, at least until reasonable agreements could be worked out. This should have been "tolerable," since the alternative would be (and indeed turned out to be) large-scale killing and destruction. This does not mean that the Spaniards had *no* just causes for war—Vitoria spells out several possible legitimate causes—but these should have been weighed against the demand for tolerance and recognition of what Vitoria calls the "invincible ignorance" of the other party.[16] It seems that for Vitoria, in the case of the encounter with the American Indians, the only truly legitimate form of war in America would be a direct reaction to widespread aggression and cruelty performed by the Indians. He held that differences of religion or political organization could not in themselves be just causes for going to war, while denial of free trade or missionary activity *could* constitute just causes, but that the disagreements in question still ought to be solved otherwise, for the reasons mentioned.

We should note that Vitoria's argument was made within the framework of a Thomistic natural law approach, which holds that natural law is in theory accessible independently of divine law (i.e., Biblical revelation), and that the political rights of the Indians were therefore not invalid simply because of religious disagreement. The fact of the Indians' "invincible ignorance" in matters of politics, religious faith, or law could not in itself be a legitimate reason for war according to natural law. The Indians, not the Pope or the Spanish crown, were the rightful owners of their land.

Vitoria and several other theologians in the century following him thus introduced an important idea: at least in theory, *reasons for war should be fully acceptable to both parties in a conflict by reference to natural law*. This is indeed an implicit call for tolerance in the face of foreign mores and cultures, yet we must note that it is neither a pacifist nor a relativist stand. It is also not a naïve utopian view that perfect agreement is achievable in the often-dramatic circumstances leading up to war. Rather, it reflects what Jürgen Habermas has come to call the idea of an "ideal speech situation,"[17] which implies a setting where both parties should be imagined as speaking (or actually being invited to speak) on the basis of mutually understandable reasons and arguments, and where all have an even chance of employing such arguments. In such a setting, tolerance is a prerequisite. In the search for reasons and arguments for one's own case, every effort must be made to understand and respect the other side's cultural soil. Otherwise there will be no discourse, merely empty-headed quarrelling. Thus, the Spaniards should have realized that, in our parlance, they did not enter with a spirit of tolerance and did not create an atmosphere amenable to civilized discourse. Therefore, war was waged on the basis of intolerance, with the reasons for war being inaccessible or incomprehensible to the side effectively under attack.

This discussion leads us naturally to the question of how we conceive of the other—the potential partner and indeed, potential enemy in a real or imagined discourse over whether and how to wage war. This is where we find the crucial break in Western political thought that precipitates the move towards tolerance as a *de facto* criterion for just war characteristic of Vitoria and his followers. Although tolerance of disagreement and difference was implied even in earlier Christian thinkers in their insistence on patience and thorough examination of motives before going to war, the potential enemy was most often seen as an *existential* enemy who, through his adherence to a certain religion or heresy, was to be seen as *morally culpable*. With Vitoria's category of "invincible ignorance," and the insistence that one is not to blame for one's religious faith *per se*, unorthodox religious faith no longer comes to be seen as primarily a moral fault, but more as a cognitive mistake. This notion of "invincible ignorance" had certainly been a staple of the tradition earlier as well, as witnessed in the oft-repeated assertion that faith is not a matter of outward pressure, but rather of inward conviction. Yet, in the context of war it is remarkable to witness the extent to which Saracens, Jews, Turks, and others came to be seen as persons who had actually made a moral mistake, at least if they had had a chance to hear the

Gospel. In the last instance, it would be perfectly just to initiate war against them since they could be morally blamed even as individuals for being enemies of the right faith. For Vitoria, the Indians may be enemies of the right faith, but they cannot be blamed for being so, and so, war cannot be waged against them merely because of difference in religion.

Thus, religious difference moved from an intolerable to a tolerable difference, one of the most significant enlargements of the category of "tolerable differences" in European and Western history, with obvious ramifications for just war theorizing. Indeed, the acceptance of religious difference may in our day be seen as the prototype of "tolerance 1."

Tolerance 2

In contrast to what we have been discussing under the heading of "tolerance 1," we now enter those differences which as such ought not to be tolerated, but which we may find ourselves forced to tolerate for specific reasons. "Tolerance 2" could also be termed "Cold War tolerance," reminding us of the superpowers' stance vis-à-vis each other in the face of a possible nuclear holocaust. Here one may stand face to face with a system of aggression and persecution, yet find solid moral and political reasons for avoiding the use of armed force because of the consequences of employing it. These reasons can usefully be divided in two:

(i) First, there is the idea of "last resort," one of the most famous ingredients of the just war idea, holding that the threat or evil one faces may be of such a kind that other options exist for dealing with it. If resort to armed force is to be just, one must be certain that the wrongdoing of the party against whom one contemplates the use of armed force is not actually tolerable. If it is, one should postpone the use of armed force until the situation becomes such that there is no reasonable choice. Along the way, one must work to make such an outcome as unlikely as possible. Of course, one may be facing a situation that will inevitably worsen, and so postponing the use of armed force could be dangerous. Many have analyzed British and French unwillingness to engage Nazi Germany in 1938 along those lines; other have held NATO resistance against intervening in Bosnia before 1995 or UN reticence about using armed force in Rwanda in the winter of 1994 as faulty applications of the last resort criterion. In the context of "tolerance 2," the criterion of last resort must be taken to apply in cases where the situation is not absolutely intolerable, and where the problem can be addressed without the use of armed force, with a reasonable hope of success. We recognize this argument from the winter of 2003 regarding the problem of possible weapons of mass destruction in Iraq, and the question whether the disarming of Iraq was a task that required violent regime change, or whether the regime could be tolerated as long as it was under close scrutiny, and weapons inspectors could continue their search for weapons.

(ii) We can also appeal to a simpler consequentialist calculus of costs in cases where the ramifications of using armed force are of a sort that cannot be morally justified, *even though one may succeed in removing the evil in question.* (We are reminded of Norwegian playwright Ludvig Holberg's sarcastic line in which a doctor excuses the death of a patient by pointing out that "The patient died, that is so, but his fever is definitely gone.") The cold war, as already mentioned, may furnish an example, where the use of armed force to topple the Moscow regime or to retaliate against the invasions in Hungary, Czechoslovakia, or Afghanistan was out of the question due to the possible ramifications in terms of world war or even nuclear holocaust. This does not mean that the use of force was excluded under all circumstances, but that the threshold for going to war was extremely high. This led the two parties to the Cold War to adopt a stance of "tolerance" vis-à-vis each other, forcing them to find ways of tolerating what they both saw as "evil."

The adoption of "tolerance 2" could also take place in cases where the international or regional support for using armed force is very low or even absent, making it politically implausible to employ armed force even if it may help eliminate an intolerable evil. The extent to which broad agreement is required for using armed force, is a matter of much dispute, a fact brought out by the Kosovo and Iraq wars in 1999 and 2003 respectively, with the United States and several NATO allies holding that unilateral action, without broad consensus in (or explicit mandate from) the United Nations, can be morally legitimate. Once again, if one chooses not to act because of a lack of broad consensus, yet faces a clear and distinct moral problem, one must find ways of living with and alleviating that problem, which makes this kind of situation fall under the category of "tolerance 2."

Tolerance 3

This leads us to a final and interesting category, theoretically related to but practically distinct from "tolerance 2." An everyday example may help illustrate the dilemma, which is very simple in structure, yet complex in reality.

In watching my four children, I see two of them quarreling ferociously, hitting and hurting each other. In order to avoid serious harm, and in order to calm down the situation, I ought to intervene. However, at the same time, I observe that another child is heading toward the kitchen, where I know that boiling water is on the stove, and her grabbing hold of that would cause great, possibly life-threatening injury. I realize that I have to prioritize one instance over the other. Thus, I leave my quarreling children and head for the kitchen.

The example seems to need little elaboration. I am faced with something that merits my intervention, morally speaking, yet has to be tolerated since I need to focus my attention elsewhere. My resources are limited, and had I concentrated on the quarrel, I would have been unable to prevent something more dangerous.

In making the decision about using armed force, political decision makers are clearly called on to make the same sort of priorities. In deciding to expend a gigantic effort to oust the Saddam Hussein regime in Baghdad, stabilize the country, and build democracy—all laudable goals, formed in reaction to what was deemed an intolerable evil—one simultaneously commits significant resources in terms of man- and womanpower, as well as money and equipment, in a way that makes it unfeasible to react similarly elsewhere. The category of "tolerance 3" forces us to evaluate such decisions critically. In truth, this category is called on all of the time in debates about world politics. When large famines or genocidal campaigns take place, with little immediate reaction from the outside world—Rwanda and Congo come to mind—it is often pointed out that no consensus could be built to commit the resources necessary to tackle the situation at hand. While morally dubious, making this sort of priority calculus is certainly understandable. With so many commitments nationally and internationally, rerouting vast amounts of money and personnel to an obscure trouble-spot far away, seems politically impossible. In light of other duties, not least to self-preservation and self-defense, one has to tolerate the fact that the atrocities or suffering in question is taking place. This is not the same as merely accepting something about which one can do nothing; it would be odd indeed to say that we "tolerate" an earthquake or the explosion of a star, simply because we accept their happening without interfering in it. What we are addressing here are situations that clearly imply a wrong or evil of some sort, and that *could* be interfered with, yet we avoid doing so because of our commitments elsewhere.

Two lessons follow from this concept of tolerance. First, every single case of using armed force should be judged according to how one's resources are spent, and whether intervening in one place could rule out addressing other and graver wrongs. By holding this, I am not implying that special responsibilities and previously accepted obligations are unimportant. If country A has accepted some special responsibility for country B, and has even entered into formal agreements to complete some aid or military mission, yet suddenly jumps the wagon because one believes that similar resources could be used better elsewhere, that would be morally unacceptable, since it would frustrate a clearly legitimate expectation, and in the long run would make long-term planning and serious development agendas totally impotent. The point is merely that priorities have to be made, and that the political attention lavished on some particular situation may not reflect the relative moral seriousness of that vis-à-vis other situations.

Second, tolerating some wrong or evil because of the urgent need to act elsewhere, also implies a challenge: How can the situation one is forced to tolerate, because one's attention has to be turned elsewhere, be tackled and restrained in other ways than by full-scale intervention? How can one find ways where the alternative to intervening is not neglect or indifference, but rather some kind of active engagement by other means? This seems common-sensical, but political history shows us that tolerated evils—from Latin America to the Balkans, from post-Soviet Afghanistan to Central Africa—often become overlooked evils.

Conclusion

Holding back on the use of armed force is often the same as tolerating what one would otherwise want to fight. The acceptance of different religions living side by side, or the agreement to give up trade privileges or territorial demands for the sake of keeping peace or observing treaties are important examples of such tolerance. In some cases, one may move—as many have in the case of religious diversity—from seeing such tolerance as a necessary evil to a positive good. Still, an attitude of tolerance is mostly associated with holding back and accepting somewhat grudgingly what one would have preferred to see otherwise.

It is interesting to note that, especially in the last ten to fifteen years, we have seen one category of behavior moved from being accepted as tolerable to being judged intolerable—namely, human rights abuse and grave human suffering of the kind that, in the oft-quoted words of the United Nations 1946 Resolution on Genocide, "shock the conscience of humanity." With the end of the Cold War, a new emphasis on the responsibility to protect the innocent from suffering and wrongdoing has come to the fore. Although the War against Terror has eclipsed the attention given to so-called humanitarian interventions, it seems true that the emergence of this category as a central concern in the discourse on the use of armed force is an example of a *limitation* rather than an enlargement of tolerance, and that this a feature that has come to stay in international politics.[18]

If we are to include tolerance as a criterion for *ius ad bellum*, as I suggest is plausible, we are, however, mainly thinking of it as a call to an acceptance of difference, and in terms of patience as a virtue in confronting such difference. As such, the criterion has its limits, since tolerance in the face of persecution and terrible human suffering is surely no virtue. Still, the majority of wars in human history can, at least in hindsight, be judged as unnecessary and immoral in terms of loss of life and material destruction weighed against whatever gains have been made. Given that assumption, there is little doubt that the virtue (and the just war criterion) that could often have restrained the bellicosity of the decision-making authorities is indeed tolerance, in the sense of a greater acceptance of difference, a greater acceptance of the limits of one's own judgment and the possible virtue of the judgment of others, and a greater acceptance of the existence of "tolerable evils" defined as tolerable slights or wounds to one's own ambitions, property, faith, or pride. As such, I find it highly reasonable to include tolerance as a meaningful and crucial just war criterion.

Above, I have attempted to delineate three versions of tolerance as a just war criterion: first, tolerance in terms of acceptance of (tolerable) differences; second, tolerance in terms of accepting evils in cases where removing them by force would cause even greater evils; and third, tolerance in terms of accepting evils because other and more pressing concerns should be attended to. In all cases, we find ourselves forced to accept that armed force may *not* be used, even though there are strong temptations and even moral pressure to do so.

The further challenge that the idea of tolerance poses to us—a challenge extending from the argument hereby made—is of course *how* we should live with the wrong or evil in question, after we have come to the realization that we actually have to live with it. Although my argument for including tolerance as a just war criterion ends here, this is where the real problems and challenges begin.

Notes

1. My thanks to the participants at the colloquium of the University of Oslo's Ethics Program on October 7, 2004, and especially to Visiting Professor Thomas Pogge, who gave many insightful comments and contributed decisively to the overall make-up of my argument. My sincere thanks also to editor Gerson Moreno-Riaño for challenging me to think through this important topic in light of the idea of tolerance.

2. For a useful overview of the just war idea as an alternative to pacifism and political realism—and also as an alternative to other ways of thinking morally about war (such as the "perpetual peace" idea)—see James Turner Johnson, *The Quest for Peace* (Princeton: Princeton University Press, 1987), and Thomas Pangle and Peter Ahrensdorf, *Justice among Nations* (Lawrence: University Press of Kansas, 1999).

3. Three texts that have helped revive just war thinking are Paul Ramsey, *The Just War: Force and Political Responsibility* (New York: Charles Scribner's Sons, 1968); Michael Walzer, *Just and Unjust Wars* (New York: Basic Books, 1977); and National Conference of Catholic Bishops, *The Challenge of Peace: God's Promise and Our Response* (Washington, D.C.: United States Catholic Conference, 1983).

4. Michael Walzer distinguishes between tolerance as an attitude and toleration as a practice; see Michael Walzer, *On Toleration* (New Haven: Yale University Press, 1997), xi. In this essay I will use the former term to denote both.

5. Maurice Cranston emphasizes just this aspect of tolerance: that tolerating is something we do vis-à-vis disagreeable things; tolerance means, in other words, "putting up with" or "enduring" something (see Cranston's essay "John Locke and the Case for Toleration," in *John Locke: A Letter concerning Toleration—in Focus*, ed. John Horton and Susan Mendus (London: Routledge, 1991).

6. It should be noted that Cicero was an important forerunner of the just war idea, and that we find elements of just war theorizing even in Plato and Aristotle.

7. See Louis Swift, ed., *The Early Fathers on War and Military Service* (Wilmington, Del.: Michael Glazier, 1983), for a good collection of texts from Ambrose, Augustine, and other early Christian writers.

8. See James Turner Johnson, *Ideology, Reason, and the Limitation of War* (Princeton: Princeton University Press, 1975); James Turner Johnson, *Just War Tradition and the*

Restraint of War (Princeton: Princeton University Press. 1981); Peter Haggenmacher, "Just War and Regular War in Sixteenth Century Spanish Doctrine," *International Review of the Red Cross* no. 290 (September-October 1992): 434-45; and Pangle and Ahrensdorf, *Justice among Nations*, for different—sometimes conflicting, sometimes complementary—portrayals of this development. For a fascinating insight into the chivalric way of describing the *ius in bello* see Christine de Pizan's work on arms and chivalry recently made available in a new English translation, Christine de Pizan, *The Book of Deeds of Arms and of Chivalry*, ed. Charity C. Willard, trans. Sumner Willard (University Park: Pennsylvania State University Press, 1999).

9. For interesting observations on the relationship between just war and international law, see Mona Fixdal and Dan Smith, "Humanitarian Intervention and Just War," *Mershon International Studies Review* 42 (1998): 283-312, and Gregory Reichberg and Henrik Syse, eds., "Special Issue on Ethics and International Law," *Journal of Military Ethics* 3, no. 2 (2004).

10. Hegel is a good example of a thinker portraying war as a positive good for a nation and culture; see, for instance, his *Philosophy of Right*, trans. T.M. Knox (Oxford: Oxford University Press, [1942] 1967), §§ 324-325. I am grateful to Endre Begby for pinpointing this and other important passages in Hegel for me.

11. This has often gone under the name of "holy war," an expression that covers a wide array of religious justifications for the use of armed force. A good overview of holy war ideas in Christianity and Islam can be found in James Turner Johnson, *The Idea of Holy War in Western and Islamic Traditions* (University Park: Pennsylvania State University Press, 1997).

12. This should not belie the fact that Augustine, while an advocate of restraint, also wrote passages, especially against the Donatists, that seemingly endorsed what would later become known as holy war. See Augustine, *Political Writings*, ed. Ernest L. Fortin and Douglas Kries (Indianapolis: Hackett, 1994), for a good selection of the relevant texts.

13. This threefold division, and especially the elaboration of "tolerance 3," is inspired by comments from Professor Thomas Pogge.

14. See Richard Miller, *Interpretations of Conflict* (Chicago: University of Chicago Press, 1991), 14, 66-67, 141-42.

15. See Johnson, *Just War Tradition*, 94-103 with reference to Vitoria's *De indis* and *De iure belli*, which are both available in Francisco de Vitoria, *Political Writings*, ed. Anthony Pagden and Jeremy Lawrance (Cambridge: Cambridge University Press, 1991). See also Pangle and Ahrensdorf, *Justice among Nations*, 88-98 for a slightly different take on Vitoria. I believe Johnson comes closer to catching the gist of Vitoria's complex texts. See also Gregory M. Reichberg, "Philosophy Meets War" in *The Classics of Western Philosophy*, ed. by Jorge Gracia, Gregory Reichberg, and Bernard Schumacher (Oxford, U.K.: Blackwell Publishers, 2003), 197–204, for a fine summary of Vitoria's ideas about war.

16. See Vitoria, *Political Writings*, 231-328 for Vitoria's most important arguments for and against Spanish titles to wage war in America.

17. See Detlef Horster, *Habermas: An Introduction*, trans. Heidi Thomson (Philadelphia: Pennbridge, 1992), 33, for a good introduction to this concept.

18. A pertinent example of this line of thinking can be found in the International Commission on Intervention and State Sovereignty, *The Responsibility to Protect* (Ottawa: International Development Research Centre, 2001), which uses just war categories to set

up a list of criteria for humanitarian interventions. However, the debate on humanitarian interventions has a long history. Ambrose's and Augustine's emphasis on protecting the innocent is certainly a precursor of the same idea, and the problem received a thorough discussion in the 19th century through John Stuart Mill, "A Few Words on Non-Intervention," in *Dissertations and Discussions* (London: Longmans, Green, Reader and Dyer, [1859]1867), 3: 153-78.

Liberal Tolerance as Robust Political Economy

Peter T. Leeson and Peter J. Boettke[1]

> Liberalism, however, must be intolerant of every kind of intolerance.
> . . . Liberalism demands tolerance as a matter of principle, not from
> opportunism. It demands toleration even of obviously nonsensical
> teachings, absurd forms of heterodoxy, and childishly silly supersti-
> tions. It demands toleration for doctrines and opinions that it deems
> detrimental and ruinous to society and even for movements that it in-
> defatigably combats. For what impels liberalism to demand and ac-
> cord toleration is not considerations for the content of the doctrine to
> be tolerated, but the knowledge that only tolerance can create and
> preserve the conditions of social peace without which humanity must
> relapse into the barbarism and penury of centuries long past.
> —Ludwig von Mises[2]

Introduction

A "robust" approach to political economy is one that compares the ability of
political-economic arrangements to cope with deviations from ideal assumptions
about agent characteristics. A robust political economy performs under high
degrees of stress. A fragile political economy collapses in the face of imperfec-
tions.

In a previous article, the authors used a robust approach to compare the capacity of liberal and socialist political economies to produce socially beneficial
outcomes under conditions of imperfect agent information and knavish agent
motivation.[3] Liberal political economy harnesses selfish behavior and transforms
selfishness through the institutions of the market to promote the interest of society as a whole. Similarly, by introducing market prices made possible by the
institution of private property, liberal political economy is able to utilize widely
dissipated information that exists as part of the "division of knowledge" to allo-
cate resources effectively and minimize the inefficiencies of informational im-

perfections. In short, liberalism constitutes a robust political-economic arrangement.

Socialism, in contrast, is fragile. Even when we assume the best of intentions on the part of socialist planners, socialism's absence of private property prevents the dispersed information embodied in market prices from coming into existence. The price system that is critical to channeling resources effectively under capitalism is eliminated, leaving those in charge of directing production without a compass to guide their decision-making. Even if we assume that planners are myopically interested in promoting the well- being of their citizens, the structural information gap generated by socialism's abrogation of market prices prevents them from doing so.

Allowing for less than perfect agent benevolence under socialism only strengthens its social welfare-destroying outcome. On the one hand, without the profit and loss system to reward productive activity and discourage destructive activity, self-interested managers will channel their energies in those directions that yield the greatest personal gain, irrespective of the connection to societal gain. Worker incentives will be similarly perverted, leading to shirking instead of work. Self-interested central planners will be led to use their political power over the economy to benefit themselves even when this runs into direct conflict with the welfare of citizens.

This paper considers the comparative robustness of liberal and socialist political economy in the face of a different less than ideal assumption regarding the agents that populate their systems. Like the robust approach taken in our previous work, this one too assumes symmetry in agent type across both systems. The reason for this is obvious. If we allowed agents to have certain characteristics in one system and different attributes in the other, we would be stacking the deck in favor of one system or another.

We consider the robustness of these systems when agent ends are multiple and different across individuals. In allowing disparate and contradictory individual desires to enter the system, we are in effect allowing a *toleration* of competing ends to play a role. Tolerance requires the plurality of individual goals within society to be accommodated by the system under consideration. In short, it requires the system to satisfy my ends and your ends in a way that reflects our relative valuations of these ends where they differ and in particular where they are in conflict. In this context, a robust political economy is one that enhances social welfare in the face of tolerance. A robust political economy tolerates tolerance. A fragile political economy, on the other hand, cannot. It folds in the face of tolerance and can only achieve its goals when the disparate wills of many are substituted for the singular will of one. Here, we argue that liberal political economy is robust in this sense, while socialist political economy is not.

The remainder of this chapter is organized as follows: Section 2 describes how liberal political economy is robust in the face of tolerance because it organizes most decision-making in a decentralized fashion through the choices of individuals in the market. Section 3 shows why socialist political economy cannot accommodate multiple and competing individual goals because it abolishes the market. We examine why, in a socialist system, it cannot work to use collective decision-making in place of the market to determine which competing goals should be pursued and to what extent. Dictatorial decision-making, which is inconsistent with tolerance, is the only means available for retaining the coherence of a central plan. Section 4 demonstrates that even if central planners are given a solution to the problem of which of the competing goals of society's members should be pursued, socialism remains unable to accommodate competing individual ends economically—i.e., in a fashion that does not result in decreased social wealth.

Liberalism, Tolerance, and Robust Political Economy

The concept of tolerance in liberal thought has several and varied forms. John Locke's work on toleration is most famously known for defending religious freedom.[4] John Stuart Mill,[5] F.A. Hayek,[6] and Robert Nozick[7] defended toleration of thought, speech, and individuality more generally, though each with their own points of emphasis. These multiple conceptions of liberal tolerance are bound together by the overriding belief that (a) individuals have different, often conflicting values about how to live, and (b) individuals should be allowed pursue their values to the greatest extent possible, free from encroachments by third parties, be they public or private. Practically speaking, this comes down to a legal (and in some conceptions, moral) right to dispose of one's property as he sees fit so long as he does not encroach on the rights of others to do the same.

In this paper we utilize a closely related but different conception of tolerance. It is similar in that it refers generally to the ability of individuals to dispose of their property as they see fit (within the bounds addressed above). It differs in that it takes a more "reductionist" approach to tolerance by defining tolerance in terms of how individuals hold different and inconsistent values *manifested in how they satisfy these values through the goods and services they seek to acquire towards their ends.* For instance, we are not concerned with toleration of differing religions among members of society except insofar as this refers to the ability of individuals to obtain the goods and services they may desire as a means of pursuing their religion. In other words, we concern ourselves with "tolerance of demands," as it were, to focus in on how various political-economic systems accommodate or fail to accommodate competing claims on scarce resources that emerge from individuals' different views about the world and how to live in it more generally.

To use one last example, imagine that there are limited plots of land and society is composed of some members who value nature, and thus want to see it preserved in its unaltered state, some members who value "luxury living," and thus want to build mansions on the property, and some individuals who are concerned primarily with education, and thus want to build a school on the property. We are interested in how the political-economic arrangement of society enables its members, with their competing values of varying intensities, to satisfy their values in a socially productive fashion (i.e., one that does not involve violent conflict or the destruction of social wealth). We explore how this arrangement allows or does not allow for competing values to peacefully co-exist, as manifested through demonstrated preferences.

Liberalism is that form of political economy based on private property and a market economy. Government in this system is limited to those functions, such as national defense, that the privately organized activities of individuals are thought to be unable to accomplish without centrally coordinated collective action. The mechanism of government in a liberal political economy is democratic, though the key issue for liberalism is not what form of collective decision-making society follows so much as the range of questions collective decision-making is asked to answer.

As writers in the classical liberal tradition have long noted, in providing each member of society the right to dispose of his property as he sees fit (so long as doing so does not violate the rights of others), liberalism provides what Hayek called the greatest free sphere of action to individuals.[8] In establishing mine and thine and thus delineating the boundaries within which one may do as he pleases, the private property institution of liberal political economy establishes maximal tolerance on two fronts. On the one hand, the private property system tells individuals that they are free to do what they want with their property and must refrain from interfering with others doing the same, even if they disagree with what others are doing. On the other hand, in establishing maximal latitude to individuals to use their property as they see fit, liberalism limits the size and scope of the government to its role as protector of individuals' property rights. Like private third parties, then, public third parties—arms of the state—are limited to acting as referees in society and cannot be active players who interfere with individuals' actions when they disagree. In these ways, as has traditionally been pointed out, the private property system upon which liberal political economy rests institutionalizes tolerance in a liberal society.

As we noted above, the fact that individuals have competing goals and resources requires liberal society to be tolerant in another fashion as well. If it is to be robust, liberalism needs to accommodate individuals' competing ends in a fashion consistent with society's beliefs about the relative importance of these ends. Concretely, this means first, establishing which competing goals among individuals should be pursued and to what extent, and second, establishing how these goals should be pursued. No more highly valued goal should go unsatisfied because the means required for its satisfaction have been devoted to some less highly valued goal.

Markets achieve these two things through the institutions of private property, prices, and profit and loss. Under liberalism, private property permits the exchange of final goods and services as well as the exchange of the means of production. Individuals with subjective valuations of various ends through exchange generate exchange ratios (individuals' relative intensity of preferences for various goals). These ratios express the relative scarcity of resources objectively in monetary prices. In bringing the most willing suppliers and demanders together to realize the mutual benefits of trade, the market process amalgamates the subjective preferences of agents over competing goals to indicate to producers through the price system what ends should be pursued and to what extent. In short, only through the institution of private property can market prices provide producers with the necessary information about consumer desires to satisfy what tolerance requires.

Prices for the factors of production similarly guide producers as to how to pursue the "correct" goals in the most economically efficient manner. By creating profits and losses, market prices create the incentive for producers to pursue various projects in a way that minimizes the use of resources and penalizes inefficiency. This effectively shrinks inefficient producers' control over resources. Market prices generated through the institution of private property thus simultaneously perform the dual functions required to effectively accommodate competing individual goals. In the face of multiple and contradictory individual ends, the market (a) identifies which ends should be pursued and to what extents and (b) satisfies these goals in a way that enhances rather than destroys social wealth.

Although any system confronted with scarcity is forced to sacrifice the pursuit of some ends for the pursuit of others, the market accommodates *any number* of competing ends—even those that directly conflict—that individuals value sufficiently. Thus, the market produces religious bookstores for Christians, pornography for hedonists, recycled goods for environmentalists, and foods for vegetarians and meat-lovers alike. Furthermore, each of these disparate lifestyle choices is produced in such a way—both in terms of quantity of the good produced and combination of resources used in its production—as to optimally satisfy society's disparate members. Liberalism thus maximizes the number of individual values that can co-exist without reducing social wealth.

Tolerance, Democracy and Dictatorship: The Fragility of Socialism Part I

Through the price system, the market reveals to producers how they should direct their activities in the face of multiple and competing consumer goals. Consumers with competing desires register their desires and the intensity of their desires, creating a coherent mechanism whereby their multiple ends are satisfied in an economically efficient manner. The price system amalgamates the disparate and competing subjective valuations of consumers' demands into an objective price that signals to producers how to proceed. In creating profits and losses, the price system simultaneously creates an incentive to accommodate these competing goals efficiently.

Without the price system, however, how will the central planners in a socialist state come to learn about consumers' goals and how they rank these goals where they compete with one another? Tolerance requires competing ends to be mutually accommodated in the magnitudes dictated by consumers' collective valuations of their importance. But clearly planning cannot work if socialism cannot determine what these demands are, let alone their relative magnitudes in consumers' eyes.

Since it explicitly precludes the market mechanism from performing this task, the only mechanisms socialism leaves to determine what ends society should aim to fulfill (and to what extent) are political ones. Concretely, this means one of two things: the socialist planning board may decide what goals will be pursued and in what amounts, or such decisions may be subjected to democratic procedure. In either event, socialism is unable to advance social welfare in the face of tolerance.

In the first instance, the wishes of those in political power are explicitly substituted for consumers' goals. This "solution" overcomes the hurdle that tolerance poses by denying it to enter the system. In this case, socialist planners simplify the problem they need to solve by pursuing their own ends rather than those of the citizens. Their welfare, instead of society's in general, receives the attention in this instance.

Putting to democratic vote decisions about what goals should be pursued and to what extent brings the ends of the public back into play. However, it fails to provide those in charge of planning with the information about individuals' valuations they need to accommodate competing desires. The reason for this is found in the intersection of arguments offered by F.A. Hayek in his seminal *Road to Serfdom*[9] and in Ken Arrow's *Social Choice and Individual Values*.[10] The authors have discussed this overlap elsewhere.[11] Here we recount some of their argument and connect it specifically to the issue of tolerance and fragility in the socialist system.

Arrow famously destroyed the idea that the voting mechanism could coherently translate individual values into a collective social choice fifty years ago. Arrow begins his discussion by contrasting an ideal dictatorship with the voting booth. Choice under dictatorship is by definition rational in the sense that any individual can be rational in his choices. A single will substitutes for all wills in determining the course of action. But Arrow wanted to figure out whether voting can make the same claim to rationality. "Can such consistency be attributed to collective modes of choice, where the wills of many people are involved?"[12] In other words, is it possible to construct a procedure beginning with a set of known individual tastes and ending in a pattern of social decision-making which would meet the basic tenets of rationality in choice? As is well known, Arrow argued that no such procedure was possible under reasonable assumptions.

Consider a situation where a vacant lot exists near downtown and the city council must decide what to do with the lot. The preferences of the three council members who must vote are given in Table 1.

If they submit the issue to democratic decision, they will find that the decision does not conform to the ordinary cannons of rational choice. If they are asked to choose between the Park (A) and the Parking Garage (B), the Park would win by a vote of two to one. If they then had to choose between the Park (A) and a School (C), the School would win by a vote of two to one. However, if they began the voting process by running the Parking Garage (B) against the School (C), the Parking would have won by a vote of two to one. The result of the vote process is not consistent, but instead, changes depending on the order in which the vote takes place. The winner, in other words, is not unambiguous and can be either A, B or C depending on how we start the pair-wise matching. This is known as the problem of cycling. Another way to put the vote paradox is to test the majority rule decision against the principle of transitivity in choice. If A > B, and B > C, then A > C. But in the example provided, majority rule will violate the principle of transitivity. A will win against B, and B will win against C, but C would win against A. Therefore, majority rule fails as a procedure for passing from individual tastes to collective choice in a rational manner.[13]

Table 12.1: Preference Scales of City Council Members

Council Member 1	Council Member 2	Council Member 3
Public Park (A)	Parking Garage (B)	Elementary School (C)
Parking Garage (B)	Elementary School (C)	Public Park (A)
Elementary School (C)	Public Park (A)	Parking Garage (B)

If democracy cannot coherently translate individuals' preferences for various ends into a collective preference, democracy cannot be used to determine what goals the central planning board in a socialist political economy should pursue. Voting is not a solution to the problem of tolerance that socialism confronts. Arrow's theorem suggests that for political decision-making to correspond to individual values, it must either take place over issues for which there is near universal agreement—i.e., individual ends are the same—or it must be dictatorial.

In severely limiting the size and scope of government, liberal political economy restricts the number of decisions it subjects to democratic decision-making to those few over which there is substantial agreement among individuals. The overwhelming majority of decisions are left up to individuals to pursue in the private sphere. Democratic decision-making under socialism, however, necessarily involves subjecting a much larger number of decisions to collective choice and, in doing so, applies majority voting to decisions about what goals should be pursued and in what ways where there is not near universal agreement among citizens. Collective decision-making cannot be used to reveal what goals society ought to pursue under socialism precisely because it involves applying collective decision-making to questions about goals over which there is no general agreement.

This point was raised by Hayek who stated:

> To direct all our activities according to a single plan presupposes that every one of our needs is given its rank in order of values which must be complete enough to make it possible to decide among all the different courses which the planner has to choose. It presupposes, in short, the existence of a complete ethical code in which all the different human values are allotted their due place.[14]

Hayek writes,

> The essential point for us is that no such complete ethical code exists. The attempt to direct all economic activity according to a single plan would raise innumerable questions to which the answer could be provided only by a moral rule, but to which existing morals have no answer and where there exists no agreed view on what ought to be done. People will have either no definite views or conflicting views on such questions because in the free society in which we have lived there has been no occasion to think about them and still less to form common opinions about them.[15]

His argument is that planning via democracy requires that we push democratic decision-making beyond its appropriate domain. In short, planning requires too much democracy.

Hayek points out that our cognitive capabilities limit our span of control and moral sympathy. The liberal doctrine:

> does not assume, as is often asserted, that man is egoistic or selfish or ought to be. It merely starts from the indisputable fact that the limits of our power of imagination make it impossible to include in our scale of values more than a sector of the needs of the whole society, and that, since, strictly speaking, scales of value can exist only in individual minds, nothing but partial scales of values exist—scales which are inevitably different and often inconsistent with each other.[16]

If we wish to avoid the problems raised by Arrow, the proper sphere of government action through democratic deliberation must therefore be determined by the extent to which individuals in society can agree to particular ends.

In other words, Hayek postulates a limit to our ability to come to agreement. Hayek argues,

> It is not difficult to see what must be the consequences when democracy embarks upon a course of planning which in its execution requires more agreement than in fact exists . . . Agreement will in fact exist only on the mechanism to be used. But it is a mechanism which can be used only for a common end; and the question of the precise goal toward which all activity is to be directed will arise as soon as the executive power has to translate the demand for a single plan into a particular plan.[17]

People may be able to come to an agreement on the desirability of a central plan, but not on the ends which that plan is to serve.

> That planning creates a situation in which it is necessary for us to agree on a much larger number of topics than we have been used to, and that in a planned system we cannot confine collective action to the tasks on which we can agree but are forced to produce agreement on everything in order that any action can be taken at all, is one of the features which contributes more than most to determining the character of a planned system.[18]

Planning thus requires submission to the unitary end of the common purpose.[19] In other words, unless we presuppose a singular rank order of values, democratic decision-making will thwart the planning process. And since such a singular rank order of values is not possible where individuals have different and competing ends, democratic outcomes will conflict with parts of the plan. If the plan is to take precedent, planning officials must be free from the strictures imposed by democratic procedures. Democratic decision-making under socialism thus faces pressure to give way to dictatorial decision-making by the planning board. As noted earlier, by doing this, socialist planners overcome the problem tolerance poses for them by eliminating tolerance from the system.

Hayek's argument presents planners with the following choices. Planners can have a coherent economic plan, but must suppress democratic procedure to achieve it. That is, they must oust tolerance and substitute the will of one for the wills of many. Alternatively, they may retain democratic procedures but suffer an incoherent plan as a result. In other words they can have tolerance, but planning in this case will not work. In the face of this choice, socialist planners opt for the latter.

Planning, Hayek argues, "leads to dictatorship because dictatorship is the most effective instrument of coercion and the enforcement of ideals and, as such, essential if central planning on a large scale is to be possible."[20] Planners overcome the problem that tolerance poses for planning by eliminating the conditions that lead to the need for tolerance—the co-existence of competing individual goals. In its place they substitute a singular goal which they decide, such as "industrial power," "military might," or some other end that is singular in its outcome. Economic decisions, those about trade-offs, are minimized and replaced with much simpler technological decisions that the system can handle.

Calculation and Toleration: The Fragility of Socialism Part II

The foregoing discussion established that the central planners in a socialist political economy are unable to deal with tolerance because they have no means of arriving at the information necessary to determine which of the multiple, competing goals of society's members it ought to pursue and to what extent. On the one hand, in abolishing private property, prices, and profit and loss, socialism cannot rely upon the decentralized decision-making of individuals to provide this information. On the other hand, socialism has no means of political decision-making to establish this information either. Democratic decision-making cannot work for this purpose where individuals have disparate and contradictory goals for the reasons described by Hayek and Arrow. Dictatorial decision-making will allow the plan to be coherent, but only because it substitutes the singular end of the planning board for the competing plans and goals of the many. In other words, it avoids the issue posed by tolerance altogether.

Confronted with the issue of tolerance, however, socialism has an even more difficult problem. This problem was raised by Ludwig von Mises in his 1920 essay, *Economic Calculation in the Socialist Commonwealth*. In this essay, Mises showed how *even if* the planning board had full knowledge of the goods and services consumers want produced, and thus the problem posed for socialism above were solved, it would still be unable to satisfy their desires without squandering scarce factors of production and in doing so harming social wealth.

Even if consumer valuations are known, the fact that consumer goals compete means that to avoid wasting resources, the planning board under socialism needs to know the most economically efficient way of satisfying those goals. For instance, if the planning board knows that consumers want a railroad, in the face of competing consumer ends, it must decide how the railroad is to be produced. Should tracks be made of steel, wood, platinum? What materials should be used to produce the train cars? If the planning board chooses the wrong materials, another goal that consumers value more highly will go unsatisfied because the means for its satisfaction will have been devoted to the production of the train.

Capitalism uses the price system to accommodate the plurality of competing consumer desires in a way that ensures these desires are satisfied in the order and quantities dictated by the intensity of consumer preferences. In abolishing private property in the means of production, however, socialism abolishes exchange in the means of production. Without exchange in the means of production, there can emerge no exchange ratios to indicate the relative scarcity of the means of production in the face of competing consumer desires. In short, there are no prices. Without prices, the planning board has no means of economic calculation to effectively accommodate the plurality of competing consumer goals. Tolerance of competing consumer ends prevents socialism from advancing material production.

Again, socialism can "overcome" this problem by substituting tolerance of competing consumer goals with a singular end determined by the planning board. In this case, the problem of scarcity, of trade-offs and competing ends, is eliminated. Here, planning can achieve what it sets out to do—maximize the achievement of the singular end. In fact, this is what war planning aims at; it reduces the numerous and competing goals of its citizens to the singular goal of more war machinery. For the reasons explained above, however, such planning is not an effective way to organize economic activity where there are multiple and competing ends. Furthermore, war economies are defined by their absence of tolerance for competing individual goals. For planning to work, disparate and contradictory individual desires must be subjugated to *the* "national good." Consumer ends and activities that conflict with this good cannot be tolerated.

If consumers have identical value scales and their goals do not compete, or what is equivalent, the ends of the planning board are substituted for the multiple, contradictory ends of individuals, socialism, and in fact *any* conceivable mode of social organization will not have a problem achieving its ends. In this event, there is no *economic* problem *per se* to be overcome. There remains a technological issue about how to ensure that the production of the selected end is maximized, but the fact that ends do not compete means that there is no economic question regarding how resources should be allocated between uses. However, tolerance introduces the specifically economic problem of how resources can be allocated in such a way that the more highly valued consumer desire is satisfied because the means required for its satisfaction have not been devoted to some less highly valued alternative. Without market prices for the means of production, however, socialism has no means of doing this. The result is economic waste, and with it, declining social wealth.

Conclusion

Robust political economy requires us to relax assumptions that make it easier for political economic arrangements to perform effectively in order to establish their relative abilities to perform well where more problematic situations are confronted. Introducing into systems individuals who seek diverse goals, and whose goals compete with one another for scarce resources, creates the distinctively economic question for the system at hand. Tolerance requires a system to accommodate multiple and competing ends in a manner consistent with the valuations of diverse individuals. A robust political economic arrangement is up to the task posed by tolerance. A fragile one is not.

In relying upon the market process to generate the necessary information for the appropriate participants, liberalism accommodates competing individual ends and does so efficiently. In abolishing the market, socialism has no means at its disposal to perform the functions required for tolerance. As we have defined it, tolerance necessitates utilizing widely dissipated information about various consumer goals including the intensity of consumers' preferences, and satisfying those goals in a way that is consistent with consumer valuations, so that the disparate ends of society's members can co-exist without destroying social wealth. Robustness in the face of tolerance can thus be viewed as a form of robustness in the face of imperfectly available information. Precisely because of their disparate abilities to handle problems of information, however, liberal and socialist political economy find themselves at polar opposite ends of the robustness spectrum in the face of tolerance.

Notes

1. The authors gratefully acknowledge the Oloffson Weaver Fellowship for financial support.
2. Ludwig von Mises, *Liberalism* (Irvington-on-the-Hudson, N.Y.: Foundation for Economic Education, 1985 [1927]), 55-57.
3. Peter Boettke and Peter Leeson, "Liberalism, Socialism, and Robust Political Economy," *Journal of Markets and Morality* 7, no. 1 (2004): 99-111.
4. John Locke, *A Letter Concerning Toleration*. (London: Printed for A. Churchill, 1689).
5. John Stuart Mill, *On Liberty* (London: J.W. Parker and Son, 1859).
6. F.A. Hayek, *The Constitution of Liberty* (Chicago: University of Chicago Press, 1960).
7. Robert Nozick, *Anarchy, State and Utopia* (New York: Harper and Row, 1974).
8. Hayek, *The Constitution of Liberty*.
9. F.A. Hayek, *The Road to Serfdom* (Chicago: University of Chicago Press, 1944).
10. Kenneth Arrow, *Social Choice and Individuals Values* (New York: Wiley and Sons, 1951).
11. Peter Boettke and Peter Leeson, "Hayek, Arrow, and the Problems of Democratic Decision-Making," *Journal of Public Finance and Public Choice* 20, no. 1 (2002): 9-21.
12. Arrow, *Social Choice and Individuals Values*, 2.
13. Arrow, *Social Choice and Individuals Values*, 3.
14. Hayek, *The Road to Serfdom*, 57.
15. Hayek, *The Road to Serfdom*, 58.
16. Hayek, *The Road to Serfdom*, 59.
17. Hayek, *The Road to Serfdom*, 61.
18. Hayek, *The Road to Serfdom*, 62.
19. William Riker, *Liberalism Against Populism* (Prospect Heights, Ill.: Waveland Press, 1982).
20. Hayek, *The Road to Serfdom*, 70.

Tolerance and the Internet
David Resnick

At its inception, the Internet was a realm of tolerance. Unlike its history in the real world, tolerance on the Internet was not achieved through long and protracted political struggle. It was written into the Internet code as a basic norm governing its operation. In no small measure, the Internet's development and growth as a space of pure tolerance was due to the fact that at the time of its creation, it was under the radar screen. It was an elite and geeky form of computer mediated communication in which governments, as well as the public at large, were simply not interested. As new, easier to use, and less expensive technology became available, the Internet attracted millions of new users. It also attracted the attention of people who thought that the tolerance of the early Net was too extensive, and who had the power to change it.

At its inception, the Internet was hailed as a savior of modern civilization. It would remake our social and political world. So-called Netizens would create free, open, and tolerant new communities. Not only would the Internet empower ordinary persons to become active citizens of Cyberspace, but it would enable them to transcend the narrow, selfish, and bigoted perspectives which dominate the institutions and practices of ordinary life. While most pundits held that it would be very beneficial, there had always been an undercurrent of doubt—a fear that this new and powerful technology would result in a more repressive and less tolerant society. Early enthusiasts and detractors alike agreed, however, that the Internet would change everything; yet, so far, both the utopians and the techno-phobes have been proven wrong. Not everything has changed; indeed, it is not clear exactly what has changed other than the Internet itself. It has turned into a highly complex and ambiguous phenomenon, and no more so than when we examine its impact on tolerance.

To explore the impact of the Internet on tolerance, I will frame the discussion in terms of tolerance/intolerance, since a particular practice might have both a positive and a negative impact. It is useful to explore the impact of the Internet from three viewpoints:

(1) Tolerance/intolerance within the Net, which refers to the life of cyber-communities and other Net activities which have little or no impact on life off the Net. It considers how Netizens interact with each other online.

(2) The impact of the Net on tolerance/intolerance, which refers to the ways that the Internet affects ordinary life in the real world. This has two aspects, the impact of the structure of the Net itself, and specific intentional uses of the Net to spread tolerance or intolerance.

(3)Tolerance/intolerance which affects the Net, which refers to the host of attempts by governments and others to make the Internet a more tolerant (or intolerant) medium.

Tolerance/Intolerance within the Net

The period before the World Wide Web and the explosion of the online population appeared to be an age of pure tolerance. There was no discrimination based on race, religion, social class, ethnic origin, gender and the like. In fact, this lack of discrimination was considered one of the great strengths of the Internet. This tolerance was captured by the famous *New Yorker* cartoon of a canine sitting at a monitor proclaiming, "On the Internet, no one knows you're a dog."[1] Identity itself was flexible. Many people enjoyed participating in role playing games in which they pretended to be whatever they wanted to be.

There were actions that could bring on sanctions. Even people who thought of themselves as extremely tolerant drew the line somewhere. There were three types of behavior which elicited intolerant responses. The first was irrelevant postings—one of the great taboos. People felt that it was a waste of already scanty bandwidth. To our surprise, some colleagues and I encountered this type of intolerance when we were accused of spamming while conducting one of the first polls on the Internet.[2]

The second type of intolerance was scorn for the *newbies*, people who were not acquainted with *netiquette*, the informal rules of the Net. Those who went online were expected to have minimal knowledge of how things were done, and if they made especially stupid mistakes, they were kicked out of groups. This was sometimes justified in terms of shortage of bandwidth, but most often it was the expression of ordinary intolerance, the refusal to suffer novices gladly. Unlike those who knew the rules but engaged in irrelevant postings anyway, these folks just didn't know the rules.

The third type of intolerance seems quaint today. The early Internet was considered a noncommercial medium. You could sell ideas, but not things. Advertising was banned. There was a famous case of two lawyers in 1994 who posted an advertisement for their service to several thousand Usenet news groups. This caused an immense uproar, and they undoubtedly became the two most hated individuals in the history of the Internet up to that time. Now, of course, ads are rampant.[3]

Though the Net prided itself on its tolerance, it also had to confront in practical terms a standard philosophical question. Must we tolerate the intolerant? The preferred libertarian way of dealing with people who wished to revel in their intolerance was to establish a special area for them so that everyone else need not be disturbed by their ranting. However, there were people who did not harbor views most of society would label intolerant, but who were themselves intolerant of views differing from their own and were all too willing to express their hostility in unacceptable ways. These two types, of course, sometimes overlapped. Some degree of civility is necessary to carry on an extended fruitful discussion. Every once in a while so-called *flame wars* would erupt. A person would respond to a communication they deemed offensive with a scathing reply, often replete with obscenities and personal denunciations. This would prompt an equally intemperate reply, and a flame war would begin. Sometimes these flame wars would burn themselves out, and the group would return to more civil discourse. At other times, the whole group would be destroyed as more and more people were turned off by the hostilities.

The Impact of the Net on Tolerance/Intolerance

It seems reasonable to assume that the Net itself has some impact on the attitudes and dispositions of those who use it. One argument on the side of tolerance suggests that using the Internet increases tolerance because it exposes people to new and different viewpoints. They can easily encounter a range of opinions and attitudes which they would not otherwise experience. This would especially be the case for those who lived in isolated, closed homogeneous societies. The entire world of diversity is open to them online. The Internet is a public space, like the public spaces of great cities in which people encounter those of dissimilar backgrounds and ethnicities in a dense urban environment. They learn that difference need not be equated with danger, and strangers need not be a threat.

Another argument counters that the cornucopia of views and perspectives on the Internet does not necessarily translate into encounters which breed tolerance. Putnam has observed that real-world interactions often force us to confront diversity, whereas interactions online can lead to homogeneity in views and outlooks: "Place-based communities may be supplanted by interest-based communities."[4] Sunstein has also argued that rather than encouraging productive encounters among those who hold different views and attitudes, the Internet engenders fragmentation. While the Internet has dramatically increased options, in practice, people do not necessarily use them. People online have the ability to filter out what does not interest them. When people tailor their encounters according to their interests, they need not confront views different from their own.

Rather than leading to tolerance, Sunstein claims that this fragmentation creates its own problems: "If diverse groups are seeing and hearing quite different points of view, or focusing on quite different topics, mutual understanding might be difficult, and it might be increasingly hard for people to solve problems that society faces together."[5] Sunstein further challenges the optimistic evaluation of the Internet by pointing to the phenomenon of group polarization. There is evidence that when a group of like-minded people deliberate about an issue, the members tend to adopt a more extreme position. As people are exposed to the views of others in a group who have the same orientation, they become more convinced that they are right.[6]

According to Sunstein, the Net is a "breeding ground for extremism" because like-minded people are debating more and more among themselves without listening to contrary views.[7] This would seem to be a bad thing, but he is careful to point out that such extremism might be good in certain circumstances. He cites civil rights, anti-slavery, and sex equality as movements that were considered extreme in their own time. He points out, however, that even if there is homogeneity of opinions within a movement, it might contribute to the diversity of ideas within society. These enclaves could serve as incubators for new attitudes, positions, and programs which would add to the overall process of democratic deliberation. In order for this to occur, however, there is a need for the committed and convinced to reach out to those who hold different views.

This argument shows some of the political complexities of tolerance. Extremists are often the means for increasing tolerance in society. Their own intolerance may generate arguments and actions leading to the modification of intolerant practices by changing the ways particular issues are discussed, or they may serve as the vanguard of political movements for change and force new issues onto the political agenda. Whether or not the fragmentation and relative isolation of the Internet population is good or bad for society in the long run, if Sunstein is correct, as currently structured, the internet tends to make people less tolerant.

A recent analysis of survey research data challenges Sunstein's position. This analysis was made possible by the fact that the General Social Survey, which has been conducted since 1974, included questions about Internet usage for the first time for the year 2000. The principal researcher for the Internet part of the survey, John P. Robinson, professor of sociology at the University of Maryland at College Park, reported that the results showed "People who are more likely to support more tolerant positions are more likely to use the Internet. What we see is not so much a digital divide as a diversity divide." However, increased usage of the Net does not result in increased tolerance. Heavy users of the Net are not significantly more tolerant than those who use it less frequently.[8]

So far we have considered structural arguments about the effect of the Internet. We now briefly look at some ways people are using the Internet to try to influence tolerance and intolerance directly. Most commentators refer to groups dedicated to increasing intolerance as "hate groups." Hate groups were online for years before the Internet and the World Wide Web. In 1985 the Anti-Defamation League published a report entitled *Computerized Networks of Hate* which described the operations of "Aryan Nation Liberty Net" which was on a computer bulletin board accessible to anyone with a modem and home computer. Even in those prehistoric years of computer mediated communication, this bulletin board used tactics which have become commonplace on hate group sites today, spreading racist propaganda, recruiting new members, soliciting money, and bypassing the prohibitions of other less tolerant nations than the U.S. Hate groups have also used Internet Relay chat channels, USENET discussion groups, and listservs, both moderated and unmoderated. Though all these types of electronic communication have been used, the preferred forum now is the World Wide Web. The first American white supremacist website, Stormfront, was launched in March of 1995, and there have been literally thousands of racist and other hate sites created since then.[9]

While the Internet has been used to further all sorts of political and social causes including the most virulent racist, sexist, and homophobic, it has also been used by those struggling to increase tolerance. This year's Webby award for the best activist web site went to Tolerance.org, which is a project of the Southern Poverty Law Center. It includes current news stories as well as numerous short articles designed to spread tolerance, such as "10 ways to fight hate," "101 Tools for Tolerance," Explore your hidden biases," and "Deconstructing biased language."[10] The Web also contains lists of sites which can be used for teaching tolerance.[11] Both pro-tolerance and anti-tolerance web sites are flourishing on the Net.

What are we to conclude? Does the Internet increase tolerance or intolerance? It's hard to say. Structural arguments such as Sunsteinn's that polarization and fragmentation lead to extremism are ambiguous. It might depend upon the predispositions of those who participate in the discussions. It is possible that the tolerant become more tolerant, and the intolerant become more intolerant. Claims that the Net increases intolerance because it enables hate groups to recruit and to spread their messages can be countered by the fact that a great many groups use the Internet to spread a message of tolerance. In terms of sheer numbers, I suspect that the anti-tolerance sites predominate. Though the number of sites cannot be equated with effectiveness, it is my impression that the Internet has given more of a boost to hate groups than to those promoting tolerance.

The Internet has certainly changed since the early days when it flourished under a policy of benign neglect. It has become a subject of government action and public policy debates around the world. We now turn to a discussion of some of the ways in which the old realm of pure tolerance has been modified by new concerns and regulations.

Tolerance/Intolerance Which Affects the Net

Different cultures and legal traditions have significant impact on the way the Net now operates. Many countries other than the United States ban racist and other extremist web sites. Because of the first amendment of the U.S. Constitution, which protects free speech, the U.S. government cannot remove such sites from the Internet. This has caused many neo-Nazi sites intended for Europeans to switch to American Internet service providers (ISPs). Some ISPs have tried to avoid being used as conduits for hate groups by creating service contracts prohibiting subscribers from setting up hate sites. Organizations like the Anti-Defamation League have urged private individuals to use filtering software to keep such sites off their home computers.[12]

While the first amendment also protects ISPs, there have been attempts, for example, by the Simon Wiesenthal Center, to convince them to remove objectionable web sites from their servers. Sometimes this effort succeeds and sometimes not. Given the expansive and international nature of the Net, sites can easily migrate from one ISP to another. Pressuring ISPs has come under criticism by civil liberties groups. While approving of the Wiesenthal Center's campaign to expose hate group sites, the American Civil Liberties Union (ACLU) has criticized their attempts to pressure ISPs. The ACLU said "It is particularly troublesome that an organization like the Wiesenthal Center that is dedicated to promoting tolerance would seek to erode the liberty most necessary for a free and tolerant society—free speech."[13] Civil liberties organizations equate tolerance with free speech, but even they recognize that free speech has its limits. They do not countenance fraud, criminal conspiracy, libel, child pornography, and other types of speech which have been recognized in our society as beyond tolerance.

What one society is willing to tolerate, another is not. This discrepancy has an impact on attempts by governments to regulate the Internet. While tolerating gambling under regulated conditions off line, the United States government has conducted a concerted campaign against online gambling. Other countries see nothing wrong with online gambling and are perfectly willing to regulate it and tax it.[14] While the United States finds it intolerable that gambling is going on, the French find using only English intolerable on a French web site. The French government once sued an English language web site in France affiliated with an American university because it offered services in English but not in French.[15]

The old realm of pure tolerance on the Internet has changed because of the regulatory activities of governments around the world. In 1966 John Perry Barlow, and Internet activist (and Grateful Dead songwriter), wrote the widely distributed so called "Declaration of Independence of Cyberspace" in which he asserted that Cyberspace exists beyond government borders. Addressing governments, he proclaimed, "You have no morel right to rule us nor do you possess any methods of enforcement we have true reason to fear."[16] In the light of history, statements proclaiming Cyberspace as a government-free zone seems hopelessly naïve. The Chinese began permitting commercial Internet accounts in 1995 and, since then, have issued at least 60 sets of regulations intended to control content. For example, Article 57 of the Telecommunications Regulations, which went into effect in September of 2000, prohibits the use of the Internet to disseminate, among other things, "material that harms the prosperity and interests of the state," "material that arouses ethnic animosities, ethnic discrimination, or undermines ethnic solidarity," "material that undermines state religious policies, or promotes cults and feudal superstitions," "material that spreads rumors, disturbs social order, or undermines social stability," and "material that spreads obscenities, pornography, gambling, violence." Violations of such regulations can lead to serious consequences. ISPs can be fined or closed, and users face severe criminal penalties.[17]

The Internet has been fundamentally altered by the attempts of governments to regulate it. While not all of these have been successful, it is still evident that in many parts of the world the intolerance of governments has molded the Internet in their own image.

On balance, is the Net more likely to have a positive or negative impact on Tolerance? Actually, it is most likely that the Net will have little effect. I believe that tolerance is another aspect of the Internet in which what I have called "the normalization thesis" will be validated. Those who are very optimistic or pessimistic about the Net exaggerate its impact as an independent factor in social change. The short history of the Net shows that, as it matures, it comes to increasingly reflect the real world, and it is implausible that, by itself, it will have a significant impact on behavior or attitudes. What people bring to the Net, rather than what they do on it, is more important in determining their fundamental attitudes and beliefs.

Notes

1. Peter Steiner, "On the Internet, no one knows you're a dog," *The New Yorker* 69, no. 20 (July 5, 1993): 61.

2. B. Fisher, M. Margolis, and D. Resnick, "Breaking ground on the virtual frontier: Surveying civic life on the Internet," *American Sociologist* (1996): 11-29; B. Fisher, M. Margolis, and D. Resnick, "Surveying the Internet: Democratic theory and civic life in cyberspace," *Southeastern Political Review* 24 (1996): 399-429.

3. David Loundy, "Lawyers' electronic ads leave bad taste," *Chicago Daily Law Bulletin*, 9 March 1995, 6, http://www.Loundy.com/CDLB/Spam.html.

4. Robert Putnam, *Bowling Alone* (New York: Simon & Schuster, 2000), 178.

5. Cass R. Sunstein, *Republic.com* (Princeton: Princeton University Press, 2001), 61.

6. Sunstein, *Republic.com*, 65-72.

7. Sunstein, *Republic.com*, 71.

8. Jeffrey R. Young, "A Study Finds That Web Users Are More Tolerant Than Non-Users," *The Chronicle of Higher Education*, 15 June 2001, http://chronicle.com/free/2001/06/2001061501t.htm.

9. Anti-Defemation League Law Enforcement Agency Resource Network, *Poisoning the Web*, 1999 Anti-Defemation League, http://www.adl.org/poisoning_web/introduction.asp.

10. The Southern Poverty Law Center, *Tolerance.org Home Page*, 2002, www.tolerance.org.

11. B. Goodman, *Teaching Tolerance, Discussing Diversity*, Wilmetter, Ill.: Wilmette Public Library, 12 March 2002, http://www.wilmette.lib.il.us/tolerance.html.

12. Anti-Defemation League, *Poisoning the Web*.

13. Kevin Anderson, "Battling Online Hate," *BBC News Online*, 30 August 2001, http://news.bbc.co.uk/1/hi/world/americas/1516271.stm.

14. Michael Margolis and David Resnick, *Politics as usual: The cyberspace "revolution"* (Thousand Oaks, Calif.: Sage, 2000), 157-81.

15. Margolis and Resnick, *Politics as usual*, 12.
16. John Perry Barlow, "A Declaration of Independence of Cyberspece," *Electronic Frontier Foundation*, 8 February 1996, http://homes.eff.org/~barlow/Declaration-Final.html.
17. "Freedom of Expression and the Internet in China," *Human Rights Watch*, 1 August 2001, http://www.hrw.org/backgrounder/asia/china-bck-0701.htm.

Selected Bibliography

"Freedom of Expression and the Internet in China." *Human Rights Watch*, 1 August 2001. http://www.hrw.org/backgrounder/asia/china-bck-0701.htm.

"Special issue: National identity in Europe." *Political Psychology* 24, no. 2. (2003).

Aboud, F. *Children and prejudice*. Oxford, U.K.: Blackwell, 1988.

Achen, Christopher H. *The Statistical Analsis of Quasi-Experiments*. Berkeley: University of California Press, 1986.

Ackerman, Bruce. *Social Justice in the Liberal State*. New Haven: Yale University, 1980.

Adelson, J. "The political imagination of the young adolescent." *Daedalus* 100 (1971): 1013-50.

Altemeyer, B. "The other 'authoritarian personality'." *Advances in Experimental Social Psychology* 30 (1998),47-92

Alvermann, D., D. O'Brien, and D. Dillon. "What teachers do when they say they're having discussions of content area reading assignments: A qualitative analysis." *Reading Research Quarterly* 24 (1990): 296-322.

American Heritage Dictionary, Fourth Edition 2000. On-line version. http://www.bartleby.com/61/31/T0253100.html.

Anderson, Kevin. "Battling Online Hate." *BBC News Online*, 30 August 2001. http://news.bbc.co.uk/1/hi/world/americas/1516271.stm.

Annan, Kofi. "Role of United Nations Development Programme Much Clearer Now." Keynote address at the Ministerial Meeting on the UN Development Program (UNDP), 11 September 2000. http://www.undp.org/execbrd/pdf/sgspeech.pdf.

Anti-Defemation League Law Enforcement Agency Resource Network. *Poisoning the Web*. Anti-Defemation League, 1999. http://www.adl.org/poisoning_web/introduction.asp.

Appadurai, A. "Disjuncture and Difference in the Global Cultural Economy." P. 324 in *The Globalization Reader*, edited by F. Lechner and J. Boli. Malden, Mass.: Blackwell Publishers, 2000.

Arrow, Kenneth *Social Choice and Individuals Values*. New York: Wiley and Sons, 1951.

Augustine. *Political Writings*. Edited by Ernest L. Fortin & Douglas Kries. Indianapolis: Hackett, 1994.

Aveneri, S., and A. de-Shalit, eds. *Communitarianism and Individualism*. Oxford: Oxford University Press, 1992.

Avery, P. G. "Political tolerance: How adolescents deal with dissenting groups." Pp. 39–51 in *The development of political understanding*, edited by H. Haste and J. Torney-Purta. San Francisco: Jossey-Bass, 1992.

Avery, P. G., and A. M. Simmons. "Civic life as conveyed in U.S. civics and history textbooks." *International Journal of Social Education* 15, no. 2 (Fall/Winter 2000/2001): 105-30.

Avery, P. G., D. Hoffman, J. L. Sullivan, E. Theiss-Morse, A. Fried, K. Bird, S. Johnstone, and K. Thalhammer. *Tolerance for diversity of beliefs: A secondary curriculum unit.* Boulder, Colo.: Social Science Education Consortium, 1993.

Avery, P. G., D. W. Johnson, R. T. Johnson, and J. M. Mitchell. "Teaching an understanding of war and peace through structured academic controversies." Pp. 260-80 in *How children understand war and peace*, edited by A. Raviv, L. Oppenheimer, and D. Bar-Tal. San Francisco: Jossey-Bass, 1999.

Avery, P. G., K. Bird, S. Johnstone, J. L. Sullivan, and K. Thalhammer. "Exploring political tolerance with adolescents: Do all of the people have all of the rights all of the time?" *Theory and Research in Social Education* 20, no. 4 (1992): 386-420.

Bai, M. "Another Contested Contest?" *The New York Times Magazine*, 31 October 2004, section 6, 20.

Baldi, S., M. Perie, D. Skidmore, E. Greenberg, and C. Hahn. *What democracy means to ninth-graders: U.S. results from the international IEA Civic Education Study (NCES 2001-096).* U.S. Department of Education, National Center for Education Statistics. Washington, D.C.: U.S. Government Printing Office, 2001.

Barlow, John Perry. "A Declaration of Independence of Cyberspece." *Electronic Frontier Foundation*, 8 February 1996. http://homes.eff.org/~barlow/Declaration-Final.html.

Barnow, Burt, Glen Cain, and Arthur Goldberger. "Issues in the Analysis of Selectivity Bias." In *Evaluation Studies Review Annual*, vol. 5, edited by E. Stromsdorfer and G. Farkas. Beverly Hills, Calif.: Sage Publications, 1980.

Basow, S. A. *Gender: Stereotypes and roles.* 3rd ed. Pacific Grove, Calif.: Brooks/Cole, 1992.

Baumeister, A. T. "Multicultural Citizenship, Identity and Conflict." Pp. 87-102 in *Toleration, Identity, and Difference*, edited by J. Horton and S. Mendus. London: MacMillan Press, 1999.

Bellah, Robert. *The Broken Covenant: American Civil Religion in Time of Trial.* New York: Crossroad, 1975.

Berger, Peter L. *The Sacred Canopy: Element of a Sociological Theory of Religion.* Garden City, N.Y.: Doubleday, 1967.

Berk, Richard A., and Subhash C. Ray. "Selection Biases in Sociological Data." *Social ScienceResearch* 11 (1982): 352-98.

Bickmore, K. "Learning inclusion/inclusion in learning: Citizenship education for a pluralistic society." *Theory and Research in Social Education* 21, no. 4 (1993): 341-84.

Bird, K., J. L. Sullivan, P. G. Avery, K. Thalhammer, and S. Wood. "Not just lip-synching anymore: Education and tolerance revisited." *The review of Education/Pedagogy/ Cultural Studies* 16, nos. 3-4 (1994): 373-86.

Blackwell, J., and P. Hart. *Cities, suburbs, and blacks: A study of concerns, distrust, and alienation.* Bayside, N.Y.: General Hall, 1982.

Bobo, Lawrence, and Frederick C. Licari. "Education and political tolerance: Testing the effects of cognitive sophistication and target group affect." *Public Opinion Quarterly* 53 (1989): 285-308.

Boettke, Peter, and Peter Leeson. "Hayek, Arrow, and the Problems of Democratic Decision-Making." *Journal of Public Finance and Public Choice* (2002): 9-21.

——. "Liberalism, Socialism, and Robust Political Economy." *Journal of Markets and Morality* (2004): 99-111.

Bogardus, Emory S. "Measuring Social Distances." *Journal of Applied Sociology* (1925): 299-308.

Booth, John, and Patricia Richards. "Civil Society, Social Capital and Democratization in Central America." *Journal of Politics* 60 (1998): 780-801.

Bork, Robert. "Neutral Principles and Some First Amendment Problems." *Indiana Law Journal* 47, no. 1 (1971).

Bratton, Michael, and Robert Mattes. "Support for Democracy in Africa: Intrinsic or Instrumental?" *British Journal of Political Science* 31 (2001): 447-74.

Bratton, Michael, Philip Alderfer, Georgia Bowser, and Joseph Temba. "The Effects of Civic Education on Political Culture: Evidence from Zambia." *World Development* 27 (1999): 807-24.

Breen, Richard, *Regression Models: Censored, Sample-Selected, or Truncated Data.* Thousand Oaks, Calif..: Sage Publications, 1996.

Brewer, Marilynn. "The psychology of prejudice: Ingroup love or outgroup hate?" *Journal of Social Issues*, 55 (1999): 429-44.

Brewer, Marilynn, and Rupert Brown. "Intergroup relations." Pp. 554-94 in *The Handbook of Social Psychology*, 4th edition, edited by Daniel T. Gilbert, Susan T. Fiske and Gardner Lindzey. New York: McGraw-Hill, 1998.

Brody, R. A. *Secondary education and political attitudes: Examining the effects on political tolerance of the "We the People..." curriculum.* Calabasas, Calif,: Center for Civic Education, 1994. ERIC Document Reproduction Service, ED 460881.

Brown, Jr., S. M. "Hobbes: The Taylor Thesis." *Philosophical Review* 68 (1959): 303-23.

Buchanan, James, and Gordon Tullock. *The Calculus of Consent.* Ann Arbor, Mich.: University of Michigan, 1962.

Budziszewski, J. "The Illusion of Moral Neutrality." *First Things* 35, (August/September 1993): 32-37.

———. Appendix 3, "Patristic Sources." In *True Tolerance.* New Brunswick, N.J.: Transaction Publishers, [1992] 2000.

———. *True Tolerance: Liberalism and the Necessity of Judgment.* New Brunswick, N.J.: Transaction Publishers, 1992.

Buffalo News, 8 May 2005, Viewpoints Section, p. 15.

Cantril, Hadley. *Public Opinion, 1935-1946.* Princeton: Princeton University Press, 1951.

Capps, Walter H. *Religious Studies: The Making of a Discipline.* Minneapolis: Fortress Press, 1995.

Carlson, Dennis. "Gayness, Multicultural Education, and Community." *Educational Foundations* 8, no. 4 (1994): 5-25.

Carothers, Thomas. *Aiding Democracy Abroad: The Learning Curve.* Washington, D.C.: Carnegie Endowment for International Peace, 1999.

———. *Assessing Democracy Assistance: The Case of Romania.* Washington, D.C.: Carnegie Endowment for International Peace, 1996.

Carroll, J., W. Broadnex, G. Contreras, T. Mann, N. Orenstein, and J. Steihm. *We the people: A review of U.S. government and civics textbooks.* Washington, D.C.: People for the American Way, 1987.

Chaiken, S., E. Pomerantz, and R. Giner-Sorolla. "Structural Consistency and Attitude Strength." Pp. 387-412 in *Attitude Strength: Antecedents and Consequences*, edited by R. Petty and J. Krosnick. Mahwah, N. J., Erlbaum, 1995.

Chong, D. "How people think, reason, and feel about rights and liberties." *American Journal of Political Science* 37, no. 3 (1993): 867-99.

Clooney, Francis X. *Thinking Ritually: Rediscovering the Purva Mimamsa of Jaimini.* Vienna: Indological Insitute of the University of Vienna, 1990.

Conover, P. J., and D. D. Searing. "A political socialization perspective." Pp. 91-124 in *Rediscovering the Democratic Purposes of Education*, edited by L. M. McDonnell, P.M. Timpane, and R. Benjamin. Lawrence, Kans.: University of Kansas Press, 2000.

Corbett, Michael. *Political Tolerance in America: Freedom and Equality in Public Attitudes*. New York: Longman, 1982.

Cornbleth, C. "Images of America: What youth do know about the United States." *American Educational Research Journal* 29, no. 2 (2002): 519-52.

Cranston, Maurice. "Toleration." *The Encyclopedia of Philosophy*. Vol. 8. Edited by Paul Edwards. New York: Macmillan, 1967.

———. "John Locke and the Case for Toleration." In *On Toleration*, edited by Susan Mendus and David Edwards. Oxford, U.K.: Clarendon Press, 1987.

Creppel, Ingrid. *Toleration and Identity: Foundations in Early Modern Thought*. New York: Routledge, 2003.

Crespi, Irving. "What Kinds of Attitude Measures Are Predictive of Behavior?" *Public Opinion Quarterly*, 35 (1971): 327-34.

Crick, Bernard. *Political Theory and Practice*. London: Allen Lane the Penguin Press, 1971.

Dalton, Russell. "Communists and Democrats: Democratic Attitudes in the Two Germanies." *British Journal of Political Science* 24, (1994): 469-93.

Davis, J. A. "Communism, conformity, cohorts, and categories: American tolerance in 1954 and 1972-73." *American Journal of Sociology* 81 (1975): 491-513.

Davis, James Allan, Tom W. Smith, and Peter V. Marsden. *General Social Survey 2002*. Chicago: National Opinion Research Center; Storrs, Conn.: The Roper Center for Public Opinion Research, University of Connecticut. Cited and discussed in *American Attitudes* (Ithaca, N.Y.: New Strategist Publications, Inc., 2005), 209-18.

De Figueiredo, Rui J.P., Jr., and Zachary Elkins. "Are patriots bigots? An inquiry into the vices of in-group pride." *American Journal of Political Science*, 47 (2003): 171-88.

de Tocqueville, Alexis. *Democracy in America*. New York: J. & H.G. Langley, 1840.

Delanty, G. *Citizenship in a Global Age*. Buckingham: Open University Press, 2000.

Delpit, L. *Other people's children: Cultural conflict in the classroom*. New York: New York Press, 1995.

Deutscher, Irwin. "Words and Deeds: Social Science and Social Policy." In *The Consistency Controversy*, edited by Allen E. Liska. New York: John Wiley & Sons, 1975.

Devine, P.G. "Stereotypes and prejudice: Their automatic and controlled components." *Journal of Personality and Social Psychology* 56, no. 1 (1989): 5-18.

Dewey, J. "The Search for the Great Community." Pp. 61-65 in *Twentieth Century Political Theory*, edited by S.E. Bronner. New York: Routledge, 1997.

———. *Democracy and Education: An Introduction to the Philosophy of Education*. New York: The MacMillan Company, 1933.

———. *Freedom and Culture*. Buffalo, N.Y.: Prometheus Books, 1989.

———. *Individualism Old and New*. New York: Minton, Balch and Company, 1930.

Diamond, Larry. *Promoting Democracy in the 1990s: Actors and Instruments, Issues and Imperatives*. New York: Carnegie Corporation of New York, 1995.

Douglas, M. "Introduction to Grid/Group Analysis." In *Essays in the Sociology of Perception*, edited by Mary Douglas. London: Routledge, 1982.

———. *Natural Symbols: Explorations in Cosmology*. New York: Pantheon Books, 1982.

———. *Risk and Blame: Essays in Cultural Theory*. London: Routledge, 1992.

———. *Thought Styles*. Thousand Oaks, Calif.: Sage, 1996.

Douglas, M., and A. Wildavsky. *Risk and Culture*. Berkeley: University of California Press, 1982.

Dovidio, J. F., G. Maruyama, and M. G. Alexander. "A social psychology of national and international group relations." *Journal of Social Issues* 54, no. 4 (1998): 831-46.

Duckitt, John. "Authoritarianism and group identification: A new view of an old construct." *Political Psychology*, 10 (1989): 63-84.

Duncan, L. E., B. E. Peterson, and D. G. Winter. "Authoritarianism and gender role: Toward a psychological analysis of hegemonic relationships." *Personality and Social Psychology Bulletin* 23, no. 1 (1997): 41-49.

Dworkin, R. "Liberal Community." Pp. 205-24 in *Communitarianism and Individualism*, edited by S. Avenevi and A. de-Shalit. Oxford: Oxford University Press, 1992.

Dworkin, Ronald. "Liberalism." In *Public and Private Morality*, edited by Stuart Hampshire. Cambridge: Cambridge University Press, 1978.

Dye, T. R., and H. L. Zeigler. *American Politics in the Media Age*. Monterey, Calif.: Brooks/Cole Publishing Company, 1983.

——. *The Few and the Many: Uncommon Readings in American Politics*. Belmont, Calif.: Duxbury Press, 1972.

Eagly, A. H. and S. Chaiken. *The Psychology of Attitudes*. Ft. Worth, Tex.: Harcourt, Brace, Jovanovich, 1993.

Edelman, M. *Politics as Symbolic Action*. Chicago: Markham Publishing Company, 1971.

——. *The Symbolic Uses of Politics*. Urbana: The University of Illinois Press, 1964.

Ehman, L. H. "The American school in the political socialization process." Review of Educational Research 50, no. 1 (1980): 99-119.

Eisenberg, A. N. "Accommodation and Coherence: In Search of a General Theory for Adjudicating Claims of Faith, Conscience, and Culture." Pp. 147-66 in *Engaging Cultural Differences : the multicultural challenge in liberal democracies*, edited by R. A. Shweder, M. Minow, and H. R. Markus. New York: Russell Sage Foundation, 2002.

Ekehammar, Bo, Nazar Akrami, and Tadesse Araya. "Gender differences in implicit prejudice." *Personality and Individual Differences* 34 (2003): 1509-23.

Ellison, Christopher G., and Daniel A. Powers. "The Contact Hypothesis and Racial Attitudes Among Black Americans." *Social Science Quarterly* 75 (1994): 385-400.

Espinal, R. "The Dominican Republic: An Ambiguous Democracy." In *Constructing Democratic Governance: Mexico, Central America and the Caribbean in the 1990s*, edited by J. Dominguez and A. Lowenthal. Baltimore: Johns Hopkins University Press, 1996.

Evans, G., and S. Whitefield. "The Politics and Economics of Democratic Commitment: Support for Democracy in Transitional Societies." *British Journal of Political Science* 25 (1995): 485-514.

Feingold, A. "Gender differences in personality: A meta-analysis." *Psychological Bulletin* 116 (1994): 429-56.

Feldman, Stanley, and Karen Stenner. "Perceived threat and authoritarianism." *Political Psychology*, 18 (1997): 741-70.

Fingarette, Herbert. *Confucius: The Secular as Sacred*. San Francisco: Harper, 1972.

Finkel, Steven E. "Can Democracy Be Taught? Adult Civic Education, Civil Society, and the Development of Democratic Political Culture." *Journal of Democracy* 14 (2003).

——. "Civic Education and the Mobilization of Political Participation in Developing Democracies." *Journal of Politics* 64 (2002): 994-1020.

Finkel, Steven E., and Howard A. Ernst. "Civic Education in Post-Apartheid South Africa: Alternative Paths to the Development of Political Knowledge and Democratic Value." *Political Psychology* 26 (2005): 333-64.

Finkel, Steven E., Christopher A. Sabatini, and Gwendolyn G. Bevis. "Civic Education, Civil Society, and Political Mistrust in a Developing Democracy: The Case of the Dominican Republic." *World Development* 28 (2000): 1851-74.

Finkel, Steven E., Lee Sigelman, and Stan Humphries. "Democratic Values and Political Tolerance." Chap. 5 in *Measures of Political Attitudes*, edited by John P.Robinson, Philip R. Shaver, and Lawrence S. Wrightman. San Diego, Calif.: Academic Press, 1999, 203-96.

Fisher, B., M. Margolis, and D. Resnick. "Breaking ground on the virtual frontier: Surveying civic life on the Internet." *American Sociologist* (1996): 11-29.

——. "Surveying the Internet: Democratic theory and civic life in cyberspace." *Southeastern Political Review* 24 (1996): 399-429.

Fixdal, Mona, and Dan Smith. "Humanitarian Intervention and Just War." *Mershon International Studies Review* 42 (1998): 283-312.

Fletcher, George. P. "The Instability of Tolerance." Pp. 158-72 in *Toleration: An Elusive Virtue*, edited by David Heyd. Princeton: Princeton University Press, 1996.

Fotion, Nick, and Gerrard Elfstrom. *Toleration*. Tuscaloosa, Ala. and London: The University of Alabama Press, 1992.

Galeotti, Anna Elizabeth. *Toleration as Recognition*. Cambridge: Cambridge University Press, 2002.

Galston, William A. "Defending Liberalism." *American Political Science Review* 76, no. 621 (1982): 625.

George, R. *The Clash of Orthodoxies*. Wilmington: ISI Books, 2001.

Gibson, James L. "A Sober Second Thought: An Experiment in Persuading Russians to Tolerate." *American Journal of Political Science* 42 (1998): 819-50.

——. "Alternative measures of political tolerance: Must tolerance be 'least-liked'?" *American Journal of Political Science* 36, no. 2 (1992): 560-77.

——. "Becoming tolerant? Short-term changes in Russian political culture." *British Journal of Political Science* 32 (2002): 309-33.

——. "Mass Opposition to the Soviet Putsch of August 1991: Collective Action, Rational Choice and Democratic Values in the Former Soviet Union." *American Political Science Review* 91 (1997): 671-84.

——. "Perceived Political Freedom in the Soviet Union: A Comparative Analysis." Paper presented at the annual meeting of the Western Political Science Association, San Francisco, Calif., March 19-21 1992.

Gibson, James L., and Amanda Gouws. "Social identities and political intolerance: Linkages within the South African mass public." *American Journal of Political Science* 44, no. 2 (2000): 272-86.

——. *Overcoming Intolerance in South Africa: Experiments in Democratic Persuasion*. Cambridge: Cambridge University Press, 2003.

Gibson, James L., and Arthur J. Anderson. "The Political Implications of Elite and Mass Tolerance." *Political Behavior*, 7 (1985): 118-46.

Gibson, James L., and Raymond Duch. "Political Intolerance in the USSR: The Distribution and Etiology of Mass Opinion." *Comparative Political Studies* 26 (1993): 286-329.

——. "Putting Up with Fascists in Western Europe: A Comparative Cross-Level Analysis of Political Tolerance." *Western Political Quarterly* 45 (1992): 237-73.

Gibson, James L., and Richard G. Bingham. *Civil Liberties and Nazis: The Skokie Free Speech Controversy*. New York: Praeger, 1985.

Gibson, James L., Raymond Duch, and Kent Tedin. "Democratic Values and the Transformation of the Soviet Union." *Journal of Politics* 54 (1992): 329-71.

Goldenson, D. R. "An alternative view about the role of the secondary school in political socialization: A field-experimental study of the development of civil liberties attitudes." *Theory and Research in Social Education* 6 (1978): 44-72.

Golebiowska, Ewa A. "Gender gap in political tolerance." *Political Behavior* 21, no. 1 (1999): 43-66.

———. "Individual value priorities, education, and political tolerance." *Political Behavior* 17, no. 1 (1995): 23-48.

Gonzales, M. H., E. Riedel, I. Williamson, P. G. Avery, J. L. Sullivan, and A. Bos. "Variations of citizenship education: a content analysis of rights, obligations, and participation concepts in high school civic textbooks." *Theory and Research in Social Education* 32, no. 3 (2004): 301-25.

Goodman, B. *Teaching Tolerance, Discussing Diversity*. Wilmetter, Ill.: Wilmette Public Library, 12 March 2002. http://www.wilmette.lib.il.us/tolerance.html.

Gouws, Amanda. "Political Tolerance and Civil Society: The Case of South Africa." *Politikon* 20 (1993): 15-31.

Gray, John. "The Virtues of Toleration." *The National Review*, (October 5, 1992): 28-36.

Greene, William. *Econometric Analysis*. New York: Prentice Hall, 1993.

Guttman, A. "Why should schools care about civic education?" Pp. 91-124 in *Rediscovering the Democratic Purposes of Education*, edited by L. M. McDonnell, P. M. Timpane, and R. Benjamin. Lawrence, Kans.: University of Kansas Press, 2000.

———, ed., *Multiculturalism: Examining the politics of recognition*. Princeton: Princeton University Press, 1994.

Habermas, J. "Struggles for Recognition in the Democratic Constitutional State." Pp. 107-48 in *Multiculturalism: Examining the politics of recognition*, edited by A. Gutmann. Princeton: Princeton University Press, 1994.

Haggenmacher, Peter. "Just War and Regular War in Sixteenth Century Spanish Doctrine." *International Review of the Red Cross* 290 (September/October 1992): 434-45.

Hahn, C. L. *Becoming political: Comparative perspectives on citizenship education*. Albany, N.Y.: SUNY Press, 1998.

Halliday, F. " Global Governance: Prospects and Problems," Pp. 431-41 in *The Global Transformations Reader*, edited by D. Held and A. McGrew. Cambridge: Polity Press, 2000.

Hartlyn, J. *The Struggle for Democratic Politics in the Dominican Republic*. Chapel Hill: University of North Carolina Press, 1998.

Hayek, F. A. *The Constitution of Liberty*. Chicago: University of Chicago Press, 1960.

———. *The Road to Serfdom*. Chicago: University of Chicago Press, 1944.

Heckman, James J. "Selection Bias and Self-Selection." Pp. 201-24 in *The New Palgrave Econometrics*, edited by John Eatwell, Murrary Milgate, and Peter Newman. London: MacMillan, 1992.

Heckman, James J., and Richard Robb. "Alternative Methods for Evaluating the Impact of Interventions." Pp. 156-245 in *Longitudinal Analysis of Labor Market Data*, edited by James J. Heckman and Burton Singer. Cambridge: Cambridge University Press, 1985.

Held, D., and A. McGrew, eds. *The Global Transformations Reader*. Cambridge: Polity Press, 2000.

Heller, Carol, and Joseph A. Hawkins. "Teaching Tolerance: Notes from the Front Line." *Teachers College Record*, 95 (1994): 337-68.

Helwig, C. C. "The role of agent and social context in judgments of freedom of speech and religion." *Child Development* 68, no. 3 (1997): 484-95.

Herek, Gregory M. "Gender gaps in public opinion about lesbians and gay men." *Public Opinion Quarterly* 66, no. 1 (2002): 40-66.

Herek, Gregory M., and Eric K. Glunt. "Interpersonal contact and heterosexuals' attitudes toward gay men: Results from a national survey." *The Journal of Sex Research* 30, no. 3 (1993): 239-44.

Herek, Gregory M., and John P. Capitanio. "Some of my best friends: Intergroup contact, concealable stigma, and heterosexuals' attitudes toward gay men and lesbians." *Personality and Social Psychology Bulletin* 22, no. 4 (1996): 412-24.

Herson, L. J. R., and C. R. Hofstetter. "Tolerance, Consensus, and the Democratic Creed: A Contextual Exploration." *The Journal of Politics* 37 (1975): 1007-32.

Hess, D. "Controversies about controversial issues in democratic education." *PS: Politics and Society* 37, no. 2 (2004): 257-61.

Hess, D., and J. Posselt. "How high school students experience and learn from the discussion of controversial public issues." *Journal of Curriculum & Supervision* 17, no. 4 (2002): 283-314.

Hewstone, Miles, and Katy Greenland. "Intergroup conflict." *International Journal of Psychology*, 35 (2000): 136-44.

Heyd, David. *Tolerance: An Elusive Virtue.* Princeton: Princeton University Press, 1997.

——, ed. Introduction to *Toleration: an Illusive Virtue.* Princeton: Princeton University Press, 1996.

Hibbing, J.R., and E. Theiss-Morse *Stealth democracy: Americans' beliefs about how government should work.* Cambridge: Cambridge University Press, 2002.

Hightower, Eugene, "Psychosocial Characteristics of Subtle and Blatant Racists as Compared to Tolerant Individuals." *Journal of Clinical Psychology* 53, no. 4 (1997): 369-74.

Horster, Detlef. *Habermas: An Introduction.* Translated by Heidi Thomson. Philadelphia: Pennbridge, 1992.

Horton, John, and Peter Nicholson, eds. "Philosophy and the practice of toleration." Pp. 1-13 in *Toleration: Philosophy and Practice.* Aldershot, U.K.: Avebury, 1992.

Horton, John, and Susan Mendus. *John Locke: A Letter concerning Toleration—in Focus.* London: Routledge, 1991.

Horton, John, ed. "Liberalism, Multiculturalism and Toleration." In *Liberalism, Multiculturalism and Toleration.* New York: St. Martin's, 1993.

——. "Tolerance as a Virtue." In *Toleration: an Illusive Virtue*, edited by David Heyd. Princeton: Princeton University Press, 1996.

Houston Chronicle, 11 April 2005, sec. A, p. 1.

Hoxter, A.L., and D. Lester. "Gender differences in prejudice." *Perception and Motor Skills* 79 (1994): 1666.

Huddy, L. "Group Identity and Political Cohesion." Pp. 511-58 in *Oxford Handbook of Political Psychology*, edited by D.O. Sears, L. Huddy, and R. Jervis Oxford: Oxford University Press, 2003.

Huntington, Samuel P. *The Clash of civilizations and the Remaking of the World Order.* New York: Simon and Schuster, 1996.

International Commission on Intervention and State Sovereignty. *The Responsibility to Protect.* Ottawa: International Development Research Centre, 2001.

Isin, E., and P. Wood. *Citizenship and Identity.* London: Sage, 1999.

Jackman, R. W. "Political Elites, Mass Publics, and Support for Democratic Principles." *The Journal of Politics* 34 (1972): 753-73.

Jain, Bawa. Speech to delegates of the UN's Millennium Peace Summit of Religious and Spiritual Leaders, 28-31 August, 2000, New York City.

Jennings, M. Kent, and Jan Van Deth et al., eds. *Continuities in Political Action*. New York: de Gruyter, 1990.

Jennings, M. Kent, and Richard Niemi. *The Political Character of Adolescence*. Princeton: Princeton University Press, 1974.

Johnson, James Turner. *Ideology, Reason, and the Limitation of War*. Princeton: Princeton University Press, 1975.

———. *Just War Tradition and the Restraint of War*. Princeton: Princeton University Press, 1981.

———. *The Idea of Holy War in Western and Islamic Traditions*. University Park: Pennsylvania State University Press, 1997.

———. *The Quest for Peace*. Princeton: Princeton University Press, 1987.

Johnson, M. E., C. Brems, and P. Alford-Keating. "Personality correlates of homophobia." *Journal of Homosexuality* 34 (1997): 57-69.

Johnson, Monica Kirkpatrick, and Margaret Mooney Marini. "Bridging the racial divide in the United States: The effect of gender." *Social Psychology Quarterly* 61, no. 3 (1998): 247-58.

Johnson, Stephen D. "Model of Factors Related to Tendencies to Discriminate Against People with Aids." *Psychological Reports* 76 (1995): 563-72.

Jones, P. "Beliefs and Identities." Pp. 65-86 in *Toleration, Identity, and Difference*, edited by J. Horton and S. Mendus. London, MacMillan Press, 1999.

Journal of Social Issues, 31 (1975).

Judd, Charles, and David Kenny. *Estimating the Effects of Social Interventions*. New York: Cambridge University Press, 1981.

Kahne, J., M. Rodriguez, B. Smith, and K. Thiede. "Developing citizens for democracy? Assessing opportunities to learn in Chicago's social studies classrooms." *Theory and Research in Social Education* 28, no. 3 (2000): 311-38.

Kautz, S. "Liberalism and the Idea of Toleration." *American Journal of Political Science* 37, no. 2 (May 1993): 610-32.

Kawakami, K., J. F. Dovidio, J. Moll, S. Hermsen, and A. Russin. "Just say no (to stereotyping): Effects of training in the negation of stereotypic associations on stereotype activation." *Journal of Personality and Social Psychology* 78, no. 5 (2000): 871-88.

Kiess, Harold O. *Statistical Concepts for the Behavioral Sciences*. Boston: Allyn and Bacon, 1989.

King, Preston. *Toleration*. New York: St. Martin's Press, 1976.

Kite, Mary E., and Bernard E. Whitley, Jr. "Sex differences in attitudes toward homosexual persons, behavior, and civil rights: A meta-analysis." *Personality and Social Psychology Bulletin* 22, no. 4 (1996): 336-53.

Kluegel, James R., and Eliot R. Smith. *Beliefs about Equality: Americans' Views of What Is and What Ought to Be*. New York: Aldine De Gruyter, 1986.

Krosnick, J., and R. Petty. "Attitude Strength: An Overview." Pp. 1-24 in *Attitude Strength: Antecedents and Consequences*, edited by R. Petty and J. Krosnick. Mahwah, N. J.: Erlbaum Press, 1995.

Kuklinski, J., and N. Hurley. "It's a Matter of Interpretation." Chap. 5 in *Political Persuasion and Attitude Change*, edited by D. Mutz, D. P. Sniderman, and R. Brody. Ann Arbor: University of Michigan Press, 1996, 125-44.

Kuklinski, J., E. Riggle, V. Ottati, N. Schwarz, and R. S. Wyer, Jr. "The Cognitive and Affective Bases of Political Tolerance Judgments." *American Journal of Political Science* 35 (1991): 1-27.

Kymlicka, W., and W. Norman. *Citzenship in Diverse Societies*. Oxford: Oxford University Press, 2000.

Kymlicka, Will. "Two Models of Tolerance and Pluralism." In *Toleration: an Illusive Virtue*, edited by David Heyd. Princeton: Princeton University Press, 1996.

LaPiere, Richard T. "Attitudes vs. Actions." *Social Forces* 13 (1934): 230-37.

Larmore, Charles E. "Liberal Neutrality." *Political Theory* 17 (1989).

——. *Patterns of Moral Complexity*. Cambridge: Cambridge University Press, 1987.

Larson, B. E., and W. C. Parker. "What is classroom discussion? A look at teachers' conceptions." *Journal of Curriculum and Supervision* 11, no. 2 (1996): 110-26.

Laursen, J. C., and C. Nederman, eds. *Beyond the Persecuting Society*. Philadephia: University of Pennsylvania Press, 1998.

Lawrence, D. "Procedural norms and tolerance: A reassessment." *American Political Science Review* 70 (1976): 80-100.

Legutko, Ryszard. "The Trouble with Toleration." *Partisan Review* 61 (1994): 610-624.

Lipset, Seymour M. "Some Social Requisites for Democracy." *American Political Science Review* 53 (1959): 69-105.

Locke, John. *A Letter Concerning Toleration*. London: Printed for A. Churchill, 1689.

Loewen, J.W. *Lies my teacher told me: Everything your American history textbook got wrong*. New York: Touchstone, 1995.

Lord Scarman. "Toleration and the Law." Pp. 49-62 in *On Toleration*, edited by Susan Mendus and David Edwards. Oxford, U.K.: Clarendon Press, 1987.

Los Angeles Times, 4 May 2005, National Desk, sec. A, p. 14.

Loundy, David. "Lawyers' electronic ads leave bad taste." *Chicago Daily Law Bulletin* 9 (March 1995): 6. http://www.Loundy.com/CDLB/Spam.html.

Lurry, C. *Cultural Rights*. London: Routledge, 1993.

Lyotard, Jean-François. *The Postmodern Condition: A Report on Knowledge*. Translated by Geoff Bennington and Brian Massumi. Minneapolis: University of Minnesota Press, [1979] 1984.

Mannheim, K. *Ideology and Utopia*. New York: Harcourt, Brace, and Company, 1936.

Marcus, George E., John L. Sullivan, Elizabeth Theiss-Morse, and Sandra L. Wood. *With Malice to Some: How People Make Civil Liberties Judgment*. Cambridge: Cambridge University Press, 1995.

Marcuse, Herbert. "Repressive Tolerance." Pp. 95-137 in *A Critique of Pure Tolerance*. Edited by Robert Paul Wolff, Barrington Moore, Jr., and Herbert Marcuse. Boston: Beacon Press, 1968.

Margolis, Michael, and David Resnick. *Politics as usual: The cyberspace "revolution"*. Thousand Oaks, Calif.: Sage, 2000.

Marshall, T. H. *Citizenship and Social Class*. London: Pluto Press, 1950, reprint 1992.

Marty, Martin E., and R. Scott Appleby, eds. *Fundamentalisms Observed*. Chicago: University of Chicago Press, 1991.

Mattes, Robert, and Hermann Thiel. "Consolidation and Public Opinion in South Africa." *Journal of Democracy* 9, no. 1 (1998): 95-110.

Maykovich, Minako K. "Correlates of racial prejudice." *Journal of Personality and Social Psychology* 32, no. 6 (1975): 1014-20.

McClosky, Herbert. "Consensus and Ideology in American Politics." *American Political Science Review* 58 (1964): 361-82.

McClosky, H., and J. Zaller. *The American ethos: Public attitudes toward capitalism and democracy.* Cambridge: Harvard University Press, 1984.

McClosky, Herbert, and Alida Brill, *Dimensions of Tolerance: What Americans Believe About Civil Liberties.* New York: Russell Sage, 1983.

McClosky, Herbert, Paul J. Hoffman, and Rosemary O'Hara. "Issue Conflict and Consensus Among Party Leaders and Followers." *American Political Science Review* 54 (1960): 406-27.

McDonald, Mary Francis. trans. *Lactantius: The Divine Institutes.* Washington, D.C.: Catholic University of America Press, 1964.

McElroy, Wendy. "The Origins of Religious Tolerance: Voltaire." *Wendy McElroy Home Page.* http://www.zetetics.com/mac/volt.htm.

McNeil, L. M. *Contradictions of control: School structure and school knowledge.* New York: Routledge, 1986.

Mead, G. H. *Mind, Self and Society.* Chicago: The University of Chicago Press, 1934.

Mendelberg, Tali. *The Race Card: Campaign Strategy, Implicit Messages and the Norm of Equality.* Princeton: Princeton Uniersity Press, 2001.

Mendus, Susan. "Toleration." *The Encyclopedia of Ethics.* Vol. 2. Edited by Lawrence C. Becker. New York: Garland Publishing, 1992.

——. *Toleration and the Limits of Liberalism.* Atlantic Highlands, N.J.: Humanities Press International, 1989.

Merelman, R. "The role of conflict in children's political learning." Pp. 47-65 in *Political socialization, citizenship education, and democracy*, edited by O. Ichilov. New York: Teachers College Press, 1990.

Mill, John Stuart. *On liberty.* Orchard Park, N.Y.: Boardview Press, 1999.

——. "A Few Words on Non-Intervention." In *Dissertations and Discussions.* Vol. 3. London: Longmans, Green, Reader, and Dyer, [1859]1867.

——. *On Liberty*, edited by Alburey Castel. Arlington Heights, Ill.: AHM Publishing, 1947.

——. *On Liberty.* London: J.W. Parker and Son, 1859.

Miller, Richard. *Interpretations of Conflict.* Chicago: University of Chicago Press, 1991.

Mills, C. W. *The Power Elite.* Oxford: Oxford University Press, 1956.

Mises, Ludwig von. *Liberalism.* Irvington-on-the-Hudson, N.Y.: Foundation for Economic Education, 1985 [1927].

Mishler, William, and Richard Rose. "Trust, Distrust, and Skepticism: Popular Evaluations of Civil and Political Institutions in Post-Communist Societies." *Journal of Politics* 59 (1997): 418-51.

Mondak, J. J., and J. Hurwitz. "Values, acts, and actors: Distinguishing generic and discriminatory intolerance." *Political Behavior* 20, no. 4 (1998): 313-39.

Mondak, Jeffery J., and Mitchell S. Sanders. "Tolerance and intolerance, 1976-1998." *American Journal of Political Science* 47, no. 3 (2003): 492-502.

Moon, J. D. *Constructing Community: Moral Pluralism and Tragic Conflicts.* Princeton: Princeton University Press, 1993.

Moore, J. W., W. E. Hauck, and T. C. Denne. "Racial prejudice, interracial contact, and personality variables." *Journal of Experimental Education* 52 (1984): 168–73.

Morduchowicz, Roxana, Edgardo Catterberg, Richard G. Niemi, and Frank Bell. "Teaching Political Information and Democratic Values in a New Democracy: An Argentine Experiment." *Comparative Politics* 28 (1996): 465-76.

Moreno-Riano, G. "The Roots of Tolerance." *Review of Politics* 65, no. 1 (Winter 2003): 111-29.

Moreno-Riano, G. *Political Tolerance, Culture, and the Individual.* Lewiston, N. Y.: The Edwin Mellen Press, 2002.

Murphy, A. *Conscience and Community.* University Park: Pennsylvania State University Press, 2001.

National Campaign for Tolerance. "Wall of Tolerance." Southern Poverty Law Center, Montgomery, Ala., 2002. Mailing.

National Conference of Catholic Bishops. *The Challenge of Peace: God's Promise and Our Response.* Washington, DC: United States Catholic Conference, 1983.

NEA Today, 13 (December 1994): 6.

Nederman, C. *World of Difference: European Discourses of Tolerance in Europe c. 1100-1500.* University Park: Pennsylvania State University Press, 2000.

Nelson, Thomas, R. A. Clawson, and Z. M. Oxley. "Media Framing of a Civil Liberties Conflict and its Effects on Tolerance." *American Political Science Review* 88 (1997): 635-52.

Neville, Robert C. "Political Tolerance in an Age of Renewed Religious Warfare." Pp. 28-42 in *Philosophy, Religion, and the Question of Intolerance,* edited by Mahdi Amin Razavi and David Ambuel. Albany, N.Y.: State University of New York Press, 1977.

——. *Boston Confucianism: Portable Tradition in the Late-Modern World* Albany, N.Y.: State University of New York Press, 2000.

——. *Normative Cultures.* Albany, N.Y.: State University of New York, 1995.

——. *Religion in Late Modernity.* Albany, N.Y.: State University of New York Press, 2002.

——. *Soldier Sage Saint.* New York: Fordham University Press, 1978.

——, ed. *The Human Condition.* Albany, N.Y.: State University of New York, 2001.

——, ed. *Ultimate Realities.* Albany, N.Y.: State University of New York, 2001.

New Straits Times (Malaysia), 25 December 2004, p. 1.

Newey, G. F. "Tolerance as a Virtue." Pp. 38-64 in *Tolerance, Identity, and Difference,* edited by J. Horton and S. Mendus. London: MacMillan Press, 1999.

——. *Virtue, Reason, and Toleration.* Edinburgh: Edinburgh University Press, 1999.

Newmann, F. M. "Qualities of thoughtful social studies classes: An empirical profile." *Journal of Curriculum Studies* 22, no. 3 (1990): 253-75.

Newmann, F. M., and Associates. *Authentic achievement: Restructuring schools for intellectual quality.* San Francisco: Jossey-Bass Publishers, 1996.

Nie, N. H., J. Junn, and K. Stehlik. *Education and democratic citizenship in America.* Chicago: University of Chicago Press, 1996.

Niebuhr, H. Richard. *Christ and Culture.* New York: Harper and Brothers, 1951.

Nielson, H. D. *Tolerating political dissent.* Stockholm: Almqvist & Wiksell International, 1977.

Niemi, R. G., and J. Junn. *Civic Education: What Makes Students Learn.* New Haven: Yale University Press, 1998.

Nieto, Sonia. "Moving Beyond Tolerance in Multicultural Education." *Multicultural Education* 1 (1994): 9-12, 35-38.

Norrander, Barbard, and Clyde Wilcox, eds. *Understanding Public Opinion.* Washington, D.C.: CQ Press, 2002.

Nozick, Robert. *Anarchy, State and Utopia.* New York: Harper and Row, 1974.

Nunn, Clyde Z., Harry J. Crockett, and J. A. Williams. *Tolerance for Nonconformity.* San Francisco: Jossey-Bass, 1978.

Oakeshott, Michael J. *On Human Conduct.* Oxford: University of Oxford Press, 1975.

Owen, D., and J. Dennis. "Preadult development of political tolerance." *Political Psychology* 8 (1987): 547-61.

Page, R. *Lower-track classrooms: A curricular and cultural perspective.* New York: Teachers College Press, 1991.

Pangle, Thomas, and Peter Ahrensdorf. *Justice among Nations.* Lawrence, Kans.: University Press of Kansas, 1999.

Parker, W. C. "Classroom discussion: Models for leading seminars and deliberations." *Social Education* 65, no. 2 (2001): 111-15.

Parker, W. C., and D. Hess. "Teaching with and for discussion." *Teaching and Teacher Education* 17 (2001): 273-89.

Peffley, Mark, Jonathan Hurwitz, and Paul M. Sniderman. "Racial stereotypes and whites' political views of blacks in the context of welfare and crime." *American Journal of Political Science* 41, no. 1 (1997): 30-60.

Persell, C. H., A. Green, and L. Gurevich. "Civil society, economic distress, and social tolerance." *Sociological Forum* 16, no. 2 (2001): 203-30.

Pettigrew, Thomas F. "Intergroup contact theory." *Annual Review of Psychology* 49 (1998): 65-85.

——. "Personality and sociocultural factors in intergroup attitudes: A cross-national comparison." Pp. 18-29 in *Intergroup Relations: Essential Readings*, edited by Michael A. Hogg and Dominic Abrams. Philadelphia: Psychology Press, 2001.

Petty, R. E., and J. T. Cacioppo. "Source Factors and the Elaboration Likelihood Model of Persuasion." *Advances in Consumer Research* 11 (1984): 668-72.

Phillips, A. "The Politicisation of Difference: Does this Make for a More Intolerant Society?" Pp. 126-45 in *Toleration, Identity, and Difference,* edited by J. Horton and S. Mendus. London: MacMillan Press, 1999.

Pizan, Christine de. *The Book of Deeds of Arms and of Chivalry*, edited by Charity C. Willard, translated by Sumner Willard. University Park: Pennsylvania State University Press, 1999.

Pratto, F., J. Sidanius, L. M. Stallworth, and B. F. Malle. "Social dominance orientation: A personality variable predicting social and political attitudes." *Journal of Personality and Social Psychology* 67 (1994): 741-763.

Pratto, Felicia, Lisa M. Stallworth and Jim Sidanius. "The gender gap: Differences in political attitudes and social dominance orientation." *British Journal of Social Psychology* 36 (1997): 49-68.

Prothro, James W., and Charles W. Grigg. "Fundamental Principles of Democracy: Bases of Agreement and Disagreement." *Journal of Politics* 22 (1960): 276-94.

Putnam, Robert. *Bowling Alone.* New York: Simon & Schuster, 2000.

Quails, R. C., M. B. Cox, and T. L. Schehr. "Racial attitudes on campus: Are there gender differences?" *Journal of College Student Development* 33 (1992),524-30.

Quigley, Kevin F. F. "Political scientists and assisting democracy: too tenuous links," *PS: Political Science & Politics* 30 (1997): 564-68.

Ramsey, Paul. *The Just War: Force and Political Responsibility.* New York: Charles Scribner's Sons, 1968.

Rawls, J. "Justice As Fairness: Political Not Metaphysical." Pp. 37-58 in *Twentieth Century Political Theory*, edited by S.E. Bronner (New York: Routledge, 1997). First published in *Philosophy and Public Affairs* 14, no. 3 (1985).

——. "Kantian Constructivism in Moral Theory." *Journal of Philosophy* 77 (1980): 543.

——. *Political Liberalism.* New York: Columbia University Press, 1993.

Reichberg, Gregory M. "Philosophy Meets War." Pp. 197–204 in *The Classics of Western Philosophy*, edited by Jorge Gracia, Gregory Reichberg, and Bernard Schumacher. Oxford, U.K.: Blackwell Publishers, 2003.

Reichberg, Gregory, and Henrik Syse, eds. "Special Issue on Ethics and International Law." *Journal of Military Ethics* 3, no. 2 (2004).

Riker, William. *Liberalism Against Populism*. Prospect Heights, Ill.: Waveland Press, 1982.

Rorty, R. *Contingency, Irony, and Solidarity*. Cambridge: Cambridge University Press, 1989.

——. *Truth and Progress*. Cambridge: Cambridge University Press, 1998.

Rose, Richard, and William Mishler. "Mass Reaction to Regime Change in Eastern Europe: Polarization or Leaders and Laggards?" *British Journal of Political Science* 24 (1994): 159-82.

Rose, Richard, William Mishler, and Christian Haerpfer. *Democracy and Its Alternatives: Understanding Post-Communist Societies*. Baltimore: The Johns Hopkins University Press, 1998.

Sagar, H. A., J. W. Schofield, and H. N. Snyder. "Race and gender barriers: Preadolescent peer behaviour in academic classrooms." *Child Development* 54 (1983): 1032–40.

Sagiv-Schifter, Tamy, and Michal Shamir. "Israel as a laboratory for the study of political tolerance." *Deot Baam* 6 (October 2002).

Sandel, M. "The Procedural Republic and the Unencumbered Self." P. 77 in *Twentieth Century Political Theory*, edited by S.E. Bronner. New York: Routledge, 1997. First published in *Political Theory* 12, no.1 (1994): 81-96.

Schuman, Howard. "Attitudes vs. Actions versus Attitudes vs. Attitudes." *Public Opinion Quarterly* 36 (1972): 347-54.

Sears, D. O. and S. Levy. "Childhood and Adult Political Development," Pp. 60-109 in *Oxford Handbook of Political Psychology*, edited by D. O. Sears, L. Huddy, and R. Jervis. Oxford: Oxford University Press, 2003.

Seligson, Mitchell, and John Booth. "Political Culture and Regime Type: Evidence from Nicaragua and Costa Rica." *Journal of Politics* 55 (1993): 777-92.

Shamir, Michal, and Keren Weinshall-Margel. "Disqualification of party lists in Israel – Were the 2003 elections unique?" In *The Elections in Israel – 2003*, edited by Asher Arian and Michal Shamir. New Brunswick, N.J.: Transaction, in press.

Shamir, Michal. *The political context of tolerance: Israel in the 1980's and 1990's*. Report to the Israel Science Foundation, 2002; grant July 11, 1999.

Shapiro, Robert Y., and H. Mahajan. "Gender differences in policy preferences: A summary of trends from the 1960s to the 1980s." *Public Opinion Quarterly* 50, no. 1 (1986): 42-61.

Shklar Judith M. *Political Thought and Political Thinkers*, edited by Stanley Hoffman. Chicago: University of Chicago Press, 1998.

Sidanius, J., and F. Pratto. *Social dominance: An intergroup theory of social hierarchy and oppression*. New York: Cambridge University Press, 1999.

Sigelman, Lee, and Susan Welch. *Black Americans' Views of Racial Inequality*. New York: Cambridge University Press, 1991.

Slomczynski, K. M., and G. Shabad. "Can Support for Democracy and the Market Be Learned in School? A Natural Experiment in Post-Communist Poland." *Political Psychology* 19 (1998): 749-79.

Smooha, Sammy. *Conflicting and shared attitudes in a divided society*. Vol. 1 of *Arabs and Jews in Israel*. Boulder, Colo.: Westview, 1989.

Sniderman, P. M., P. E. Tetlock, J. M. Glaser, D. P. Green, M. Hout. "Principled Tolerance and the American Mass Public." *British Journal of Political Science* 19 (1989): 25-45.

Sniderman, Paul M., and Michael Hagen. *Race and Inequality: A Study in American Values.* Chatham, N.J.: Chatham House, 1985.

Sniderman, Paul M., and Thomas Piazza. *The Scar of Race.* Cambridge: Harvard University Press, 1993.

Sniderman, Paul M., Pierangelo Peri, Rui J. P.de Figueiredo, Jr., and Thomas Piazza. *The Outsider – Prejudice and Politics in Italy.* Princeton: Princeton University Press, 2000.

Sniderman, Paul, J. F. Fletcher, P. E. Tetlock, and R. M. Boyd. *The Clash of Rights.* New Haven: Yale University Press, 1996.

Sniderman, Paul, R. Brody, and P. E. Tetlock. *Reasoning and Choice: Explorations in Political Psychology.* New York: Cambridge University Press, 1991.

Special issue: National identity in Europe. *Political Psychology* 24 (2003).

Sprinzak, Ehud. *Political Violence in Israel.* Jerusalem: The Jerusalem Institute for Israel Studies, 1995.

Steiner, Peter. "On the Internet, no one knows you're a dog," *The New Yorker* 69, no. 20 (July 5, 1993): 61.

Stevenson, N. *Culture and Citizenship.* London: Sage, 2001.

Stouffer, Samuel A. *Communism, Conformity and Civil Liberties.* New York: Doubleday, 1955.

Strauss, Leo. *What is Political Philosophy and Other Studies.* Chicago: The University of Chicago Press, 1988.

Street, J. *Politics and Popular Culture.* Cambridge: Polity Press, 1997.

Sullivan, John L., James E. Piereson, and George E. Marcus. *Political Tolerance and American Democracy.* Chicago: The University of Chicago Press, 1982.

Sullivan, John L., Michal Shamir, Patrick Walsh, and Nigel S. Roberts. *Political Tolerance in Context: Support for Unpopular Minorities in Israel, New Zealand, and the United States.* Boulder, Colo.: Westview, 1985.

Sullivan, John, and John Transue. "The Psychological Underpinnings of Democracy: A Selective Review of Research on Political Tolerance, Interpersonal Trust, and Social Capita." *Annual Review of Psychology* (1999): 625-xxx.

Sumner, William Graham. *Folkways: A Study of the Sociological Importance of Usages, Manners, Customs, Mores and Morals.* Boston: Ginn, 1906.

Sunstein, Cass R. *Republic.com.* Princeton: Princeton University Press, 2001.

Swift, Louis, ed. *The Early Fathers on War and Military Service.* Wilmington: Michael Glazier, 1983.

Tajfel, Henri, Michael Billig, R. P. Bundy, and Claude Flament. "Social categorization and intergroup behavior." *European Journal of Social Psychology* 1 (1971): 149-77.

Tajfel, Henri. *Human Groups and Social Categories.* Cambridge: Cambridge University Press, 1981.

Taylor, A. E. "The Ethical Doctrine of Hobbes." *Philosophy* 13 (1938): xxx.

Taylor, C. "Atomism." Pp. 29-50 in *Communitarianism and Individualism*, edited by S. Aveneri and A. de-Shalit. Oxford: Oxford University Press, 1992.

———. "The Politics of Recognition." Pp. 25-74 in *Multiculturalism: Examining the politics of recognition*, edited by A. Gutmann. Princeton: Princeton University Press, 1994.

Thalhammer, K., S. L. Wood, K. Bird, P. G. Avery, and J. L. Sullivan, "Adolescents and political tolerance: Lip-synching to the tune of democracy." *Review of Education, Pedagogy, and Cultural Studies* 16 (1994): 325-47.

The Advertiser (Australia), 15 February 2003, Sports p. 113.

The Financial Times, 5 April 2005, Europe Section, p. 8.

The Gazette (Montreal, Quebec), 20 December 2003, News A4.

The Gazette (Montreal, Quebec), 28 February 2004, News A12.

The New York Times, 31 October 2004.

The New York Times, 7 November 2004.

The Southern Poverty Law Center. *Tolerance.org Home Page*. 2002. www.tolerance.org.

Tillich, Paul. *Systematic Theology*. Vol. 1. Chicago: University of Chicago Press, 1952.

Torney, J. V., A. N. Oppenheim, and R. F. Farnen. *Civic education in ten countries: An empirical study*. New York: John Wiley and Sons, 1975.

Torney-Purta, J., R. Lehmann, H. Oswald, and W. Schulz. *Citizenship and education in twenty-eight countries: Civic knowledge and engagement at age fourteen*. Amsterdam: IEA, 2001.

Tully, J. "Identity Politics." P. 526 in *The Cambridge History of Twentieth-Century Political Thought*, edited by T. Ball and R. Bellamy. Cambridge: Cambridge University Press, 2003.

UNESCO, *Declaration of Principles of Tolerance*, 1995, http://www.unesco.org/tolerance/declaeng.htm.

Vella, Francis. "Estimating Models with Sample Selection Bias: A Survey." *The Journal of Human Resources* 33 (1998): 127-69.

Verba, Sidney, Nancy Burns, and Kay Schlozman. "Knowing and caring about politics: Gender and political engagement." *Journal of Politics* 59, no. 4 (1997): 1051-72.

Vitoria, Francisco de. *Political Writings*, edited by Anthony Pagden & Jeremy Lawrance. Cambridge: Cambridge University Press, 1991.

Vogt, W. P. *Tolerance and education: Learning to live with diversity and difference*. Thousand Oaks, Calif.: SAGE Publications, 1997.

Wainryb, Cecilia, Leigh A. Shaw, Marcie Langley, Kim Cottam, and Renee Lewis. "Children's thinking about diversity of belief in the early school years: Judgments of relativism, tolerance, and disagreeing persons." *Child Development* 75, no. 3 (2004): 687-703.

Waldron, J. "Liberalism, Political and Comprehensive." Pp. 89-99 in *Handbook of Political Theory*, edited by G. F. Gaus and C. Kukathas. Thousand Oaks: Sage Publications, 2004.

Walzer, M. *Thick and Thin: Moral Argument at Home and Abroad*. Notre Dame: University of Notre Dame Press, 1994.

———. *Just and Unjust Wars*. New York: Basic Books, 1977.

———. *On Toleration*. New Haven: Yale University Press, 1997.

Washington Post, 1 June 2004, Editorial A23.

Washington Post, 13 May 2005, sec. A, p. 4.

Wechsler, Herbert. "Toward Neutral Principles of Constitutional Law." In *Principles, Politics, and Fundamental Law: Selected Essays*. Cambridge: Harvard University, 1961.

Weil, F. D. "The Development of Democratic Attitudes in Eastern and Western Germany in a Comparative Perspective." *Research on Democracy and Society* 1 (1993): 195-225.

Weissberg, Robert. *Political Tolerance: Balancing Community and Diversity*. Thousand Oaks, Calif.: Sage, 1998.

Welch, S., L. Sigelman, T. Bledsoe, and M. Combs. *Race & place: Race relations in an American city.* Cambridge: Cambridge University Press, 2001.

Whitley, Bernard E. "Right-wing authoritarianism, social dominance orientation, and prejudice." *Journal of Personality and Social Psychology* 77, no. 1 (1999): 126-34.

Wilcox, Laird. *Crying Wolf: Hate Crime Hoaxes in America.* Olathe, Kans.: Laird Wilcox Editorial Research Service, 1994.

Wildman, Wesley J. "Theological Literacy: Problem and Promise." Pp. 335-51 in *Theological Literacy in the 21st Century.* Grand Rapids: Eerdmans, 2002.

Williams, Bernard. "Toleration: An Impossible Virtue." In *Toleration: an Illusive Virtue,* edited by David Heyd. Princeton: Princeton University Press, 1996.

Winship, Christopher, and Stephen L. Morgan. "The Estimation of Causal Effects from Observational Data." *Annual Review of Sociology* 25 (1999): 659-706.

Wolff, Robert Paul, *In Defense of Anarchism.* New York: Harper Row, 1970.

Young, Jeffrey R. "A Study Finds That Web Users Are More Tolerant Than Non-Users." *The Chronicle of Higher Education* 15 June 2001. http://chronicle.com/free/2001/06/2001061501t.htm.

Zaller, John R. *The Nature and Origins of Mass Opinion.* New York: Cambridge University Press, 1992.

List of Contributors

PAT AVERY—*Professor of Education, University of Minnesota.* Avery's publications and research focus on the areas of civic education, diversity and tolerance, and political socialization. She has served on the Expert Panel on Civic Education for the International Association for the Evaluation of Education Achievement (IEA) between 1995 and 2001. Avery currently coordinates the evaluation of the Deliberating in a Democracy Project, a study in which models for discussing controversial public issues are implemented in secondary classrooms in three U.S. cities (Chicago, Los Angeles, and Washington, DC), and three countries (Azerbaijan, Czech Republic, and Lithuania).

PETER J. BOETTKE—*Deputy Director, James M. Buchanan Center for Political Economy; Senior Research Fellow, Mercatus Center; Professor of Economics, George Mason University.* Boettke has edited numerous books and is the author of several books on the history, collapse, and transition from socialism in the former Soviet Union with his most recent work entitled *Calculation and Coordination: Essays on Socialism and Transitional Political Economy* (Routledge, 2001). Boettke is also the editor of the *Review of Austrian Economics* (Kluwer Academic Publishers).

J. BUDZISZEWSKI—*Professor of Government and Philosophy, University of Texas at Austin.* Budziszewski specializes in the relations among ethical theory, political theory, and Christian theology. One of America's foremost authorities in natural law, the focus of his current research is natural law and moral self-deception. Author of several books and articles, Budziszewski's most recent work is entitled *What We Can't Not Know: A Guide* (Spence, 2003).

STEVEN E. FINKEL—*Professor and Daniel Wallace Chair in Political Science, University of Pittsburgh; Professor of Quantitative and Qualitative Methods at the Hertie School of Governance, Berlin, Germany.* Finkel's research interests are in the areas of political participation, voting behavior, the development of democratic attitudes and values, and research methodology. He has conducted research extensively on these topics in the United States, as well as in new and established democracies such as Germany, South Africa, Kenya, and the Dominican Republic. He has published numerous articles in journals such as the *American Political Science Review, American Journal of Political Science, Journal of Politics*, and *Journal of Democracy*, as well as a monograph, *Causal Analysis with Panel Data*, for the Sage Series on Quantitative Applications in the Social Sciences.

NICK FOTION—*Professor of Philosophy, Emory University*. A Fulbright Professor (1984, 1988, and 1991-1992), Fotion has written extensively in the area of ethics and moral philosophy and authored a work on the American philosopher John Searle (Princeton University Press, 2000). His most recent work is a co-edited volume entitled *Moral Constraints on War: Principles and Cases* (Lexington Books, 2003).

EWA GOLEBIOWSKA—*Associate Professor of Political Science, Wayne State University*. Golebiowska's interests focus on intergroup attitudes, including political tolerance, homophobia, racism, and anti-Semitism. Her recent publications have appeared in *The Journal of Politics, Political Behavior*, and *Journal of Applied Social Psychology*.

PETER T. LEESON—*Assistant Professor of Economics, West Virginia University*. Leeson has been a visiting fellow at Harvard University (2004) and a F.A. Hayek Fellow at the London School of Economics (2005). Leeson has published numerous articles and book chapters in economics and political economy. Besides numerous forthcoming articles, his most recent and forthcoming work is a co-edited volume entitled *The Legacy of Ludwig von Mises: Theory and History*. 2 vols. Aldershot: Edward Elgar Publishing.

GERSON MORENO-RIAÑO—*Associate Professor of Political Science, Cedarville University; Fellow, Center for the Study of Democratic Citizenship, University of Cincinnati*. Moreno-Riaño's interests lie in the fields of political theory with particular emphasis in early modern political thought, Liberalism, and natural law. His most recent and forthcoming work is an edited work entitled *The World of Marsilius of Padua* (Brepols Press).

ROBERT CUMMINGS NEVILLE—*Professor of Philosophy, Religion, and Theology; Dean Emeritus of the School of Theology; Dean of Marsh Chapel and Chaplain of the University, Boston University*. Neville has written close to twenty books and many articles in the field of philosophy and religious studies. His most recent work is entitled *Religion in Late Modernity* (SUNY Press, 2002).

DAVID RESNICK—*Professor of Political Science and Director of the Center for the Study of Democratic Citizenship, University of Cincinnati*. His research interests included the history of political theory, citizenship theory, and Internet politics. He co-authored *Politics as Usual: The Cyberspace 'Revolution'* (Sage 2000). His articles appeared in the *American Political Science Review, Harvard International Journal of Press/Politics, American Journal of Political Science, Polity, The Review of Politics, Political Theory* and other leading scholarly journals.

TAMMY SAGIV-SCHIFTER—teaches at Tel-Aviv University and at the Academic College of Tel-Aviv-Yaffo. Her main area of specialization is medical sociology. Since the assassination of Prime Minister Rabin in November 1997, she is involved in the conduction of periodical national surveys measuring political tolerance in Israel.

MICHAL SHAMIR—*Alvin Z. Rubinstein Professor of Political Science at Tel Aviv University*. Shamir specializes in democratic politics, including elections, party systems, public opinion, tolerance, and democratic culture. She has published several books and numerous articles in these areas and is involved in major national and international research projects, such as the Israel National Election Study (INES) and the Comparative Study of Electoral Systems project (CSES), coordinated by the University of Michigan. Her most recent work is a co-edited volume entitled The Elections in Israel, 2003 (Transaction Publishers, 2005).

HENRIK SYSE—*Senior Researcher PRIO; Research fellow at the Ethics Program of the University of Oslo*. Syse has just completed writing a book on the relationship between ethical theory and moral practice, published in Norwegian by Aschehoug in 2005. He is currently writing several research articles on the ethics of war and peace, with special attention to questions of responsibility and authority; and co-editing a major anthology on classical works of the ethics of war and peace, and an anthology on ethics, nationalism, and just war. In 2005, Norges Bank appointed Syse to build up its new Investment Management (NBIM) unit by outlining the ethical foundations of the huge petroleum fund investments.

ROBERT WEISSBERG—*Professor of Political Science, Emeritus, University of Illinois-Urbana*. A summer fellow at the Social Philosophy and Public Policy Center, Bowling Green State University (2001, 2003), Weissberg is the author of close to a dozen books and scores of professional articles. His latest and forthcoming book is entitled *The Limits of Political Activism: Some Cautionary Tales on the Use of Politics*. New Brunswick: Transactions Press.

Index